Network Computing System Reference Manual

Mike Kong

Terence H. Dineen
Paul J. Leach
Elizabeth A. Martin
Nathaniel W. Mishkin
Joseph N. Pato
Geoffrey L. Wyant

Apollo Computer Inc.
a subsidiary of Hewlett-Packard Company
Chelmsford, Massachusetts

Prentice Hall
Englewood Cliffs, New Jersey 07632

Editorial/production supervision: *Jacqueline A. Jeglinski*
Cover design: *Lundgren Graphics*
Manufacturing buyer: *Ray Sintel*

Published by Prentice-Hall, Inc.
A Division of Simon & Schuster
Englewood Cliffs, New Jersey 07632

Printed in the United States of America
10 9 8 7 6 5 4 3 2 1

ISBN 0-13-617085-4

Prentice-Hall International (UK) Limited, *London*
Prentice-Hall of Australia Pty. Limited, *Sydney*
Prentice-Hall Canada Inc., *Toronto*
Prentice-Hall Hispanoamericana, S.A., *Mexico*
Prentice-Hall of India Private Limited, *New Delhi*
Prentice-Hall of Japan, Inc., *Tokyo*
Simon & Schuster Asia Pte. Ltd., *Singapore*
Editora Prentice-Hall do Brasil, Ltda., *Rio de Janeiro*

Contents

Figures

Tables

Preface

This book describes Version 1.5.1 of the Network Computing System (NCS), a set of tools for heterogeneous distributed computing. We have organized the book as follows:

Chapter 1   Introduces NCS and the Network Computing Architecture.

Chapter 2   Describes the basic concepts of NCS.

Chapter 3   Surveys NCS software.

Chapter 4   Describes how to define interfaces in Network Interface Definition Language (NIDL).

Chapter 5   Describes how to develop distributed applications that use NCS.

Chapter 6   Describes the C syntax of NIDL.

Chapter 7   Describes the Pascal syntax of NIDL.

Chapter 8   Covers special topics.

Chapter 9   Contains reference descriptions of the **error_$** calls.

Chapter 10   Contains reference descriptions of the **lb_$** calls.

Chapter 11   Contains reference descriptions of the **pfm_$** calls.

Chapter 12   Contains reference descriptions of the **pgm_$** calls.

Chapter 13   Contains reference descriptions of the **rpc_$** calls.

Chapter 14   Contains reference descriptions of the **rrpc_$** calls.

Chapter 15   Contains reference descriptions of the **socket_$** calls.

Chapter 16   Contains reference descriptions of the **uuid_$** calls.

Chapter 17	Contains reference descriptions of the NCS daemons and utilities.
Chapter 18	Contains reference descriptions of NCS configuration files.
Appendix A	Describes how to use NCS with FORTRAN programs.
Appendix B	Describes considerations for using NCS on Apollo Domain systems.
Appendix C	Describes considerations for using NCS on SunOS systems.
Appendix D	Describes considerations for using NCS on ULTRIX systems.
Appendix E	Describes considerations for using NCS on VAX/VMS systems.
Appendix F	Describes considerations for using NCS on MS-DOS® systems.

A glossary and an index appear after the appendixes.

Summary of Technical Changes

Version 1.5.1 of NCS incorporates the following major changes from previous versions:

- The Network Computing Kernel (NCK) products for SunOS and ULTRIX systems now contain the replicatable version of the Global Location Broker daemon.

- Enhancements to Location Broker software provide support for a wider variety of network and internet configurations.

- We now supply system interface definitions, and header files derived from them, with both the NCK product and the NIDL product. We also supply a new header file for a portable Process Fault Manager (PFM) interface.

- NCK and NIDL now support servers that export more than one version of an interface or implement an interface for more than one type.

- Enhancements to the NIDL Compiler improve the performance and robustness of stubs.

- NIDL syntax has been extended and rationalized.

These and other changes, along with their implications for compatibility, are described further in the *Release Document* for each NCK and NIDL product.

Using this Book

This book is a reference manual for programmers developing applications based on NCS. If you are only running, rather than developing, NCS-based applications, you should not need this book; instead, see *Managing NCS Software*, which explains how to establish and maintain the runtime support necessary for running NCS applications.

NCS is designed for use with a wide variety of programming languages, operating systems, and hardware architectures. However, it is impossible to cover the full range of these possibilities in documentation. In general, the body of this book shows examples written in C for Apollo workstations and other UNIX® systems. Appendixes discuss how to use NCS with FORTRAN programs and how to use NCS on various operating systems.

Related Manuals

For more information on topics related to NCS, see the following documents, which we list with their Apollo order numbers:

- *Managing NCS Software* (011895)
  This book, formerly titled *Managing the NCS Location Broker*, explains how to set up and administer NCS runtime software, including the Location Broker.

- *Network Computing Architecture* (010201)
  This book contains technical specifications for the Network Computing Architecture.

- *Concurrent Programming Support (CPS) Reference* (010233)
  This book describes Concurrent Programming Support (CPS), a set of routines that manage a multitasking environment within a process. Use of CPS on Apollo systems is also described in the *Domain/OS Call Reference* (007196 and 012888).

The Apollo order number for the *Network Computing System Reference Manual* is 010200.

The *Release Document* for each NCK and NIDL product contains information specific to a particular release of the product. This information includes instructions for installation, descriptions of new or changed functionality, and lists of bugs and bug fixes.

Documentation Conventions

In the body of this book, we adopt the following conventions to avoid names or syntaxes that are specific to particular systems:

- We refer to NCS daemons and utilities by leaf names, not full names. For example, we say **llbd** rather than **/etc/ncs/llbd**.

- We omit filename suffixes that are specific to particular systems. For example, we say **llbd** rather than **llbd.exe**.

- We use the symbolic names *idl*, for the system **idl** directory, and *examples*, for the online examples directory.

- In examples that show interaction between the user and the system, we use a dollar sign ($) as a generic prompt.

In the appendixes that address various operating systems, we give names and syntaxes that are correct for each system.

Except where otherwise noted, we use the following typographic conventions:

literal Bold type indicates names, keywords, identifiers, pathnames, or other items that you should supply literally. We also use bold type when we define a new term.

symbolic Italic type indicates symbols for which you should substitute a value. We also use italic type for titles of books and for figure and table captions.

output/code In examples, output that the system displays appears in typewriter font. We also use this font for program source code.

CTRL/ This notation indicates a control character sequence.

| In syntax descriptions and shell command descriptions, a vertical bar separates items in a list of choices.

. . . In syntax descriptions and shell command descriptions, ellipsis points indicate that the preceding item can be repeated one or more times. In source code examples, they indicate that code has been omitted.

[   ] In shell command descriptions, square brackets enclose optional items.

{   } In shell command descriptions, braces enclose a list from which you choose an item.

———— 🔲 ———— This symbol indicates the end of a chapter or a part of the manual.

Mike Kong is a technical writer in the network computing group at Apollo Computer Inc.

Terence H. Dineen, Paul J. Leach, Elizabeth A. Martin, Nathaniel W. Mishkin, Joseph N. Pato, and Geoffrey L. Wyant are the designers of the Network Computing Architecture and the developers of the Network Computing System.

Chapter 1

Introduction to NCS

The Network Computing System (NCS) is a set of tools for heterogeneous distributed computing. These tools conform to the Network Computing Architecture. This chapter introduces the Network Computing Architecture and NCS.

1.1 NCS and the Network Computing Architecture

NCS is an implementation of the Network Computing Architecture, an architecture for distributing software applications across heterogeneous collections of computers, networks, and programming environments. Programs based on NCS can take advantage of computing resources throughout a network or internet, with different parts of each program executing on the computers best suited for the tasks.

The Network Computing Architecture supports distributed programs of many kinds. One program might perform graphical input and output on a workstation while it does intense computation on a supercomputer. Another program might perform many independent calculations on a large set of data; it could distribute these calculations among any number of available processors on the network or internet. On Apollo systems, the Domain/OS network registry uses NCS to implement a distributed database of account information; requests for information are automatically directed to registry servers that manage the database.

For technical definitions of the components in the Network Computing Architecture, see *Network Computing Architecture*. The Preface contains more information about this and other related books.

1.2 NCS Components

The components of NCS are written in portable C wherever possible. They are available in source code and in several binary formats. Currently, the NCS components are

NCK

- The Remote Procedure Call (RPC) runtime library

- The Location Broker

- The Network Interface Definition Language (NIDL) Compiler

The RPC runtime library and the Location Broker provide runtime support for network computing. These two components, along with various utilities and files, make up the Network Computing Kernel (NCK), which contains all the software you need to run a distributed application. On Apollo systems, NCK is part of standard system software.

The NIDL Compiler is a tool for developing distributed applications.

1.2.1 Remote Procedure Call Runtime Library

The RPC runtime library is the backbone of the Network Computing System. It contains the calls that enable local programs to execute procedures on remote hosts. These calls transfer requests and responses between **clients** (the programs calling the procedures) and **servers** (the programs executing the procedures).

When you write NCS applications, you usually do not use many RPC runtime library calls directly. Instead, you write interface definitions in Network Interface Definition Language and use the NIDL Compiler to generate most of the required calls to the runtime library.

1.2.2 Location Broker

A **broker** is a server that provides information about resources. The Location Broker enables clients to locate specific **objects** (for example, databases) or specific **interfaces** (for example, data retrieval interfaces). Location Broker software includes the Global Location Broker (GLB), the Local Location Broker (LLB), a client agent through which programs use GLB and LLB services, and administrative tools.

The GLB stores in a global database the locations of objects and interfaces throughout a network or internet; clients can use the GLB to access an object or interface without knowing its location beforehand. The LLB stores in a local database similar information about resources on the local host; it also implements a forwarding facility that provides access via a single address to all of the objects and interfaces at the host.

Managing NCS Software describes the administration of the Location Broker.

1.2.3 Network Interface Definition Language Compiler

The NIDL Compiler takes as input an **interface definition** written in NIDL. From this definition, the Compiler generates source code in portable C for client and server **stub** modules. An interface definition specifies the interface between a user of a service and the provider of the service; it defines how a client "sees" a remote service and how a server "sees" requests for its service.

The stubs produced by the NIDL Compiler contain nearly all of the "remoteness" in a distributed application. They perform data conversions, assemble and disassemble packets, and interact with the RPC runtime library. It's much easier to write an interface definition in NIDL than it would be to write the stub code that the NIDL Compiler generates from your definition.

1.2.4 Concurrent Programming Support

Concurrent Programming Support (CPS) is a set of routines that create and manage a multitasking environment within a process. Though it is not strictly part of the Network Computing System, CPS supports many distributed programs, including the replicatable version of the Global Location Broker.

In the multitasking environment that CPS manages, several threads of execution run within one process and address space; each thread is called a **task**. Task creation and switching require less overhead than process creation and switching. CPS allows you to divide a complex program into separate pieces that run in parallel; it is especially useful in servers that simultaneously manage several remote requests.

CPS is implemented on only a subset of the systems for which NCS is available. On Apollo systems, CPS is part of standard operating system software. For information about CPS on other systems, see the *Release Document* for each NCK product.

The *Concurrent Programming Support Reference* describes CPS in detail.

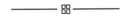

Chapter 2

NCS Concepts

This chapter describes the basic concepts of the Network Computing System. Some of these concepts are unique to the Network Computing Architecture; others, such as sockets and ports, apply to networking software in general.

2.1 Object Orientation

The Network Computing Architecture is object oriented. Programs access objects through interfaces and are cast in terms of the objects they manipulate rather than the machines with which they communicate. Object-oriented programs are easy to design and can readily accommodate changes to hardware and network configurations.

2.1.1 Objects, Types, and Interfaces

An **object** is an entity accessed via well-defined operations. A file, a directory, a database, a serial line, a printer, and a processor can all be objects.

Every object has a **type**. Programs can access any object of a given type through one or more **interfaces**; each interface is a set of **operations** that can be applied to any of those objects. For example, you can classify several printer queues as objects of one type; any of these objects can be accessed through a **directory** interface that includes operations to add, delete, and list jobs in the queues.

As another example of how objects, types, and interfaces apply to NCS, consider databases as objects. Programs can access databases through two interfaces: an **update** interface with operations such as **update$add** and **update$delete** and a **lookup** interface with operations such as **lookup$byname** and **lookup$bynumber**.

2.1.2 UUIDs

NCS identifies every object, type, and interface by a **Universal Unique Identifier**
(UUID). The Network Computing Architecture defines a UUID as a 16-byte quantity
indicating the host on which the UUID is created and the time at which it is created.
Six bytes indicate the time, two are reserved, and eight indicate the host.

NCK contains a **uuid_gen** utility that generates UUIDs as text strings or as data structures
defined in C or Pascal. The string representation used by the NIDL Compiler and by the
NCK utilities consists of 28 hexadecimal characters arranged as in this example:

```
3a2f883c4000.0d.00.00.fb.40.00.00.00
```

2.1.3 Clients and Servers

A **client** is a program that makes remote procedure calls. A remote procedure call requests
that a particular operation be performed on a particular object.

A **server** is a program that implements one or more interfaces and provides access to one
or more objects. A server accepts requests for operations in any of its interfaces. When a
server receives a request from a client, it executes procedures to perform the operation
and it sends a response to the client.

All NCS applications involve communication between clients and servers through interfaces.
However, some applications do not involve specific objects and types. If your application
operates on only one object, you can specify **uuid_$nil**, the nil UUID, as the identifier for
its type. If your application does not operate on any object, you can specify **uuid_$nil** for
both the type and the object.

2.1.4 Replicated Objects

An object can be **replicated**. Replicas are copies of an object; all replicas of an object
have the same UUID. The Global Location Broker database, which we describe in Section
2.6, can be a replicated object. On Apollo systems, the network registry and the network
root directory (//) are replicated objects. Replicating an object can ensure the availability
of information or services despite hardware or network failure.

Replicas can be **weakly consistent** or **strongly consistent**. Weak consistency allows access
to replicas even at times when they are not identical. Weak consistency is preferred when
high availability of an object is desired and small discrepancies among its replicas can be
tolerated; a change made to one replica will eventually be propagated to the other replicas,
but while propagation is pending, all replicas remain accessible. Strong consistency requires
that all replicas be identical whenever they are accessible; this ensures uniformity at the
cost of reduced availability. Replicated GLB databases are weakly consistent.

2.2 RPC Communications

The RPC runtime library is independent of any underlying communications protocol. An application based on NCS can therefore use several different protocols transparently. The destination address of a message automatically determines the protocol to be used; both the sending host and the receiving host must support the protocol.

Currently, the RPC runtime library can use both the Domain protocols (**DDS**) and the DARPA Internet Protocols (**IP**). An NCS application that runs on an Apollo workstation, for example, can access foreign hosts via IP and can access other Apollo workstations via either IP or DDS, because Apollo workstations support both DDS and IP. The program selects the protocol simply by specifying it in the destination address.

2.2.1 Sockets

NCS RPC uses the Berkeley UNIX **socket** abstraction for interprocess communications. A socket is an endpoint for communications, in the form of a message queue. An RPC server "listens" on one or more sockets: it receives any message delivered to a socket on which it is listening.

Figure 2-1 illustrates RPC communications. Two servers run on one host and three clients run on other hosts. One server listens on an IP socket. The other server listens on both an IP socket and a DDS socket.

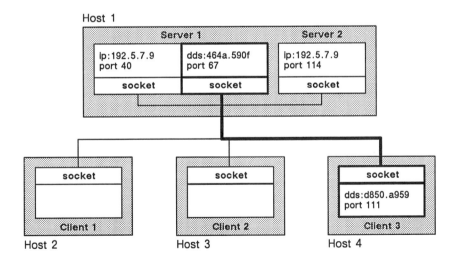

Figure 2-1. RPC Communications

2.2.2 Socket Addresses

Each socket is identified uniquely by a **socket address**. A socket address, sometimes called a **sockaddr**, is a data structure that specifies the socket's

- Address family

- Network address

- Port number

The **address family**, also called the **protocol family**, determines the communications protocol used to deliver messages and the structure of the addresses used to represent communications endpoints.

The **network address**, given the address family, uniquely identifies a host and contains information sufficient to establish communication with the host. Hosts also have **host IDs**; a host ID uniquely identifies a host but may not be sufficient to establish communication. In the IP family, the network address and the host ID are identical. In the DDS family, a network address consists of a network ID and a host ID.

The **port number** specifies a communications endpoint within a host. The terms "port" and "socket" are synonymous, but "port number" and "socket address" are not. A port number is one of the three parts in a socket address. For example, a port number might be represented as the character string "77", while a socket address might be represented as "ip:wooster[77]".

Figure 2-2 illustrates the structure of socket addresses in the DDS and IP families.

DDS Socket Address

Family	Port	Network Address	
		Network ID	Host ID
16-bit Integer	16-bit Integer	32-bit Integer	32-bit Integer

IP Socket Address

Family	Port	Network Address
		Host ID
16-bit Integer	16-bit Integer	32-bit Integer

Figure 2-2. DDS and IP Socket Address Structures

A socket address can be represented textually by a string of the form *family:host*[*port*], where *family* is the textual name of an address family, *host* is either a textual host name or a numeric host ID preceded by a #, and *port* is a port number. Several of the NCS calls and utilities accept textual representations of socket addresses as input or produce them as output.

The following examples are textual representations of socket addresses for the IP and DDS address families:

```
ip:capsicum[57]
ip:#192.5.7.9[53]
dds://allium[101]
dds:#88f99.114a[120]
```

2.2.3 Well-Known and Opaque Ports

It is possible to design an interface with a specific port number "built in." Clients of the interface always send to that port; servers always listen on that port. The port used in such an interface is called a **well-known** port. Some well-known ports are assigned to particular servers by the administrators of a protocol. For example, the administrators of the Internet Protocols have assigned the port number 23 to the **telnet** remote login facility; all telnet servers listen on this well-known port and all telnet user programs send to it.

For very widely used services such as telnet, well-known ports offer a simple way to coordinate communication between clients and servers. For most applications, however, well-known ports are impractical. Each protocol family has a limited number of ports, so unless you obtain an assignment from a central administrator, your application's well-known port number is liable to conflict with that of another program.

The NCS Location Broker solves this problem by enabling clients to locate servers easily without direct use of well-known ports. A server can use ports that the RPC runtime library assigns dynamically. The server registers its socket address, including the assigned port, with the Location Broker; a client can then use Location Broker lookup calls to obtain the socket address of the server. The dynamically assigned port is said to be **opaque**, since there is no need for either the client or the server to know the port number.

Although the RPC runtime library supports both kinds of ports, we strongly recommend that you use opaque ports, so that your application can always coexist with other services.

The Local Location Broker itself uses one well-known port to listen for requests. Clients and servers find Global Location Brokers by broadcasting to this port.

Section 2.6 describes the Location Broker.

2.3 The RPC Paradigm

Remote procedure calls extend the procedure call mechanism from a single computer to a distributed computing environment. They enable you to distribute the execution of a program among several computers in a way that is transparent to the application code.

Figure 2–3 shows the flow of ordinary local procedure calls between a calling client and called procedures. Figure 2–4 shows the flow of remote procedure calls and illustrates how the RPC paradigm hides the remote aspects of a call from the calling client. A client uses ordinary calling conventions to request execution of a procedure, as if the procedure were part of the local program, but the procedure is executed by a remote server. The client stub acts as the "local representative" of the procedure; it uses RPC runtime library calls to communicate with the server. Similar activities occur in the server process.

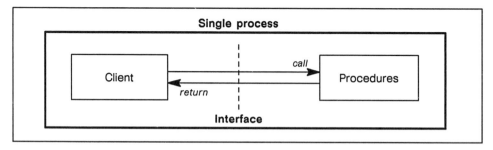

Figure 2–3. Ordinary Local Procedure Call Flow

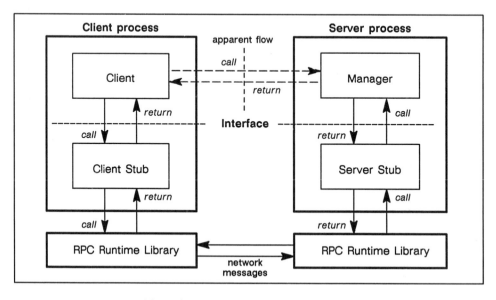

Figure 2–4. Remote Procedure Call Flow

2.3.1 Interfaces

The definition of an interface determines the calling syntax—the **signature**—for each of its operations; client and server procedures use the same syntax. The interface is independent of the mechanism that conveys requests between client and server. It is also independent of the way the operations are implemented. A server that implements the operations in an interface is said to **export** the interface. A client that requests the operations is said to **import** the interface.

For example, suppose that a matrix arithmetic package is running as a server on an array processor. Servers on array processor hosts export a **vector** interface containing operations such as **vector$add** and **vector$cross**. Clients on other hosts import the **vector** interface by calling **vector$add** or **vector$cross**. The client programs run on their local hosts, but the matrix operations run on the remote array processor.

2.3.2 Clients, Servers, and Managers

An RPC client is a program that makes remote procedure calls to request operations. A client does not know how an interface is implemented and might not know the location of a server exporting the interface.

An RPC server is a program that performs the operations in one or more interfaces. It executes these operations on objects of one or more types. A server receives requests for operations from clients and it sends responses containing the results of the operations. A server can export interfaces for one object or for several objects. In the array processor example, there is only one object, the array processor. A file server, however, might manage many file objects.

A server can also be a client; it can even be a client of itself. For example, a server that maintains a replica of an object is a client of all other servers that maintain replicas of the object. We discuss some implications of replicated servers in Subsection 2.4.3.

A **manager** is a set of procedures that **implement** the operations in one interface for objects of one type. It is possible for a server to export several interfaces or to export an interface for several types of objects; each combination of interface and type has its own manager.

Figure 2–4 showed the simplest case, a server that exports one interface for objects of one type. Figure 2–5 illustrates a server that exports two interfaces. Figure 2–6 shows a server that exports one interface to objects of more than one type.

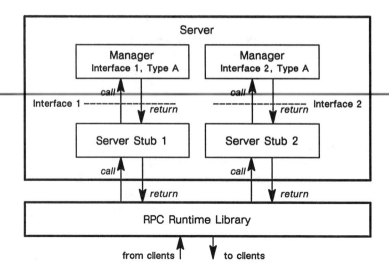

Figure 2-5. An RPC Server Exporting Two Interfaces

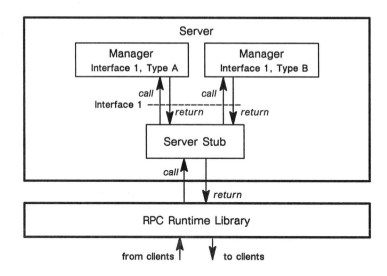

Figure 2-6. An RPC Server Exporting One Interface for Two Types

2.3.3 Handles

When a client makes a remote procedure call, requesting that a particular operation be performed on a particular object, the RPC runtime library needs the following information to transmit the call:

- The object on which the operation is to be performed

- The location of a server that can perform the operation

The client process represents this information about the object and the server location in a **handle**. NCS provides several calls to create and manage handles. Once created, a handle always represents the same object; however, it may represent different servers at different times, or it may not represent a server at all. The server location represented in a handle is called the **binding**. To **bind** a handle is to set its server location.

RPC Handles

An RPC handle is a pointer to an opaque data structure that contains the information needed to access an object. The name for this pointer type is **handle_t**. We use the term **RPC handle** for handle variables of this type and the term **generic handle** for handle variables of other types.

Clients and servers manipulate RPC handles indirectly, through RPC runtime library calls.

Figure 2–7 shows an RPC handle.

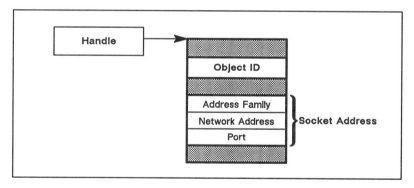

Figure 2–7. An RPC Handle

Binding States for RPC Handles

An RPC handle can exist in three **binding states**:

- An **unbound** handle (also called an **allocated** handle) identifies an object but does not identify a location. When a client uses an unbound handle to make a remote procedure call, the RPC runtime library broadcasts the request to all hosts on the local network. Any server that exports the requested interface and supports the requested object can respond. The client accepts the first response it receives. This mechanism is inefficient and has other disadvantages which we discuss in Subsection 5.3.4.

- A **bound-to-host** handle identifies an object and a host but does not identify the port number of the server that exports the requested interface. When a client uses a bound-to-host handle to make a remote procedure call, the RPC runtime library sends the request to the host identified in the handle. If the requested interface specifies a well-known port, the request goes to that port; otherwise, the request goes to the Local Location Broker forwarding port, and the LLB forwards the request to the server.

- A **fully bound** handle (also called a **bound-to-server** handle) identifies an object and the complete socket address of a server. When a client uses a fully bound handle to make a remote procedure call, the RPC runtime library sends the message directly to the socket address identified by the handle.

In all cases, when the client RPC runtime library receives a response from a server, it binds the handle to the server socket address. Therefore, RPC handles are always fully bound when a remote procedure call returns, and the client does not need to use the broadcasting or forwarding mechanism for subsequent calls to the server.

Table 2–1 shows, for each possible binding state of a handle when a remote procedure call is made, the information that the handle represents, the delivery mechanism of the remote procedure call, and the binding state when the procedure call returns.

Table 2–1. RPC Binding States

Binding State On Call	Information Represented	Delivery Mechanism	Binding State On Return
Unbound	Object	Broadcast to all hosts on the local network	Fully Bound
Bound-to-Host	Object Host	Sent to LLB forwarding port at host	Fully Bound
Fully Bound	Object Host Port	Sent to specific port at host	Fully Bound

2.3.4 Handle Representations and Binding Techniques

NCS offers a choice of handle representations and binding techniques. It allows applications to use

- Explicit or implicit handles

- Manual or automatic binding

The **handle representation**, explicit or implicit, determines whether the client represents handle information with a parameter in each operation or with a global variable. The **binding technique**, manual or automatic, determines whether the client uses RPC handles directly or uses generic handles that are then converted to RPC handles by automatic binding routines. Table 2-2 summarizes the effects of the handle representation and the binding technique on the handle variable.

Table 2-2. Handle Representations and Binding Techniques

	Manual Binding	**Automatic Binding**
Explicit Handle	*Data Type:* **handle_t** *Representation:* Operation parameter	*Data Type:* Generic, user defined *Representation:* Operation parameter
Implicit Handle	*Data Type:* **handle_t** *Representation:* Client global variable	*Data Type:* Generic, user defined *Representation:* Client global variable

Explicit and Implicit Handles

In an application that uses **explicit handles**, each operation in the interface must have a handle variable as its first parameter. This parameter passes explicitly from the client to the server, through the client stub, the client and server RPC runtime libraries, and the server stub. (The server runtime library manipulates the location information in the handle so that on the server side of the application only, the handle specifies the location of the client making the call. The server can thereby identify its client. Of course, the handle always represents the same object.)

In an application that uses **implicit handles**, the handle identifier is a global variable in the client. The operations do not include a handle parameter, and the server does not receive a handle. When the client stub delivers a remote procedure call, it uses the implicit handle variable to supply the handle information needed by the client RPC runtime library.

An implicit handle makes remote procedure calls look more like ordinary procedure calls, since there is no need to pass "special" information in each call. However, this added simplicity comes at the expense of reduced flexibility. Applications that use implicit handles have two major limitations:

- Because the server does not receive the object identifier that a handle contains, the client can access only one object at any time, unless it explicitly passes some other form of object identifier, such as a pathname, as an operation parameter.

- Because all operations in an interface use the same global variable, the client can access only one server at any time. For example, you cannot use implicit handles in applications that divide computation in parallel among several hosts.

Figure 2–8 illustrates the differences between explicit and implicit handles.

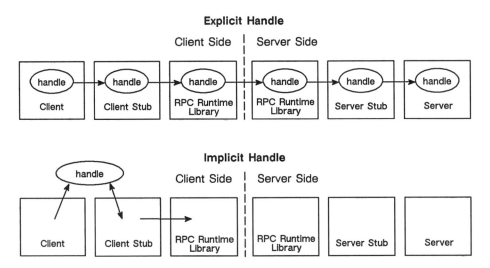

Figure 2–8. Explicit and Implicit Handles

Manual and Automatic Binding

In an application that uses **manual binding**, the handle variable is an RPC handle, and the client directly invokes RPC runtime library calls to create and bind the handle.

In an application that uses **automatic binding**, the handle variable is generic, and the application developer must supply **autobinding** and **autounbinding** routines that convert generic handles (used by the client) to RPC handles (used by the RPC runtime library). The client stub invokes the autobinding routine each time the client makes a remote procedure call; it invokes the autounbinding routine after the remote call returns. The generic handle variable must contain information sufficient for the autobinding routine to generate an RPC handle.

Automatic binding offers convenience at the expense of performance. In an application that uses automatic binding, each time the client stub processes a remote procedure call, it must invoke the autobinding routine to convert the generic handle to an RPC handle. In an application that uses manual binding, the client might bind the RPC handle only once and reuse the handle with each call. The difference in performance is smallest in applications where each call is likely to require rebinding of the handle.

Table 2–3 shows the differences between manual and automatic binding when a client makes a remote procedure call.

Table 2–3. Manual and Automatic Binding in a Remote Procedure Call

Manual Binding	Automatic Binding

1. *Client:*
   Generates RPC handle
   Binds handle as necessary
   Makes procedure call to stub
 	
2. *Client stub:*
   Sends request to server
   Receives response from server
   Returns to client
 	
3. *Client:*
   Receives call return from stub
   Frees RPC handle as necessary
	1. *Client:*
	   Using generic handle,
	     makes procedure call to stub
	
	2. *Client stub:*
	   Calls autobinding routine
	
	3. *Autobinding routine:*
	   Generates RPC handle from
	     generic handle
	   Binds RPC handle as necessary
	   Returns RPC handle to stub
	
	4. *Client stub:*
	   Sends request to server
	   Receives response from server
	   Calls autounbinding routine
	
	5. *Autounbinding routine:*
	   Frees handles as necessary
	   Returns to stub
	
	6. *Client stub:*
	   Returns to client
	
	7. *Client:*
	   Receives call return from stub

2.3.5 Stubs

Both clients and servers are linked (in the sense of combining object modules to form executable files) with stubs. The client stub takes the place of the remote procedures in the client process; the server stub takes the place of the client in the server process. Stubs make remote procedure calls resemble local calls, enabling clients and servers to use the RPC facilities almost transparently.

When a client calls an operation in an interface, it invokes a routine in the client stub. The client stub then

1. **Marshalls** the input parameters into an RPC packet

2. Calls **rpc_$sar**, an RPC runtime library routine called only by stubs, to send the request to the server stub and await a reply

3. Receives the reply packet

4. **Unmarshalls** the output parameters from the reply packet into the data types expected by the client (that is, the data types specified in the interface definition)

5. Converts the output data to the client's native representation, if the server's native representation is different (for example, converts characters from EBCDIC to ASCII)

6. Returns to the client

Similarly, the RPC runtime library at a server host calls a server stub routine when the server receives a request from the client. The server stub then

1. Unmarshalls the input parameters from the request packet into the data types expected by the server (that is, the data types specified in the interface definition)

2. Converts the input data to the server's native representation, if the client's native representation is different (for example, converts characters from ASCII to EBCDIC)

3. Calls the manager procedure that implements the operation

4. Marshalls the output parameter values into an RPC packet

5. Returns the packet to the RPC runtime library for transmission to the client stub

As the preceding summary shows, stub procedures in both the client and the server check the data representation format in incoming packets. Each side uses its native format when it marshalls parameters. A label in the header of each transmitted packet indicates the sender's data representation format for integers, characters, and floating-point numbers. If the sender's representation of a data type is different from the receiver's representation, the receiving stub converts that data type when it unmarshalls values.

Since the Network Computing Architecture supports multiple canonical formats for data representation, there is no conversion of data if the sending and receiving hosts have identical representations. This technique allows heterogeneity at minimum cost.

NCS provides a compiler that automatically generates source code for the client and server stubs from a definition of the interface written in Network Interface Definition Language (NIDL). Section 2.4 gives more information about the NIDL Compiler and the stubs that it generates. Chapters 6 and 7 describe NIDL syntax in detail.

2.4 Interface Definitions and the NIDL Compiler

The Network Computing Architecture defines the Network Interface Definition Language (NIDL). An interface definition written in NIDL defines the signatures for each operation in an interface. The NIDL Compiler takes this definition as input and generates C source code for stubs that you can use in building an application.

2.4.1 Interface Definitions

An interface definition describes the constants, types, and operations associated with an interface. NIDL contains constructs for specifying all of this information, but it contains no executable constructs. NIDL is strictly a declarative language. You can write NIDL in either of two syntaxes, one that resembles C and one that resembles Pascal; most of the examples in this book are in the C syntax.

Chapters 6 and 7 describe the C and Pascal syntaxes of NIDL, and Chapter 4 explains how to write an interface definition. Here, we introduce interface definitions with a simple example. We supply source code for this and several other NCS examples as part of the NIDL product. We refer to the directory where the examples reside as *examples*; the Appendixes specify the location of this directory for particular systems.

The *examples*/**binopwk** directory contains source code files for **binopwk**, an application that performs integer additions on a remote server. This application uses explicit handles and manual binding. The **binopwk.idl** file, shown in Figure 2-9, defines the **binopwk** interface. Section 2.5 describes the **binopwk** client and server programs.

```
%c
[uuid(4448ecb46000.0d.00.00.fe.da.00.00.00),
    port(dds:[19], ip:[6677]), version(1)]
interface binopwk
{
[idempotent]
void binopwk$add(
    handle_t [in] h,
    long [in] a,
    long [in] b,
    long [out] *c
    );
}
```

Figure 2-9. The binopwk/binopwk.idl Interface Definition

The first line of the interface definition states that the definition uses the C syntax of NIDL. The next three lines specify the UUID, well-known ports, version, and name of the interface.

The remainder of the definition defines the signature of **binopwk$add**, the one operation in the interface. The first parameter is an RPC handle. The next two are inputs. The last parameter is an output. This operation has the **idempotent** attribute, which specifies that the operation can safely be executed more than once and allows the RPC runtime library to employ more efficient calling semantics.

Since the **binopwk** example imports no other interface definitions, defines no constants, and uses only predefined data types, it does not illustrate the NIDL import, constant, and type declarations; we give examples of these constructs in Chapters 6 and 7.

To keep the client and server for **binopwk** very simple, we specified well-known ports in the interface definition. However, as we discussed in Subsection 2.2.3, we recommend that you avoid well-known ports in real applications and use opaque ports instead. Section 2.7 describes the **binoplu** example, which uses opaque ports via Location Broker lookups. In Chapters 4 and 5, we develop the **binopfw** example, which uses opaque ports via Location Broker forwarding.

2.4.2 Files Generated by the NIDL Compiler

The NIDL Compiler translates a NIDL interface definition into stub modules that you then link with clients and servers. As we described in Subsection 2.3.5, these modules facilitate remote procedure calls by copying arguments to and from RPC packets, converting data representations as necessary, and calling the RPC runtime library.

The NIDL Compiler generates source code in C that is compatible with other languages. If you write your client or server in Pascal, for example, use a Pascal compiler to compile your source files, use a C compiler to compile the stub source files, and link the resulting object files together. You can also link stubs with FORTRAN programs. (Appendix A discusses FORTRAN considerations).

In addition to stub files, the NIDL Compiler generates header files in C and, optionally, Pascal. To compile the **binopwk** interface definition, set your working directory to *examples*/**binopwk** and run the NIDL Compiler as follows:

```
$ nidl binopwk.idl −m
```

The −m option causes the NIDL Compiler to produce stub and header files that can support multiple interface versions and/or multiple managers within a single server. Most of the examples in this book must be compiled with this option.

Figure 2–10 shows the input and output files involved in the compilation of binopwk.idl.

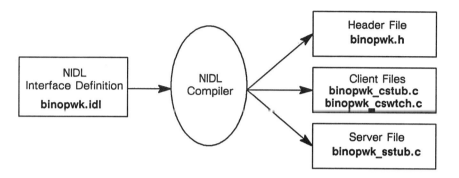

Figure 2–10. Input and Output Files in the binopwk.idl Compilation

On most systems, the NIDL Compiler derives names for its output files by replacing the .idl of the interface definition file with the suffixes **.h**, **_cstub.c**, **_cswtch.c**, and **_sstub.c**. On MS-DOS systems, the default suffixes are **.h**, **c.c**, **w.c**, and **s.c**.

The **binopwk.h** header file declares the **binopwk$add** procedure, initializes the **binopwk_v1$if_spec** interface specifier, and defines the **binopwk_v1$epv_t** data type. It also contains directives to include the standard NCS header files that define basic data types and declare RPC runtime library calls.

An **if_spec** is a data structure that servers pass to the RPC runtime library when they register an interface. An **epv_t** is the data type for an **entry point vector** (EPV), a record of function pointers to the operations in an interface. The NIDL Compiler appends the version number, in this case **_v1**, to the interface name when it generates identifiers for interface specifiers and EPV types.

The **binopwk_cstub.c** and **binopwk_cswtch.c** modules together implement the client stub. They contain a procedure named **binopwk$add**. This procedure marshalls its two input arguments, *a* and *b,* into an RPC packet and calls **rpc_$sar** to send a remote procedure call; when **rpc_$sar** returns, the result is unmarshalled from the returned packet into the output argument, *c.* We explain the roles of stub and switch files in the next subsection.

The **binopwk_sstub.c** module is the server stub. It unmarshalls *a* and *b* from the packets sent by clients, then passes those values to the manager procedure **binopwk$add**. It marshalls the result, *c,* into an RPC packet and returns control to the RPC runtime library, which sends the packet back to the waiting client.

2.4.3 Client Switches and Replicated Servers

As Figure 2–10 showed, the NIDL Compiler generates two client files for an interface: a stub file, *interface*_**cstub.c**, and a switch file, *interface*_**cswtch.c**. This scheme makes possible the creation of **replicated servers**. A replicated server provides access to a replicated object (see Subsection 2.1.4) and works with other servers to maintain consistency among all replicas of the object.

A replicated server functions as both a client and a server of the interface that performs replication. It therefore must call both client stub code (to request operations) and server manager code (to execute operations); this requirement could produce naming conflicts between stub routines and corresponding manager procedures. For example, suppose that a replicated database server implements the **repdb$add** operation. The server program must contain a **repdb$add** manager procedure to execute the operation and a **repdb$add** client stub procedure to request the operation. The server manager and the client stub could not be linked together in the same program.

The introduction of a **client switch** solves this problem. The client switch contains "public" procedures (such as **repdb$add**), while the client stub contains only "private" procedures whose names are not visible outside of the _cstub.c file. The client stub defines an EPV containing function pointers to the private procedures, and the client switch invokes these procedures through the EPV (for example, by calling **repdb_v1$client_epv.repdb$add**).

To build an ordinary client, you link both the client switch and the client stub with the client. The client calls the procedures by their ordinary public names, as specified in the NIDL definition; these procedures are contained in the client switch, which then calls the client stub procedures through the client EPV.

To build a replicated server, you link it with the client stub, but not with the switch. The client code in the server invokes operations not by their public names, but directly through the EPV. Conversely, when the server stub receives a remote procedure call, it invokes the requested operation by its public name, and the local manager code executes the call.

Figure 2–11 illustrates schematically the relationships among clients, client switches, and client stubs, in ordinary clients and in replicated servers.

```
┌─────────────────────────────┐        ┌─────────────────────────────┐
│          Normal             │        │                             │
│        Client Code          │        │      Replicated Server      │
│  if$op(h,a,b,c);            │        │        Client Code          │
│                             │        │                             │
├─────────────────────────────┤        │  (*if_v1$client_epv.if$op)(...);│
│        Client Switch        │        │                             │
│  if$op(h,a,b,c)             │        │                             │
│  {                          │        ├─────────────────────────────┤
│  (*if_v1$client_epv.if$op)(...);│    │                             │
│  }                          │        │         Client Stub         │
├─────────────────────────────┤        │                             │
│        Client Stub          │        │  if_v1$epv_t                │
│  if_v1$epv_t                │        │    if_v1$client_epv = { if$op };│
│    if_v1$client_epv = { if$op };│    │                             │
│                             │        │  static if$op(h,a,b,c)      │
│  static if$op(h,a,b,c)      │        │  {                          │
│  {                          │        │  rpc_$sar(...);             │
│  rpc_$sar(...);             │        │  }                          │
│  }                          │        │                             │
└─────────────────────────────┘        └─────────────────────────────┘
        Ordinary Client                        Replicated Server
```

Figure 2–11. Relationships Among Clients, Client Switches, and Client Stubs

2.5 A Simple Application: binopwk

To build a distributed application, you combine code that the NIDL Compiler generates with code that you write. In Subsection 2.4.2, we described the compiler-generated files for the simple **binopwk** example. Here, we describe the user-written files: **client.c**, the main client module; **server.c**, the main server module; and **manager.c**, the manager.

We present **binopwk** in this section and **binoplu** in Section 2.7 only to give you a glimpse of how NCS is used in practice; we leave many details unexplained. Chapter 5 describes application development more thoroughly.

In this book, to save space, we omit most error-handling code from the source code illustrations, and we do not show any header, stub, or switch files generated by the NIDL Compiler.

The *examples*/**binopwk** directory contains complete source code for **binopwk**.

2.5.1 The Client

The **binopwk** application uses well-known ports, explicit handles, and manual binding. The client code generates and binds an RPC handle that it passes as the first argument in its remote procedure calls.

Figure 2–12 shows the client module **client.c**. This program takes two arguments: the network address of a host where a server is running and the number of passes to execute.

To convert the network address of the server host into a socket address, the client calls **socket_$from_name**, part of the socket address manipulation interface in the RPC runtime library. Because the port parameter for **socket_$from_name** is the predefined constant **socket_$unspec_port**, the resulting socket address specifies a host, but not a particular port at that host.

The client then supplies this socket address to the **rpc_$bind** library call, which creates an RPC handle and binds this handle to the socket address. Because the socket address does not specify a port, the **rpc_$bind** call generates a bound-to-host handle. Note that the first argument to **rpc_$bind**, the object identifier, is **uuid_$nil**, since **binopwk** does not operate on any particular object.

When the client issues its first call to **binopwk$add**, the RPC runtime library at the client host extracts the well-known port number for the server from the **binopwk_v1$if_spec** interface specifier, so that the handle is fully bound when the runtime library sends the request. The handle remains fully bound for all subsequent calls.

The source code for **binopwk** illustrates some programming practices that can help make NCS applications portable to a wide range of systems:

- For portability to VAX C, we use the **globalref** declaration, which for other C compilers we define as a synonym for **extern**. Some of our examples also use the VAX C **globaldef** declaration, which for other C compilers we define as a macro with no replacement text.

- Since C data types can assume different sizes on different systems, we sometimes specify types such as **ndr_$short_int** and **ndr_$char**; these are defined by the Network Data Representation (NDR) protocol, part of the Network Computing Architecture. Section 5.2 gives more information about the NDR types.

```
#include <stdio.h>
#include "binopwk.h"
#include "socket.h"
#include <ppfm.h>
#define CALLS_PER_PASS 100

globalref uuid_$t uuid_$nil;
extern long time();

main(argc, argv)
int argc;
char *argv[];
{
    handle_t h;
    status_$t st;
    socket_$addr_t loc;
    unsigned long llen;
    ndr_$long_int i, n;
    int k, passes;
    long start_time, stop_time;

    if (argc != 3) {
        fprintf(stderr, "usage: client hostname passes\n");
        exit(1);
    }
    passes = atoi(argv[2]);

    pfm_$init((long) pfm_$init_signal_handlers);

    socket_$from_name((long)socket_$unspec, (ndr_$char *)argv[1],
        (long)strlen(argv[1]), (long)socket_$unspec_port,
        &loc, &llen, &st);

    h = rpc_$bind(&uuid_$nil, &loc, llen, &st);

    for (k = 1; k <= passes; k++) {
        start_time = time(NULL);
        for (i = 1; i <= CALLS_PER_PASS; i++) {
            binopwk$add(h, i, i, &n);
            if (n != i+i)
                printf("Two times %ld is NOT %ld\n", i, n);
        }
        stop_time = time(NULL);
        printf("pass %3d; real/call: %2ld ms\n",
            k, ((stop_time - start_time) * 1000) / CALLS_PER_PASS);
    }
}
```

Figure 2-12. The binopwk/client.c Module

2.5.2 The Server

Figure 2–13 shows the server module **server.c**. This program takes one argument, the name of an address family. It calls **socket_$family_from_name** to convert this name into the integer representation of the family, returned as **family**. The server supplies **family** and the **binopwk** interface specifier to **rpc_$use_family_wk**, which creates a socket for the server at its well-known port. The **loc** variable stores this socket address.

In order to communicate with clients, a server must register with the RPC runtime library at its host. The **binopwk** server calls **rpc_$register_mgr** to tell the runtime library that it exports the **binopwk_v1** interface. The first argument to **rpc_$register_mgr**, the type identifier, is **uuid_$nil**, since **binopwk** does not operate on an object.

If a server manages objects of several types, as in Figure 2–6, it registers its managers by calling **rpc_$register_mgr** once for each type, and it registers its objects by calling **rpc_$register_object** once for each object.

After registering with the RPC runtime library, the **binopwk** server calls **socket_$to_name** to extract a textual network address and a port number from its socket address, and it uses this information to print an announcement of its registration. Finally, it invokes **rpc_$listen** to begin handling remote procedure calls. The first argument to **rpc_$listen**, in this case 5, indicates the maximum number of calls that the server is allowed to handle concurrently; this argument is ignored on systems that do not have Concurrent Programming Support (CPS).

The *Concurrent Programming Support Reference* describes CPS. To find out whether CPS is available for a particular operating system, see the *Release Document* for the appropriate NCK product.

```
#include <stdio.h>
#include "binopwk.h"
#include "socket.h"
#include <ppfm.h>

globalref uuid_$t uuid_$nil;
globalref binopwk_v1$epv_t binopwk_v1$manager_epv;

main(argc, argv)
int argc;
char *argv[];
{
    status_$t st;
    socket_$addr_t loc;
    unsigned long llen;
    unsigned long family;
    socket_$string_t name;
    unsigned long namelen = sizeof(name);
    unsigned long port;

    if (argc != 2) {
        fprintf(stderr, "usage: server family\n");
        exit(1);
    }

    pfm_$init((long)pfm_$init_signal_handlers);

    family = socket_$family_from_name(
        (ndr_$char *)argv[1], (long)strlen(argv[1]), &st);

    rpc_$use_family_wk(
        family, &binopwk_v1$if_spec, &loc, &llen, &st);

    rpc_$register_mgr(
        &uuid_$nil,
        &binopwk_v1$if_spec,
        binopwk_v1$server_epv,
        (rpc_$mgr_epv_t)&binopwk_v1$manager_epv,
        &st);

    socket_$to_name(&loc, llen, name, &namelen, &port, &st);
    name[namelen] = 0;
    printf("Registered: name='%s', port=%ld\n", name, port);

    rpc_$listen((long)5, &st);
}
```

Figure 2–13. The binopwk/server.c Module

2.5.3 The Manager

The manager module **manager.c**, shown in Figure 2–14, defines the manager EPV **binopwk_v1$manager_epv** and contains the actual implementation of the **binopwk$add** procedure. This code is linked with the server module.

```
#include "binopwk.h"

globaldef binopwk_v1$epv_t binopwk_v1$manager_epv = {binopwk$add};

void binopwk$add(h, a, b, c)
handle_t h;
ndr_$long_int a, b, *c;
{
    *c = a + b;
}
```

Figure 2–14. The binopwk/manager.c Module

2.5.4 Building and Running the binopwk Programs

The **binopwk** client program is the result of compiling **client.c**, **util.c**, **binopwk_cstub.c**, and **binopwk_cswtch.c**. The server program is the result of compiling **server.c**, **util.c**, **manager.c**, and **binopwk_sstub.c**. All of these modules contain an **#include** directive to incorporate the definitions in **binopwk.h**.

The *examples*/**binopwk** directory contains scripts named **build.bat**, **build.com**, and **build.sh** for MS-DOS, VMS, and UNIX systems, respectively. These scripts run the NIDL Compiler to generate stub, switch, and header files, then run a C compiler to build the client and server programs. To create **binopwk** programs on your system, execute the appropriate script.

To run **binopwk**, first start the server, specifying the address family to use (for example, **dds** or **ip**):

```
$ server ip
Registered: name='ip:elektra', port=6677
```

After the server has registered itself, run the client, specifying the network address of the server host and the number of passes to execute:

$ client ip:elektra 4
```
pass   1; real/call: 20 ms
pass   2;' real/call: 20 ms
pass   3; real/call: 10 ms
pass   4; real/call: 10 ms
```

On most systems, you can stop the server by typing the kill character, often CTRL/C.

2.6 The Location Broker

The Location Broker provides clients with information about the locations of objects and interfaces. Servers register with the Location Broker their socket addresses and the objects and interfaces to which they provide access. Clients issue requests to the Location Broker for the locations of objects and interfaces they wish to access; the broker returns database entries that match an object, type, interface, or combination of these, as specified in the request.

The Location Broker also implements the RPC message forwarding mechanism. If a client sends a remote procedure call to the Location Broker forwarding port on a host, the broker automatically forwards the call to the appropriate server on the host.

This section describes the structure and function of the Location Broker software and databases. *Managing NCS Software* explains how to configure the Location Broker.

2.6.1 Location Broker Software

The Location Broker consists of the following components:

- The Local Location Broker (LLB)

- The Global Location Broker (GLB)

- The Location Broker Client Agent

The **Local Location Broker (LLB)** is a server that maintains a database of information about objects and interfaces located on the local host. The LLB runs as the daemon **llbd**. The LLB provides access to its database for application programs and also provides the Location Broker forwarding service. An LLB must run on any host that runs NCS servers. (On MS-DOS systems, which can run only one process at a time, LLB functionality is automatically incorporated into every server.)

The **Global Location Broker (GLB)** is a server that maintains information about objects and interfaces throughout the network or internet. There are two versions of the GLB daemon: **glbd** and **nrglbd**. The two versions provide the same functionality to clients, but **glbd** is replicatable, while **nrglbd** is not. We provide **glbd** only for Apollo, SunOS, and ULTRIX systems. For other systems, we provide **nrglbd**.

The **Location Broker Client Agent** is a set of library routines that application programs call to access LLB and GLB databases. When a program issues any Location Broker call, the call goes to the Client Agent at the local host. The Client Agent performs the actual remote lookup or update of information in the appropriate Location Broker database.

2.6.2 Location Broker Data

Each entry in a Location Broker database contains information about an object, an interface, and the location of a server that exports the interface to the object. Table 2-4 describes the fields in a database entry.

Table 2-4. Location Broker Database Entry

Field	Description
Object UUID	The unique identifier of the object
Type UUID	The unique identifier that specifies the type of the object
Interface UUID	The unique identifier of the interface to the object
Flag	A flag that indicates whether the object is global (and therefore should be registered in the GLB database)
Annotation	64 characters of user-defined information
Socket Address Length	The length of the Socket Address field
Socket Address	The location of the server that exports the interface to the object

Because a database entry contains only one object UUID, one interface UUID, and one socket address, a Location Broker database must have an entry for each possible combination of object, interface, and socket address. For example, if a server

- Listens on two sockets, **ip:strudel[387]** and **dds://strudel[898]**

- Exports the **update** interface for the **sacherdb** and **dehmeldb** objects

- Exports the **lookup** interface for the **dehmeldb** object

the database must have six entries for this server.

When you look up Location Broker information, you specify any combination of the object UUID, type UUID, and interface UUID as keys, and you request the information from the GLB database or from a particular LLB database. Thus, for example, you can obtain information about all objects of a specific type, all hosts with a specific interface to an object, or all objects and interfaces at a specific host.

2.6.3 Location Broker Registrations and Lookups

Here we describe how servers register their locations with the Location Broker and how clients use Location Broker lookups to locate servers.

Figure 2–15 illustrates a typical case in which a client requires a particular interface to a particular object but does not know the location of a server exporting the interface to the object. In this figure, an NCS server registers itself with the Location Broker by calling the Location Broker Client Agent in its host (1a). The Client Agent registers the server with the LLB at the server host (1b) and with the GLB (1c). To locate the server, the client issues a Location Broker lookup call (2a). The Client Agent on the client host sends the lookup request to the GLB, which returns it through the Client Agent to the client (2b). The client can then communicate directly with the located server (3a, 3b).

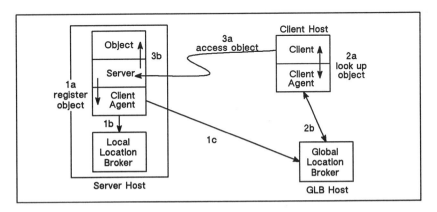

Figure 2–15. Client Agents and Location Brokers

2.6.4 The Local Location Broker

The LLB manages information about servers running on the local host. It also acts as a forwarding agent for remote procedure calls.

The forwarding facility of the LLB eliminates the need for a client to know the specific port that a server uses and thereby helps to conserve well-known ports. The LLB listens on one well-known port per address family. It forwards any messages that it receives to the local server that exports the requested object. Forwarding is particularly useful when the client requesting a service already knows the host where the server is running. The server can use a dynamically assigned opaque port; it needs to register only with the LLB at its local host, not with the GLB. To access the server, the client needs to specify the object, the interface, and the host, but not a specific port.

We recommend that an **llbd** run on every host. However, it is absolutely required only on hosts that run NCS servers.

Managing NCS Software describes Location Broker configuration in detail.

2.6.5 The Global Location Broker

The GLB manages information about servers running anywhere in the network or internet. Clients typically issue lookup calls to the GLB when they do not know at which host a server is running.

As we mentioned in Subsection 2.6.1, there are replicatable (**glbd**) and non-replicatable (**nrglbd**) versions of the GLB daemon. These two versions cannot interoperate on the same network or internet. We recommend that you use **glbd** if possible.

Managing NCS Software describes how to configure the Location Broker and how GLB replication works.

2.7 Using Location Broker Lookups: binoplu

In Sections 2.4 and 2.5, we described **binopwk**, an application that uses well-known ports to coordinate communication between client and server. Here, we modify this application to use opaque ports via Location Broker lookup. The modified example is called **binoplu**. We omit most error-handling code from the illustrations; the *examples*/**binoplu** directory contains complete source code.

2.7.1 The Interface Definition

The interface definition for **binoplu** (Figure 2–16) is identical to the definition for **binopwk** (Figure 2–9) except for the interface UUID, the interface and operation names, and the absence of well-known ports.

```
%c
[uuid(4448ef8ac000.0d.00.00.fe.da.00.00.00), version(1)]
interface binoplu
{
[idempotent]
void binoplu$add(
    handle_t [in] h,
    long [in] a,
    long [in] b,
    long [out] *c
    );
}
```

Figure 2–16. The binoplu/binoplu.idl Interface Definition

2.7.2 The Client

The **binoplu** client program takes only one argument, the number of passes to execute. Unlike the **binopwk** client, which converts a host name to a socket address, the **binoplu** client looks up a server address in the Location Broker database. There is no need for the user to specify a host.

The **lb_$lookup_interface** call in the **binoplu** client program (Figure 2–17) takes the place of the **socket_$from_name** call in the **binopwk** client (Figure 2–12). This lookup call returns a GLB database entry that matches the **binoplu** interface UUID. The returned entry contains, in its **saddr** field, the socket address of a server. The client program uses **socket_$valid_family** to check that the address family in this socket address is valid.

Addresses in Location Broker entries always specify a port number, so the handle that **rpc_$bind** returns is fully bound. The client uses **rpc_$inq_binding** and **socket_$to_name** to obtain information about the server.

```
#include <stdio.h>
#include "binoplu.h"
#include "lb.h"
#include "socket.h"
#include <ppfm.h>

#define CALLS_PER_PASS 100

globalref uuid_$t uuid_$nil;
extern long time();

main(argc, argv)
int argc;
char *argv[];
{
    handle_t h;
    status_$t st;
    lb_$entry_t entry;
    lb_$lookup_handle_t ehandle = lb_$default_lookup_handle;
    unsigned long nresults;
    socket_$addr_t loc;
    unsigned long llen;
    socket_$string_t name;
    unsigned long namelen = sizeof(name);
    unsigned long port;
    ndr_$long_int i, n;
    int k, passes;
    long start_time, stop_time;
```

(continued)

Figure 2–17. The binoplu/client.c Module

```
    if (argc != 2) {
        fprintf(stderr, "usage: client passes\n");
        exit(1);
    }
    passes = atoi(argv[1]);

    pfm_$init((long)pfm_$init_signal_handlers);

    do {
        lb_$lookup_interface(
            &binoplu_v1$if_spec.id, &ehandle, 1L,
            &nresults, &entry, &st);
        if (nresults < 1) {
            fprintf(stderr,
                "interface on valid family not found in lb lookup\n");
            exit(1);
        }
    } while (!socket_$valid_family((long)entry.saddr.family, &st));

    h = rpc_$bind(&uuid_$nil, &entry.saddr, entry.saddr_len, &st);

    rpc_$inq_binding(h, &loc, &llen, &st);

    socket_$to_name(&loc, llen, name, &namelen, &port, &st);
    name[namelen] = 0;

    printf("Bound to port %ld at host %s\n", port, name);

    for (k = 1; k <= passes; k++) {
        start_time = time(NULL);
        for (i = 1; i <= CALLS_PER_PASS; i++) {
            binoplu$add(h, i, i, &n);
            if (n != i+i)
                printf("Two times %ld is NOT %ld\n", i, n);
        }
        stop_time = time(NULL);
        printf("pass %3d; real/call: %2ld ms\n",
            k, ((stop_time - start_time) * 1000) / CALLS_PER_PASS);
    }
}
```

Figure 2-17. The binoplu/client.c Module (continued)

2.7.3 The Server

The **binoplu** server (Figure 2-18) differs from the **binopwk** server (Figure 2-13) in two important ways.

It calls **rpc_$use_family** rather than **rpc_$use_family_wk** to obtain the socket on which it listens. This call requests the RPC runtime library to dynamically assign an available port.

It calls **lb_$register** to register its interface and its socket address with the Global Location Broker. The first two arguments to **lb_$register**, the object and type identifiers, are both **uuid_$nil**, since **binopwk** does not operate on an object. The server supplies the text string "binoplu example" as an annotation for its Location Broker database entry.

The **binoplu** client and server both call **pfm_$init** to initialize the Process Fault Manager (PFM) package that we supply with NCK. Before it begins listening for requests, the server calls **pfm_$cleanup** to set a cleanup handler, a piece of code that executes when a program receives a fatal error. The cleanup handler ensures that the server unregisters from the RPC runtime library and the Location Broker before it exits. (We omitted the PFM initialization and the cleanup handler from the figures for **binopwk**.)

```
#include <stdio.h>
#include "binoplu.h"
#include "lb.h"
#include "socket.h"
#include <ppfm.h>

globalref uuid_$t uuid_$nil;
globalref binoplu_v1$epv_t binoplu_v1$manager_epv;
extern char *error_text();

main(argc, argv)
int argc;
char *argv[];
{
    status_$t st;
    socket_$addr_t loc;
    unsigned long llen;
    unsigned long family;
    boolean validfamily;
    socket_$string_t name;
    unsigned long namelen = sizeof(name);
    unsigned long port;
    lb_$entry_t lb_entry;
    pfm_$cleanup_rec crec;
```

(continued)

Figure 2-18. The binoplu/server.c Module

```
    if (argc != 2) {
        fprintf(stderr, "usage: server family\n");
        exit(1);
    }

    pfm_$init((long)pfm_$init_signal_handlers);

    family = socket_$family_from_name(
        (ndr_$char *)argv[1], (long)strlen(argv[1]), &st);

    rpc_$use_family(family, &loc, &llen, &st);

    rpc_$register_mgr(
        &uuid_$nil,
        &binoplu_v1$if_spec,
        binoplu_v1$server_epv,
        (rpc_$mgr_epv_t)&binoplu_v1$manager_epv,
        &st);

    lb_$register(
        &uuid_$nil, &uuid_$nil, &binoplu_v1$if_spec.id,
        0L, (ndr_$char *)"binoplu example",
        &loc, llen, &lb_entry, &st);

    socket_$to_name(&loc, llen, name, &namelen, &port, &st);
    name[namelen] = 0;
    printf("Registered: name='%s', port=%ld\n", name, port);

    st = pfm_$cleanup(&crec);
    if (st.all != pfm_$cleanup_set) {
        status_$t stat;
        fprintf(stderr,
            "Server received signal - %s\n", error_text(st));
        lb_$unregister(&lb_entry, &stat);
        rpc_$unregister(&binoplu_v1$if_spec, &stat);
        pfm_$signal(st);
    }

    rpc_$listen((long)5, &st);
}
```

Figure 2-18. The binoplu/server.c Module (continued)

2.7.4 The Manager

Except for name changes, the **binoplu** manager (Figure 2–19) is the same as its counterpart in **binopwk** (Figure 2–14).

```
#include "binoplu.h"

globaldef binoplu_v1$epv_t binoplu_v1$manager_epv = {binoplu$add};

void binoplu$add(h, a, b, c)
handle_t h;
ndr_$long_int a, b, *c;
{
    *c = a + b;
}
```

Figure 2–19. The binoplu/manager.c Module

2.7.5 Building and Running the binoplu Programs

The *examples*/**binoplu** directory contains build scripts like those for **binopwk**. To build the **binoplu** programs on a UNIX system, execute **build.sh**; on VMS, **build.com**; and on MS-DOS, **build.bat**.

You must set up Location Broker services on your network or internet before you can run the **binoplu** client and server. A Global Location Broker daemon should be running on at least one host. A Local Location Broker daemon should be running on every host where you intend to run a server. *Managing NCS Software* contains guidelines for configuring the Location Broker and procedures for starting Location Broker daemons.

After you have set up Location Broker services, start the **binoplu** server, specifying the address family to use (for example, **dds** or **ip**):

```
$ server ip
Registered: name='ip:elektra', port=1330
```

Your port number may differ, since **binoplu** uses dynamically assigned opaque ports.

After the server has registered itself, run the client, specifying how many passes to execute:

```
$ client 4
pass   1; real/call: 20 ms
pass   2; real/call: 20 ms
pass   3; real/call: 10 ms
pass   4; real/call: 10 ms
```

———— 🔳 ————

Chapter 3

NCS Software

NCS software includes daemons and utilities, configuration files, interface definition files, header files, and calls. In this chapter, we survey the NCS software to give you a general background for the tutorial information in Chapters 4 and 5.

Table 3–1 lists each piece of NCS software with the name of the product that contains it. On Apollo systems, NCK is part of standard software rather than a separate product.

Table 3–1. NCS Software

Software	Description	Product
nidl	Network Interface Definition Language Compiler	NIDL
uuid_gen	UUID generator	NCK
llbd	Local Location Broker Daemon	NCK
glbd	Global Location Broker Daemon (replicatable)	NCK
nrglbd	Global Location Broker Daemon (non-replicatable)	NCK
drm_admin	Data Replication Manager administrative tool	NCK
lb_admin	Location Broker administrative tool	NCK
stcode	Status code translator	NCK
configuration files	**glb_obj.txt, glb_site.txt,** and **uuidname.txt**	NCK
.idl files	Interface definitions	NCK, NIDL
.h and **.ins.pas** files	C header files and Pascal insert files	NCK, NIDL
calls	**rpc_$, rrpc_$, socket_$, lb_$, uuid_$, error_$, pfm_$,** and **pgm_$** calls	NCK

3.1 Daemons and Utilities

The NCS programs described in this section run as shell commands. The utilities **nidl** and **uuid_gen** help you to develop distributed applications. The Location Broker daemons **glbd** and **llbd** enable client applications to locate servers on remote hosts. The administrative tools **drm_admin** and **lb_admin** help you to maintain Location Broker databases. The **stcode** utility translates status codes.

Chapter 17 contains reference documentation for these daemons and utilities.

3.1.1 NIDL Compiler

The NIDL Compiler, **nidl**, compiles interface definitions. It takes as input an interface definition written in NIDL. It produces as output a server stub, a client stub, and a client switch (all in C), together with header files (in C and/or Pascal).

3.1.2 UUID Generator

The **uuid_gen** utility generates a UUID. Depending on the options you specify, **uuid_gen** produces as output a character string representing a UUID, a C or Pascal initialization for the UUID, or a skeletal interface definition in the C or Pascal syntax of NIDL.

3.1.3 Location Broker Daemons

NCK includes daemons that manage the Local Location Broker (LLB) database and the Global Location Broker (GLB) database.

Any host that runs an RPC server must also run the LLB daemon, **llbd**. (On MS-DOS systems, which can run only one process at a time, LLB functionality is automatically incorporated into every server.)

On any network or internet that supports NCS activity, at least one host must run a GLB daemon. There are two versions of the GLB daemon: **glbd** and **nrglbd**. We provide the replicatable version, **glbd**, only for Apollo, SunOS, and ULTRIX systems. For other systems, we provide the non-replicatable version, **nrglbd**.

The Location Broker daemons typically run as background processes. On most UNIX systems, they start at boot time from the **/etc/rc** file. See *Managing NCS Software* for more information on Location Broker configuration and administration.

3.1.4 Location Broker Administrative Tools

NCK includes utilities that administer the Location Broker: **lb_admin**, the Location Broker administrative tool, and **drm_admin**, the Data Replication Manager administrative tool.

The **lb_admin** tool allows you to inspect or modify the contents of a Location Broker database. It provides lookup, register, unregister, and garbage collection operations. It can perform these operations on any LLB or GLB database.

The **drm_admin** tool manages the replication of the GLB database. It can inspect or modify replica lists, merge databases to force convergence among replicas, stop servers, and delete replicas. It does not look up, register, or unregister database entries. Note that we do not supply **drm_admin** for systems that use **nrglbd**, the non-replicatable version of GLB daemon.

See *Managing NCS Software* for procedures to administer NCS software.

3.1.5 Status Code Translator

The **stcode** utility translates hexadecimal status codes into textual error messages.

3.2 Configuration Files

NCS uses configuration files to administer some aspects of its distributed application environment.

glb_obj.txt

This file specifies an alternate object UUID for the GLB. It is used only in special configurations that require several disjoint GLB databases.

glb_site.txt

This file lists network addresses of hosts where a GLB daemon may be running. It assists hosts that cannot locate a GLB by the usual broadcast mechanism.

uuidname.txt

This file associates textual names with UUIDs. The **lb_admin** tool can use these names to identify objects, types, and interfaces; it accepts names as input and displays names as output whenever possible.

Chapter 18 contains reference descriptions of these files. *Managing NCS Software* contains detailed information and procedures for configuration and administration of NCS software.

3.3 The rpc_$ Calls

The **rpc_$** calls constitute the interface to the RPC runtime library. Some of these calls are used only by clients, some only by servers, and some by either clients or servers.

Chapter 13 contains reference descriptions of the **rpc_$** calls.

3.3.1 Client Calls

Most of the **rpc_$** client calls either create a handle or manage its binding state.

rpc_$alloc_handle
  Allocate an RPC handle that identifies a specific object but not a specific server.

rpc_$set_binding
  Set the binding in an allocated handle so that it specifies a socket address.

rpc_$bind
  Allocate an RPC handle and set its binding. This call has the same effect as an **rpc_$alloc_handle** call followed by an **rpc_$set_binding** call.

rpc_$clear_server_binding
  Remove the association of an RPC handle with a server, but retain the association with a host. If a client uses this handle to make a remote procedure call, the call is sent either to a well-known port or to the Local Location Broker forwarding port on the remote host.

rpc_$clear_binding
  Remove the association of an RPC handle with a server and a host. This call saves the handle for reuse in accessing the same object, possibly via a different server. If a client uses this handle to make a remote procedure call, the call is broadcast.

rpc_$dup_handle
  Make a copy of an RPC handle. For clients that use CPS, this call allows each thread of execution within the process to use its own copy of the handle and allows the threads to share the resources that the handle identifies.

rpc_$free_handle
  Free an RPC handle.

rpc_$set_async_ack
  Set or clear asynchronous-ack mode in a client. Asynchronous-ack mode allows a client to acknowledge its receipt of replies from servers asynchronously, for greater efficiency. This call has no effect on MS-DOS systems and on systems with CPS; these systems always use asynchronous-ack mode.

rpc_$set_short_timeout

Set or clear short-timeout mode on a handle. If a client uses a handle in short-timeout mode to make a remote procedure call, but the server shows no signs of life, the call fails quickly.

rpc_$sar

Send a remote procedure call request and await a reply from the server. This call is for use only by client stubs that the NIDL Compiler generates, so we do not provide a reference description for it in Chapter 13.

3.3.2 Server Calls

Most of the **rpc_$** server calls initialize the server so that it has a socket on which to listen and is registered with the RPC runtime library on its host.

rpc_$use_family

Create a socket that the server will use to communicate with clients. You specify the address family. The RPC runtime library assigns an available port number for the socket.

rpc_$use_family_wk

Create a socket that uses a well-known port. You specify both the address family and the port number.

rpc_$register

Register an interface with the RPC runtime library. This call is obsolete; use instead **rpc_$register_mgr** and **rpc_$register_object**.

rpc_$register_mgr

Register a manager with the RPC runtime library. You specify an interface, a type for which the server exports the interface, and a set of manager procedures that implement the interface for the type. Any server that contains more than one manager or more than one version of a manager must use this call rather than **rpc_$register**.

rpc_$register_object

Register an object with the RPC runtime library. You specify an object for which the server exports interfaces and specify the type of the object.

rpc_$unregister

Unregister an interface that was previously registered with the server via an **rpc_$register_mgr** or **rpc_$register** call. The server will not respond to requests for the unregistered interface.

rpc_$listen
Listen for remote procedure call requests from clients. When a request is received, call the manager procedure for the requested operation and send the result in a reply to the client.

rpc_$inq_object
Return the UUID of the object represented by an RPC handle. This call enables manager procedures to determine the specific object that they must access.

rpc_$shutdown
Shut down. The server stops processing incoming requests and **rpc_$listen** returns.

rpc_$allow_remote_shutdown
Allow or disallow remote shutdown via **rrpc_$shutdown**.

rpc_$set_fault_mode
Control handling of faults that occur in server routines. By default, a server reflects faults back to the client and continues processing. You can use this call to set the mode of fault handling so that the server sends a "communications failure" fault to the client and exits.

3.3.3 Calls for Clients or Servers

The following **rpc_$** calls can be used by either clients or servers.

rpc_$inq_binding
Return the socket address identified by an RPC handle. Typically, a client uses this call to identify the specific server that responded to a remote procedure call.

rpc_$inq_object
Return the UUID of the object represented by an RPC handle.

rpc_$name_to_sockaddr
Given a host name and port number, return the equivalent socket address. This call is obsolete; use instead the **socket_$from_name** call.

rpc_$sockaddr_to_name
Given a socket address, return the equivalent host name and port number. This call is obsolete; use instead the **socket_$to_name** call.

3.4 The rrpc_$ Calls

The **rrpc_$** calls enable a client to request information about a server or to shut down a server.

rrpc_$are_you_there
> Check whether a server is answering requests.

rrpc_$inq_stats
> Obtain statistics about a server.

rrpc_$inq_interfaces
> Obtain a list of the interfaces that a server exports.

rrpc_$shutdown
> Shut down a server, if the server allows it. See **rpc_$allow_remote_shutdown**.

Chapter 14 contains reference descriptions of the **rrpc_$** calls.

3.5 The socket_$ Calls

The **socket_$** calls manipulate socket addresses. Unlike the calls that operating systems typically provide, the **socket_$** calls operate on addresses of any protocol family.

socket_$equal
> Compare two socket addresses.

socket_$to_name
> Convert a socket address to a textual host name and port number.

socket_$to_numeric_name
> Convert a socket address to a numeric host name and port number.

socket_$from_name
> Convert a textual host name and port number to a socket address.

socket_$family_to_name
> Convert the integer representation of a protocol family to its textual name.

socket_$family_from_name
> Convert the textual name of a protocol family to its integer representation.

socket_$valid_family
    Check whether an address family is okay to use.

socket_$valid_families
    List the address families that are okay to use.

socket_$inq_hostid
    Return the host ID part of a socket address.

socket_$set_hostid
    Set the host ID part of a socket address.

socket_$inq_port
    Return the port field in a socket address.

socket_$set_port
    Set the port field in a socket address.

socket_$set_wk_port
    Set the port field in a socket address to a well-known value.

socket_$inq_my_netaddr
    Return the primary network address of the local host for the specified protocol
    family.

socket_$inq_netaddr
    Return the network address part of a socket address.

socket_$set_netaddr
    Set the network address part of a socket address.

socket_$inq_broad_addrs
    Return a list of broadcast addresses that the local host can use.

socket_$max_pkt_size
    Return the maximum packet size for the specified protocol family.

socket_$to_local_rep
    Convert a socket address of type **socket_$addr_t** to a socket address of a type
    specific to the local system. This call is used only on systems with non-standard
    socket address structures.

socket_$from_local_rep
    Convert a socket address from a local type to **socket_$addr_t**. This call is used
    only on systems with non-standard socket address structures.

Chapter 15 contains reference descriptions of the **socket_$** calls.

3.6 The lb_$ Calls

The **lb_$** calls constitute the interface to the Location Broker Client Agent. These calls direct the Client Agent to look up, register, or unregister entries in a Location Broker database.

lb_$lookup_object
> Find entries in the GLB database that match the specified object identifier.

lb_$lookup_type
> Find entries in the GLB database that match the specified type identifier.

lb_$lookup_interface
> Find entries in the GLB database that match the specified interface identifier.

lb_$lookup_object_local
> Find entries in the specified LLB database that match the specified object identifier.

lb_$lookup_range
> Find entries in the specified database (LLB or GLB) that match the specified combination of object, type, and interface UUIDs.

lb_$register
> Register a specific object and interface, that is, create an entry in the Location Broker database. You can specify an entry as local or global. If it is local, it will be registered only in the LLB. If it is global, it will also be registered in the GLB.

lb_$unregister
> Unregister a specific object and interface, that is, remove an entry from the Location Broker database.

Chapter 10 contains reference descriptions of the **lb_$** calls.

3.7 The uuid_$ Calls

The **uuid_$** calls generate and manipulate Universal Unique Identifiers.

uuid_$gen
Generate a new UUID.

uuid_$decode
Convert a character-string representation of a UUID (as generated by the **uuid_gen** program) into a **uuid_$t** value (usable by a program).

uuid_$encode
Convert a UUID into its character-string representation.

uuid_$from_uid
Convert a Domain Unique Identifier (UID) into the equivalent UUID. This call is available only on Apollo systems. It is useful if you want to generate UUIDs for objects that already have Domain UIDs, such as files.

uuid_$to_uid
Convert a UUID into the equivalent Domain UID. This call is available only on Apollo systems. Not all UUIDs can be converted to UIDs.

uuid_$equal
Compare two UUIDs.

Chapter 16 contains reference descriptions of the **uuid_$** calls.

3.8 The error_$ Calls

Most of the NCS calls indicate their completion status via status codes. The **error_$** calls convert these status codes into textual error messages.

error_$c_get_text
Return subsystem, module, and error texts for a status code.

error_$c_text
Return an error message for a status code.

Chapter 9 contains reference descriptions of the **error_$** calls.

3.9 The pfm_$ Calls

We supply with NCS software a portable subset of the Domain/OS **pfm_$** calls. These calls allow programs to manage signals, faults, and exceptions by establishing cleanup handlers.

pfm_$cleanup
> Establish a cleanup handler.

pfm_$enable
> Enable asynchronous faults after they have been inhibited by a call to **pfm_$inhibit**.

pfm_$enable_faults
> Enable asynchronous faults after they have been inhibited by a call to **pfm_$inhibit_faults**.

pfm_$inhibit
> Inhibit asynchronous faults.

pfm_$inhibit_faults
> Inhibit asynchronous faults but allow time-sliced task switching.

pfm_$init
> Initialize the PFM package.

pfm_$reset_cleanup
> Reset a cleanup handler.

pfm_$rls_cleanup
> Release a cleanup handler.

pfm_$signal
> Signal the calling process.

Chapter 11 contains reference descriptions of the **pfm_$** calls.

3.10 The pgm_$exit Call

We supply with NCS software a portable version of the Domain/OS **pgm_$exit** call. This call is often used at the end of a cleanup handler to terminate a program.

pgm_$exit
> Exit from the calling program.

Chapter 12 contains a reference description of this call.

3.11 The System idl Directory

The "system **idl** directory" contains several interface definition files distributed by Apollo. Some of these files define only types and constants; others define local or remote interfaces.

In this book, we sometimes use the symbolic name *idl* for the system **idl** directory. On Apollo systems and other UNIX systems, this directory is usually **/usr/include/idl**.

3.11.1 Interface Definition Files for Types and Constants

The following files in the system **idl** directory define only data types and constants, not operations:

- **base.idl** defines some basic types and constants.

- **nbase.idl** defines types and constants used in network interfaces.

- **ncastat.idl** defines status codes specified by the Network Computing Architecture.

Several of the interface definitions described in the following subsections import one or more of these files.

3.11.2 Interface Definition Files for Local Interfaces

The following files in the system **idl** directory define local interfaces:

- **lb.idl** defines the interface to the Location Broker Client Agent.

- **rpc.idl** defines the interface to the RPC runtime library. The NIDL Compiler automatically imports **rpc.idl** when it compiles the definition for any remote interface.

- **socket.idl** defines types, constants, and operations pertaining to socket addresses and protocol families.

- **uuid.idl** defines types, constants, and operations pertaining to UUIDs.

- **uuid_uid.idl** defines operations that convert UUIDs to Domain UIDs and vice versa. These operations are available only on Apollo systems.

The operations in these interfaces cannot be called remotely. We use NIDL to define the interfaces so that header files in C and Pascal can be generated from a common source. We intend that the NIDL files, rather than the generated header files, serve as readable descriptions of the interfaces.

3.11.3 Interface Definition Files for Remote Interfaces

The following files in the system **idl** directory define remote interfaces:

- **conv.idl** defines operations that manage client-server conversations.

- **glb.idl** defines the interface to the Global Location Broker.

- **llb.idl** defines the interface to the Local Location Broker.

- **rrpc.idl** defines operations that a client can use to request information about a server or to shut down a server.

You should not ordinarily need to call operations in the **conv_**, **glb_**, and **llb_** interfaces, since you can access most of their functionality through the **lb_** and **rpc_** interfaces.

The **rrpc_** interface is automatically exported by every RPC server. Its operations are implemented by the runtime support for the server and are not part of the server proper.

3.12 Header Files and Insert Files

For each of the interface definition files described in the previous section, we supply a corresponding header file in C. We supply two additional header files that are hand coded, not generated from interface definitions:

- **idl_base.h** defines primitives that are present in NIDL but lacking in C, such as the **boolean** type; it also declares or defines data types, external functions, and macros used by stubs.

- **ppfm.h** defines a portable interface to the Apollo Process Fault Manager package.

The C header files reside in the **c** subdirectory of the system **idl** directory. Many C compilers support options that allow you to specify this directory as a place to look for header files.

On Apollo systems, we also supply insert files in Domain Pascal. These **.ins.pas** files reside in the **pas** subdirectory of the system **idl** directory. The Domain Pascal compiler has an option that allows you to specify this directory as a place to look for insert files.

———— 🔠 ————

Chapter 4

Writing Interface Definitions

The first step in developing a distributed application is to define its interface or interfaces in Network Interface Definition Language (NIDL). A NIDL interface definition contains

- A heading

- Import declarations

- Constant declarations

- Type declarations

- Operation declarations

The NIDL Compiler uses the information in an interface definition to generate header files and client and server stubs.

In this chapter, we explain how to write an interface definition in NIDL and illustrate the most important features of NIDL. We develop an interface definition for **binopfw,** an application that uses the Location Broker forwarding facility to perform integer additions on a remote server. In the next chapter, we will develop and build the **binopfw** client and server programs.

We introduce NIDL through examples rather than syntax specifications. All of these examples are in the C syntax of NIDL. For detailed descriptions of NIDL, see Chapter 6 (for the C syntax) and Chapter 7 (for the Pascal syntax). For a formal specification of NIDL grammar, see *Network Computing Architecture.*

4.1 Generating Interface UUIDs

Every object, type, and interface has a Universal Unique Identifier (UUID). When you define a new interface, you must generate a new UUID for it.

Typically, you run **uuid_gen** with the **–c** or the **–p** option to generate a skeletal interface definition file in the C syntax or the Pascal syntax of NIDL, as in this example:

```
$ uuid_gen –c > binopfw.idl
$ cat binopfw.idl
%c
[
uuid(4448ee491000.0d.00.00.fe.da.00.00.00),
version(1)
]
interface INTERFACENAME {

}
```

The first line of the skeletal definition is the syntax identifier, which can be either **%c** or **%pascal**. The next part of the definition is the heading, which specifies a name, a UUID, and a version number for the interface. The last part of the definition is an empty pair of braces; import, constant, type, and operation declarations will go between these braces.

By convention, the names of interface definition files end with the suffix **.idl**. To generate names for header, stub, and switch files, the NIDL Compiler replaces the suffix with **.h**, **_cstub.c**, **_cswtch.c**, and **_sstub.c**.

4.2 The Heading

The heading of an interface definition specifies the name and attributes of the interface.

4.2.1 Interface Names

After you have used **uuid_gen** to generate a skeletal interface definition, replace the dummy string "INTERFACENAME" with the name of your interface.

By convention, interfaces for Apollo software have names that end with an underscore, such as **rpc_** and **socket_**, and operations in Apollo interfaces have names such as **rpc_$listen** and **socket_$equal**. Applications have interface names such as **bank** and **primes** and operation names such as **bank$deposit** and **primes$gen**.

4.2.2 Interface Attributes

There are five interface attributes. Any interface that contains operations must have at least the **uuid** attribute or the **local** attribute.

uuid   The Universal Unique Identifier assigned to the interface. No other object, type, or interface can be assigned this UUID.

version   The version number of the interface. If you want several versions of an interface to coexist, you can distinguish them with version numbers.

port   The well-known port or ports on which servers exporting this interface will listen. In most cases, you should not use the **port** attribute; instead, you should allow the RPC runtime library to assign ports dynamically. See the discussion in Subsection 2.2.3.

implicit_handle The global variable containing handle information. If you do not specify this attribute, the handle must be passed as an explicit parameter to each operation.

local   A flag indicating that the NIDL Compiler should generate only header files and insert files (**.h** and **.ins.pas** files), not stubs. If you specify the **local** attribute, the NIDL Compiler ignores any other interface attributes.

4.2.3 Examples of Interface Headings

The heading for the **binopfw** interface definition specifies only an interface UUID, a version number, and the interface name:

```
[uuid(4448ee491000.0d.00.00.fe.da.00.00.00), version(1)]
interface binopfw
```

The heading for the **binopwk** interface definition (see Subsection 2.4.1) specifies well-known ports for the DDS and IP address families:

```
[uuid(4448ecb46000.0d.00.00.fe.da.00.00.00),
    port(dds:[19], ip:[6677]), version(1)]
interface binopwk
```

4.3 Import Declarations

The NIDL **import** declaration specifies another interface definition whose types and constants are used by the importing interface.

The **import** declaration allows you to collect the declarations for types and constants that are used by several interfaces into one common file. For example, if you are defining two database interfaces named **lookup** and **update,** and these interfaces have many constants in common, you can declare those constants in a **dbconstants.idl** file and import this file in the **lookup.idl** and **update.idl** interface definitions:

```
import "dbconstants.idl";
```

Interface definitions can also use the import declaration to import one or more of the files that we supply in the system **idl** directory. (You should never need to explicitly import **rpc.idl**, the interface definition for the RPC runtime library, because the NIDL Compiler automatically imports **rpc.idl** when it compiles any interface without the **local** interface attribute.)

The **–idir** option of the NIDL Compiler allows you to specify a directory from which the Compiler will resolve the pathnames of imported files. You can thereby avoid putting absolute pathnames in your interface definitions.

4.4 Constant Declarations

The NIDL **const** declaration allows you to declare integer, character, or character string constants, as in the following examples:

```
const int ARRAY_SIZE = 100;
const char JSB = "Johann Sebastian Bach";
```

4.5 Type Declarations

NIDL provides a wide variety of data types, including simple types (such as integers, floating-pointing numbers, characters, and enumerations), constructed types (such as sets, strings, structures, unions, arrays, and pointers), and the **handle_t** type. The NIDL type declaration lets you give a name to any of these types.

The general form of a type declaration is

typedef [*type_attribute_list*] *type_specifier type_declarator_list* ;

The *type_attribute_list* is optional.

The following type declaration defines **integer32** as a name for a 32-bit integer type:

```
typedef long integer32;
```

4.5.1 Type Attributes

The type attributes **handle** and **transmit_as** specify characteristics of a named type.

The handle Attribute

The **handle** attribute specifies that a type can serve as a generic handle. You supply an autobinding routine to convert the generic handle type to the RPC handle type.

Section 8.3 discusses automatic binding and describes an example that uses UUIDs as generic handles.

The transmit_as Attribute

The **transmit_as** attribute associates a **transmitted type** that stubs pass over the network with a **presented type** that clients and servers manipulate. You supply routines to perform conversions between the presented and transmitted types.

One use of this attribute is to help applications pass complex data types such as trees, linked lists, and records that contain pointers. The NIDL Compiler cannot generate code to marshall and unmarshall these data types, but the **transmit_as** attribute allows you to supply routines to convert the complex types into simpler types that can be marshalled and unmarshalled.

You can also use a transmitted type to pass data more efficiently. The application in the *examples*/**sparse** directory illustrates this technique. The application provides routines that convert between sparse arrays and packed arrays. Stubs transmit packed arrays over the network but present sparse arrays to the client and server programs.

Section 8.2 contains more information on data type conversion.

4.5.2 Field Attributes

The field attributes **last_is** and **max_is** can apply either to members of structures or to parameters of operations. These attributes enable you to pass **open arrays** between clients and servers. An open array is an array whose length is determined at runtime, when an operation that uses it is called. The **last_is** and **max_is** attributes control the amount of data transmitted between client and server and the amount of storage allocated at the server.

The type declaration for a structure containing an open array must specify **last_is** and can also specify **max_is**. Subsections 6.5.3 and 7.5.3 describe the **last_is** and **max_is** attributes; Subsection 8.1.1 discusses them in further detail and presents an example.

4.5.3 Examples of Type Declarations

The following declaration defines the type **sockhandle_t** as the textual representation of a socket address and specifies that this type is to be used as a generic handle:

```
typedef [handle] socket_$string_t sockhandle_t;
```

The interface definition for the **sparse** example declares the type **compress_t** as a structure containing an open array, then declares two array types, **compress_array** and **no_compress_array**:

```
/* a run-length-encoded representation of an array */
typedef struct {
    int last;
    int [last_is(last)] data[CARRAY_SIZE];
} compress_t;

/* this type will be transmitted as a more compact type */
typedef [transmit_as(compress_t)] int compress_array[ARRAY_SIZE];

/* this type will be transmitted as is */
typedef int nocompress_array[ARRAY_SIZE];
```

The complete definition for the **sparse** interface is in the file *examples*/**sparse/sparse.idl**.

4.6 Operation Declarations

Operation declarations specify the signature of each operation in the interface, including the operation name, the type of data returned (if any), and the types of all parameters passed in a call. They also specify various field, parameter, and operation attributes.

The general form of an operation declaration is

[*operation_attribute_list*] *type_specifier operation_declarator* (*parameter_list*) ;

The *operation_attribute_list* is optional. Each entry in the *parameter_list* specifies the type, attributes, and name of a parameter.

The interface definition for the **sparse** example contains the following declaration for the operation **sparse$compress_sum**:

```
[idempotent]
int sparse$compress_sum(
    handle_t [in] h,
    compress_array [in] array
    );
```

4.6.1 Operation Attributes

The operation attributes **idempotent, broadcast, maybe,** and **comm_status** describe characteristics of an operation.

The **idempotent** attribute specifies that an operation can be executed any number of times, not just once. This attribute allows the RPC runtime library to forego enforcement of the default "at most once" semantics. You should specify **idempotent** for any operation that can safely be executed more than once. The **binopfw$add** operation is idempotent.

The **broadcast** attribute specifies that an operation should always be broadcast to all hosts on the local network, rather than delivered to a specific host. The RPC runtime library automatically applies idempotent semantics to any operation with the **broadcast** attribute. We discourage use of this attribute; see the discussion in Subsection 5.3.4.

The **maybe** attribute specifies that there is no need for confirmation that an operation has been executed. You can apply this attribute only if an operation has no output parameters and returns no value.

The **comm_status** attribute specifies that an operation returns a completion status. If a communications error occurs while the operation is executing, a cleanup handler in the client stub will catch the error and return the error code to the client.

4.6.2 Parameters

If an interface uses explicit handles, you must supply a handle as the first parameter in each operation declaration, as in the following example:

```
void exp$op(
    handle_t [in] h,
    int [in] a,
    int [in] b,
    int [out] *c
    );
```

If an interface uses an implicit handle, you must specify the handle variable in an **implicit_handle** attribute of the interface, and the operations in the interface do not require handle parameters:

```
void imp$op(
    int [in] a,
    int [in] b,
    int [out] *c
    );
```

The **in** and **out** keywords in the preceding examples are parameter attributes. Subsections 4.6.5 and 4.6.6 describe the attributes that you can apply to parameters.

4.6.3 Pointers as Parameters

NIDL pointers are really references: they must point to something and cannot be null.

In the C syntax of NIDL, specify a pointer by preceding the parameter name with an asterisk (*). This construct is used primarily for output parameters, which, as in C, must be passed by reference. You can also use pointers to denote input parameters passed by reference.

In the Pascal syntax of NIDL, precede the type name with a circumflex (^) to denote an output passed by reference, but use the **ref** parameter attribute to denote an input passed by reference. Output parameters typically are not pointers in the Pascal syntax.

The NIDL Compiler generates code that can marshall and unmarshall pointers only "at top level" and not within any constructed types. Section 8.2 describes the data type conversion mechanism that allows you to overcome this restriction.

4.6.4 Arrays as Parameters

In the C syntax of NIDL, specify an array by placing the array length in brackets after the parameter name. Array subscripts start at 0. Arrays are always passed by reference, so an output array does not require a preceding asterisk. The following example specifies an array of 13 integers, indexed from 0 to 12, named **outputs**:

```
long [out] outputs[13]
```

In the Pascal syntax of NIDL, the array type constructor specifies an array. Lower and upper bounds indicate the length and the subscripting.

NIDL also supports multidimensional arrays and open arrays. Subsections 6.5.4 and 7.7.2 explain array syntax in more detail.

4.6.5 Parameter Attributes

Characteristics of an operation parameter are specified by **parameter attributes**:

in   The parameter is an input. It passes from client to server.

out   The parameter is an output. It passes from server to client. In the C syntax of NIDL, an output parameter must be a pointer marked by the * operator.

ref (Pascal syntax)   The parameter is passed by reference. Note that **ref** is defined only in the Pascal syntax of NIDL; passing by reference is specified in the C syntax by the * operator.

comm_status   The parameter is a **status parameter**. If a communications error occurs, a fault handler in the client stub will handle the error and pass the error code to the client in this parameter.

For every parameter, you must specify at least **in** or **out**. If a parameter passes in both directions between client and server, specify both **in** and **out**.

4.6.6 Field Attributes

If you pass an open array as an operation parameter, you should use the **last_is** and **max_is** field attributes to control how many elements are transmitted between client and server and how much storage is allocated at the server. In operation declarations, field attributes appear together with parameter attributes, preceding the parameter.

Subsections 6.5.3 and 7.5.3 describe the field attributes. Subsection 8.1.1 discusses them in further detail and presents an example.

4.6.7 Examples of Operation Declarations

The **binopfw** interface definition declares one operation, **binopfw$add**:

```
[idempotent]
void binopfw$add(
    handle_t [in] h,
    long [in] a,
    long [in] b,
    long [out] *c
    );
```

The interface definition for the **primes** example, *examples*/**primes/primes.idl**, declares a **primes$gen** operation:

```
[idempotent]
void primes$gen(
    handle_t    [in] h,
    int         [in, out] *last,
    int         [in] max,
    status_$t   [comm_status, out] *st,
    int         [in, out, last_is(last), max_is(max)] values[]
    );
```

4.7 The binopfw Interface Definition

Figure 4-1 shows *examples*/**binopfw/binopfw.idl**, the complete definition for the **binopfw** interface.

```
%c
[uuid(4448ee491000.0d.00.00.fe.da.00.00.00), version(1)]

interface binopfw
{
[idempotent]
void binopfw$add(
    handle_t [in] h,
    long [in] a,
    long [in] b,
    long [out] *c
    );
}
```

Figure 4-1. The binopfw/binopfw.idl Interface Definition

4.8 Running the NIDL Compiler

After you have written an interface definition, run the NIDL Compiler to generate stub and header files:

$ **nidl** *filename* **–m|–s** [*other options*]

The *filename* argument is the pathname of the interface definition file.

You should specify either the **–m** option or the **–s** option. These options determine how stubs generated by the Compiler will dispatch remote procedure calls. If you specify **–m**, the stubs will support multiple versions and/or multiple interfaces within a single server, enabling you to build a server that exports more than one version of interface and/or implements an interface for more than one type. If you specify **–s**, the stubs will support only one version of one interface. Most of our examples use **–m**, and we recommend that you use this option in your applications.

The reference description of **nidl** in Chapter ,17 describes all of the NIDL Compiler options.

The *examples*/**binopfw** directory contains scripts that build the **binopfw** programs for various systems. The **build.sh** script, intended for use on Apollo workstations and other UNIX systems, invokes the NIDL Compiler as follows:

$ **nidl binopfw.idl –m –idir /usr/include/idl –no_cpp**

The **–idir** option specifies a directory from which the Compiler should resolve pathnames of imported files. The **–no_cpp** option specifies that the interface definition should not be run through a C preprocessor before it is compiled.

On UNIX systems, the compilation of **binopfw.idl** generates files named **binopfw.h**, **binopfw_cstub.c**, **binopfw_cswtch.c**, and **binopfw_sstub.c**. We will use these files to build the **binopfw** client and server programs.

Chapter 5

Developing Distributed Applications

After you have written interface definitions for a distributed application, you write a client program, write a server program, and build the application. In this chapter, we follow the **binopfw** example, whose interface definition we presented in Chapter 4. To illustrate the use of Location Broker lookups, we show excerpts from the **binoplu** example, which we presented in Chapter 2.

We have organized this chapter as follows:

Section 5.1   Introduces the **binopfw** example, compares it with the **binopwk** and **binoplu** examples, and discusses some general considerations for designing distributed applications.

Section 5.2   Contains general advice on using data types portably.

Section 5.3   Explains how to write NCS client programs.

Section 5.4   Describes the **binopfw** client and shows the **client.c** and util.c source code modules.

Section 5.5   Explains how to write NCS server programs.

Section 5.6   Describes the **binopfw** server and shows the **server.c** and **manager.c** source code modules.

Section 5.7   Explains how to build a distributed application.

Complete source code for **binopfw** resides online in the directory *examples*/**binopfw**.

5.1 The binopfw Application

Table 5-1 compares the **binopfw** example with the **binopwk** and **binoplu** examples. In **binopfw**, the user of the client program specifies a server host on the command line, and the server listens on an opaque port dynamically allocated by the RPC runtime library; the server registers with the Local Location Broker on its host so that the LLB can forward calls to the server port. All three **binop** examples use explicit handles and manual binding; the client code generates and binds an RPC handle that it passes as the first argument in its remote procedure calls.

Table 5-1. The binopwk, binoplu, and binopfw Examples Compared

Example	Server Host	Server Port	LB Registration	Call Delivery
binopwk	specified on command line	well-known	none	direct to server port
binoplu	obtained via LB lookup	opaque	global and local	direct to server port
binopfw	specified on command line	opaque	local only	via server host forwarding port

For applications in which the client knows where a server is running, you should use Location Broker forwarding, as illustrated in **binopfw**. The server listens on an opaque port and is not required to register with the GLB. When the client makes its first remote procedure call, the server host LLB forwards the call to the server port. On return, the handle is fully bound, so that any subsequent calls go directly to the server port.

For applications in which the client does not know where a server is running, you should use Location Broker registration and lookup, as illustrated in **binoplu**. The server listens on an opaque port and registers its objects, interfaces, and socket address with the GLB. The client uses a Location Broker lookup call to obtain the server socket address and fully binds the handle to this address.

We recommend that your applications use opaque ports via one of these two techniques rather than well-known ports. See the discussion in Section 2.2.3.

We supply complete source code for all three **binop** examples in the *examples* directory. Sections 2.4 and 2.5 describe **binopwk**; Section 2.7 describes **binoplu**.

5.2 Data Types and Portability

When you develop distributed applications, the client and manager code that you write must conform to the interfaces that you define. The C data types used by your code must therefore be equivalent to the NIDL data types specified in your interface definitions.

Many systems (including most systems with Motorola MC680x0, Intel 80x86, Digital VAX, or IBM System/370 processors) support C scalar types that correspond straightforwardly and exactly to the NIDL scalar types. On other systems, however, C types that match the NIDL types may not exist. A NIDL type may also be matched by different C types on different systems.

The NIDL Compiler generates C code that uses data types defined by the Network Data Representation (NDR) protocol, part of the Network Computing Architecture. Every NIDL scalar type maps to one NDR scalar type; this mapping is the same for all systems. The header file *idl*/c/*idl_base.h* contains C definitions of the NDR types for particular systems.

To ensure portability, you can use NDR data types to declare variables that correspond to scalars specified in your interface definitions. In our examples, we often use the NDR types **ndr_$char**, **ndr_$short_int**, and **ndr_$long_int**.

Network Computing Architecture contains technical specifications for NDR.

5.3 Writing Clients

This section explains how to write an NCS client program. Section 5.4 presents the **binopfw** client code.

5.3.1 Client Structure

The source code for a client program consists of the following elements:

- The header file generated from your interface definition by the NIDL Compiler

- The client application itself, that is, the user-written code that implements the client program and calls the remote procedures

- The client switch generated from the interface definition by the NIDL Compiler

- The client stub generated from the interface definition by the NIDL Compiler

- Any user-written code that performs automatic binding (see Section 8.3) or data type conversion (see Section 8.2)

If a client imports several interfaces, the client source code must include the header file, client switch, client stub, any automatic binding routines, and any type conversion routines for each interface.

The client in the **binopfw** example is built from the following source files:

- **binopfw.h**, the header file generated from **binopfw.idl** by the NIDL Compiler

- **client.c**, the main program

- **binopfw_cswtch.c**, the client switch generated from **binopfw.idl** by the NIDL Compiler

- **binopfw_cstub.c**, the client stub generated from **binopfw.idl** by the NIDL Compiler

- **util.c**, a module containing utility routines that are used by both the client and the server.

5.3.2 Managing RPC Handles

When a client makes a remote procedure call, it must specify to the RPC runtime library the object that it is trying to access. The client uses an RPC handle to represent the object and the location of a server that can execute the call.

Binding Techniques

NCS offers two binding techniques:

- Manual binding, where the client creates and uses RPC handles directly.

- Automatic binding, where the client uses generic handles instead of RPC handles. Whenever the client makes a remote procedure call, the stub calls a user-written autobinding routine that converts the generic handle into an RPC handle.

Like most of the examples in this book and in the online *examples* directory, **binopfw** uses manual binding. Subsection 2.3.4 describes manual and automatic binding and discusses the advantages and disadvantages of these techniques. Section 8.3 presents an example of automatic binding.

Overview of RPC Handle Management Calls

The RPC runtime library contains several calls that client applications can use to create handles, free handles, or change their binding states. Figure 5–1 illustrates the effects of these calls and shows the information represented in each possible binding state of an RPC handle. (See Subsection 2.3.3 for more information about RPC binding states.)

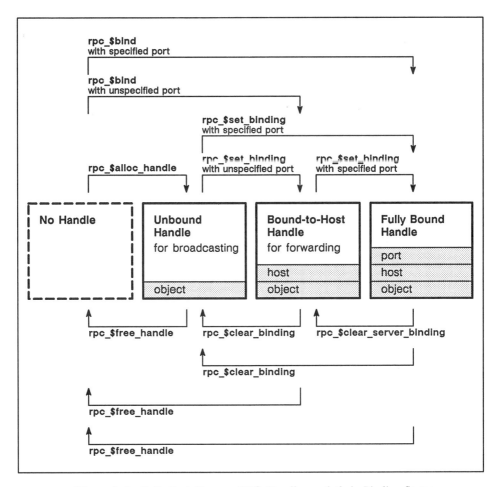

Figure 5-1. Calls that Manage RPC Handles and their Binding States

Creating Handles

As Figure 5-1 illustrates, the **rpc_$bind** and **rpc_$alloc_handle** calls enable you to create an RPC handle in any binding state: fully bound, bound-to-host, or unbound.

The **rpc_$bind** call takes as input an object UUID and a socket address. It creates a handle to represent the object and binds the handle to the address. To obtain a fully bound handle, call **rpc_$bind** with a fully specified address. To obtain a bound-to-host handle, call **rpc_$bind** with a socket address whose port number is **socket_$unspec_port**.

The **rpc_$alloc_handle** call takes as input an object UUID. It creates an unbound handle to represent the object. You can use this handle to broadcast a remote procedure call, or you can invoke **rpc_$set_binding** to set its binding.

Changing Binding States

The **rpc_$set_binding** call sets or resets the binding state in a handle. This call enables a client to change the binding state without freeing and recreating the handle. For example, if an application sequentially accesses several locations of an object, the client can

1. Use **rpc_$alloc_handle** to create a handle

2. Use **rpc_$set_binding** to bind to a server

3. Make the remote procedure call to access the object

4. Repeat steps 2 and 3, binding to servers on each host in sequence, to access the other locations of the object

The client does not need to call **rpc_$clear_binding** before it rebinds the handle to the next server, because **rpc_$set_binding** replaces any existing binding.

As with **rpc_$bind**, you can use **rpc_$set_binding** to obtain a bound-to-host handle, if you supply as input a socket address with a port number of **socket_$unspec_port**. You can use **rpc_$clear_binding** or **rpc_$clear_server_binding** to remove parts of the binding information in a handle.

5.3.3 Obtaining Socket Addresses

To obtain the socket address that **rpc_$bind** and **rpc_$set_binding** require as input, you can use a Location Broker lookup call or a **socket_$from_name** call.

Using Location Broker Lookup Calls

The Location Broker Client Agent offers calls that perform Location Broker lookups by object, type, interface, or any combination of these identifiers. Each lookup call returns as output an array of database entries that match the specified criteria.

Chapter 10 describes all of the Location Broker calls in detail. Here, we illustrate the use of **lb_$lookup_interface**, which looks up servers by interface. The syntax for this call is

lb_$lookup_interface (*&interface*, *&lookup_handle*, *max_results*,
        &num_results, *&results*, *&status*)

where *interface* is an interface UUID, *lookup_handle* indicates a position in a Location Broker database, *max_results* is the maximum number of database entries that can be returned, *num_results* is the number actually returned, *results* is an array of the returned entries, and *status* is the completion status.

A client usually specifies **lb_$default_lookup_handle** as the value for *lookup_handle* in its first Location Broker lookup call; this value indicates that the lookup should start at the beginning of the database. If a lookup operation finds *max_results* entries before it has searched the entire database, it returns a value for *lookup_handle* that indicates the start of the unsearched part of the database. If a lookup operation reaches the end of the database, it returns **lb_$default_lookup_handle** as the value of *lookup_handle*. A client can thus obtain all entries that match the lookup criteria by repeating the lookup call, supplying at each iteration the *lookup_handle* returned by the previous call, until the call returns **lb_$default_lookup_handle**.

Under normal conditions, a series of lookup calls will obtain all matching entries in a database. However, some conditions can cause entries to be skipped or duplicated: two lookup calls might be received by two different GLB replicas, or the database might be modified between lookup calls. Thus, when a client issues uses a series of lookup calls, it might obtain an inconsistent or inaccurate view of the database.

In Section 2.7, we described the **binoplu** example, in which the client uses the Location Broker to find a server for the **binoplu** interface. The client calls **lb_$lookup_interface** as follows:

```
status_$t st;
lb_$entry_t entry;
lb_$lookup_handle_t ehandle = lb_$default_lookup_handle;
unsigned long nresults;
...
do {
    lb_$lookup_interface(&binoplu_v1$if_spec.id, &ehandle, 1L,
        &nresults, &entry, &st);
    if (nresults < 1) {
        fprintf(stderr,
            "interface on valid family not found in lb lookup\n");
        exit(1);
    }
} while (!socket_$valid_family((long)entry.saddr.family, &st));
```

The **binoplu** client initializes **ehandle** to the constant **lb_$default_lookup_handle**, which on input indicates that the lookup should begin at the start of the GLB database. The value 1L for *max_results* indicates that the call can return at most one result; **nresults** is the number of entries actually returned.

If the lookup call returns an entry, the **binoplu** client uses **socket_$valid_family** to check that the address family for that entry is valid for the client host. A client on a DDS host cannot communicate with a server on an IP host, for example, so an entry for such a server should be rejected.

Once the client has obtained the Location Broker entry for a server with a valid address family, it can use the socket address information in the entry to bind its handle. The **binoplu** client calls **rpc_$bind** as follows:

```
h = rpc_$bind(&uuid_$nil, &entry.saddr, entry.saddr_len, &st);
if (st.all != status_$ok) {
    fprintf(stderr, "Can't bind - %s\n", error_text(st));
    exit(1);
}
```

Converting Names to Addresses

If a client knows the name and the address family of the host it wishes to access, it can call **socket_$from_name** to obtain a socket address without using the Location Broker.

The **socket_$from_name** call requires a port number as one of its parameters. Unless the client knows the port number for a server, specify **socket_$unspec_port**. The RPC runtime library will determine the port at runtime, as we describe in the next subsection.

The **binopfw** client, which knows the name of a host where a server is running but not a port number, uses **socket_$from_name** to convert the name into a socket address, then calls **rpc_$bind**:

```
socket_$from_name((long)socket_$unspec, (ndr_$char *)argv[1],
    (long)strlen(argv[1]), (long)socket_$unspec_port, &loc, &llen, &st);
h = rpc_$bind(&uuid_$nil, &loc, llen, &st);
```

5.3.4 Using RPC Binding States

As we explained in Subsection 2.3.4, the RPC runtime library has a different delivery mechanism for each of the three RPC binding states. In this section, we describe how and why an RPC client might use fully bound, bound-to-host, and unbound handles.

Fully Bound Handles

When a client uses a fully bound handle to make a remote procedure call, the RPC runtime library sends the call directly to the host and port identified in the handle.

To obtain a fully bound handle, supply a fully specified socket address to either **rpc_$bind** or **rpc_$set_binding**. Any socket address obtained from a Location Broker will be fully specified. A socket address converted from a host name will not be.

Fully bound handles are always a direct and efficient means of communicating with a server.

Bound-to-Host Handles

When a program uses a bound-to-host handle to make a remote procedure call, the RPC runtime library sends the call to the host identified in the handle.

If a well-known port was specified in the definition of the requested interface, the call is delivered to that port.

Otherwise, the call is delivered to the LLB forwarding port. The LLB—provided a server for the requested object and interface has registered with it—forwards the call to the port on which the server is listening. When the call returns, the RPC runtime library at the client host binds the handle to that port, and any subsequent calls are sent directly to the server.

You can obtain a bound-to-host handle in two ways:

- By calling **rpc_$bind** or **rpc_$set_binding** with an unspecified port in the socket address input parameter

- By calling **rpc_$clear_server_binding** on a fully bound handle

A client typically uses the first method, invoking **rpc_$bind** or **rpc_$set_binding**, after it has used **socket_$from_name** to generate a socket address. For example, the following code sends a matrix multiplication call to a server at the host identified by **hostname**:

```
socket_$from_name (socket_$internet, hostname, hlen,
    socket_$unspec_port, &saddr, slen, &st);
h = rpc_$bind (&matrix_id, &saddr, slen, &st);
matrix$multiply (h, a, b, result, &st);
```

A client typically uses the second method, invoking **rpc_$clear_server_binding**, after it has received an **rpc_$wrong_boot_time** error. If a client is fully bound to a server that exits and then restarts, listening on a new port, the client can reset the binding to the new port by calling **rpc_$clear_server_binding** on the existing handle; the handle will be rebound when the server responds to the next call.

Bound-to-host handles are most efficient when a client already knows the name or address of a host that is running the server it needs. For example, the client might be seeking a service that is provided by all hosts in the network, or the client might have been given the name of a particular host to access. The client does not need to do a Location Broker lookup. The server needs to register with the LLB on its host, but not with the GLB.

Unbound Handles

When a program uses an unbound handle to make a remote procedure call, the RPC runtime library broadcasts the call to all hosts on the local network. If a well-known port was specified in the definition of the requested interface, the call is broadcast to that port. Otherwise, the call is broadcast to the LLB forwarding port.

You can obtain an unbound handle in two ways:

- By calling **rpc_$alloc_handle** to generate a new unbound handle

- By calling **rpc_$clear_binding** on an existing handle to clear the binding

You can also cause an operation to be broadcast by specifying the **broadcast** attribute in its NIDL declaration. If you make a remote procedure call to request an operation that has the **broadcast** attribute, the call is always broadcast, because the RPC runtime library automatically clears any binding of the handle before it issues the call. The client does not need to clear the binding before broadcasting again.

We strongly recommend that you avoid using unbound handles or specifying the **broadcast** attribute. It is preferable, whenever possible, to determine the address of a server host via a Location Broker lookup or the **socket_$from_name** call. The broadcast delivery mechanism has several disadvantages:

- Not all systems and networks support broadcasting.

- Broadcasts are limited to hosts on the local network.

- Broadcasts make inefficient use of network bandwidth and processor cycles.

- Broadcast operations are given short timeout periods and are never retried. They are therefore more likely to produce communications failures.

- The RPC runtime library does not support "at most once" semantics for broadcast operations; it applies idempotent semantics to all such operations.

All of these disadvantages pertain both to **broadcast** operations and to any operations that are called with unbound handles.

The NIDL Compiler issues a warning if you specify the **broadcast** operation attribute without also specifying the **idempotent** attribute. We discuss broadcast and idempotent calling semantics in Subsection 6.6.1.

5.3.5 Identifying Servers

If a client application uses an unbound or bound-to-host handle to make a call, it may wish to identify the particular server that responded, for use in diagnostic or logging output. Because the handle is automatically bound to the responding server when the call returns, you can derive the location of the server from information in the returned handle.

The **rpc_$inq_binding** call extracts a socket address from a handle. The **socket_$to_name** call converts a socket address to a textual hostname. For example, a client might issue the following calls to report the location to which its handle is bound:

```
rpc_$inq_binding(h, &loc, &llen, &st);
socket_$to_name(&loc, llen, name, &namelen, &port, &st);
name[namelen] = 0;
printf("Bound to port %ld at host %s\n", port, name);
```

This technique works even for operations with the **broadcast** attribute. After a client receives a reply to a broadcast, the handle is fully bound, and the RPC runtime library does not clear the binding until the client uses that handle to issue another call.

5.3.6 Errors

Distributed applications handle some errors in much the same way as local applications. For example, if a client issues a remote procedure call to request an operation, and the manager routine for the operation encounters a divide-by-zero error, that error is reflected to the client as if the server had been locally linked with the client.

However, a distributed application can also encounter errors that a purely local application would not. In this subsection, we consider three kinds of errors that are specific to remote procedure calls: communications errors, server crashes, and interface mismatches.

Communications Errors

Communications errors occur in the underlying communications mechanisms, resulting in the failure of a client's request to reach the server or the failure of a server's response to reach the client. Communications errors are usually indicated by the **rpc_$comm_failure** status. We list other RPC runtime library statuses in the **rpc_$intro** section of Chapter 13. To recover, a client can retry the failed call or try to find another server.

You can use a status parameter, identified by the NIDL **comm_status** parameter attribute, to check for communications errors. We describe status parameters in Subsection 5.3.8.

Server Crashes

If a server crashes while handling a remote procedure call, an **rpc_$comm_failure** status is signaled to the client. To the client, the server crash is a form of communications error.

If a server crashes and restarts between remote calls, the failure is usually indicated by an **rpc_$wrong_boot_time** status. (A client can also receive an **rpc_$wrong_boot_time** status if one server fails and a different server starts, using the same port number as the failed server.) Recovery techniques depend on whether the client and the server maintain any state information between procedure calls:

- In a "connectionless" application, one that maintains no state between calls, the client needs only to rebind the handle. The client can clear the port information in the handle by calling **rpc_$clear_server_binding**; then it can check whether the server has restarted. If the server has not restarted, the client should unbind completely by calling **rpc_$clear_binding**, locate a new server, and rebind to the new server.

- In an application that does maintains some state between calls, the client must first clear the state—by unwinding to the point at which it bound to the server, for example—then rebind as in the connectionless case.

Interface Mismatches

An interface mismatch occurs when the interface definition used to build a server differs from the interface definition used to build a client. If you increment the version number in the **version** interface attribute every time you change the interface definition, mismatches are easily detected and are indicated by an **rpc_$unk_if** status. If you do not increment the version number, the resulting errors may be difficult to diagnose.

In most cases, programs cannot recover from interface mismatch errors. To eliminate the errors, you should rebuild the out-of-date client or server.

If you want some clients to import an old version of an interface and some clients to import a new version, you can build one server that exports both versions of the interface. Section 8.4 describes how to build such a server.

You can add operations to an interface and maintain some backward compatibility without changing the version number, provided you do not change the signature or implementation of any existing operation. When you modify the interface definition, place declarations for new operations after all declarations for existing operations; that is, add new operations "at the end" of the interface, not "in the middle." Clients built with the old definition and servers built with the new definition will interoperate correctly. However, if a "new" client requests a new operation from an "old" server, the RPC runtime library will signal an **rpc_$op_rng_error** status. Subsection 5.3.7 shows how you can use a cleanup handler to check for an **rpc_$op_rng_error** status.

5.3.7 Using Cleanup Handlers

The RPC runtime library always signals a fault if an error occurs while it is handling a remote procedure call. You can set cleanup handlers around remote procedure calls to catch and handle any such faults. Support for cleanup handlers is part of the PFM fault management package that we supply with NCK.

Initializing the PFM Package

A client or server should always invoke **pfm_$init** to initialize the PFM package before it invokes any other NCS calls. This call causes C signals to be translated into PFM signals. Attempts to use C signal handlers in the same program as PFM cleanup handlers can therefore result in unexpected behavior.

Setting and Releasing Cleanup Handlers

The **pfm_$cleanup** call sets a cleanup handler. The initial call to **pfm_$cleanup** returns as its value **pfm_$cleanup_set**, a status indicating that the cleanup handler is set; this call also returns as its output a **cleanup record**, a record of the context when the cleanup handler was set.

If a fault is signaled while a cleanup handler is set,

1. The process stack is unwound to the most recent **pfm_$cleanup** call.

2. The cleanup handler is released.

3. The **pfm_$cleanup** call returns the status code for the error that caused the fault.

4. Execution proceeds with the code that immediately follows the **pfm_$cleanup** call.

After you call **pfm_$cleanup**, you should test its return value, so that fault handling code executes only if the value is an error status (indicating that an error has occurred), not if the value is **pfm_$cleanup_set** (indicating that the cleanup handler has just been set).

A cleanup handler typically ends either with code to continue back into the program or with a call to **pfm_$signal** or **pgm_$exit**. If the program will continue, it should call either **pfm_$reset_cleanup** or **pfm_$enable**.

The **pfm_$rls_cleanup** call releases a cleanup handler. You should release a cleanup handler as soon as it is no longer necessary, so that fault handling code is not executed inappropriately. For example, suppose a cleanup handler is set before a remote procedure call, and the cleanup handler contains code that prepares to retry the call. If you do not release the cleanup handler immediately after the call, a fault that occurs later in the program could cause the call to be executed again, unnecessarily.

In NCS applications, a cleanup handler is typically set just before a remote procedure call and released just after the call.

An Example

In Subsection 5.3.6, we explained how to add new operations to an interface and maintain compatibility between "old" clients (which call only the old operations) and "new" servers (which export both old and new operations). Of course, an "old" server cannot execute new operations for a "new" client; when such a client calls a new operation, it should be prepared to receive an **rpc_$op_rng_error** status.

The following example shows how a client might use a cleanup handler to check for **rpc_$op_rng_error** errors:

```
pfm_$cleanup_rec clrec;              /* set the cleanup handler */
st = pfm_$cleanup(&clrec);           /* test the return value */
/*
 * if an error occurred, clean up
 */
if (st.all != pfm_$cleanup_set) {
    if (st.all == rpc_$op_rng_error) {
        found an out-of-date server; find another one and rebind
        pfm_$reset_cleanup(&clrec, &st);
    }
    else {
        some other error occurred; report the error and exit
        pfm_$signal(st);
    }
}
/*
 * otherwise, proceed normally
 */
if$newop(h, input, &output);         /* call the operation */
pfm_$rls_cleanup(&clrec, &st);       /* release the cleanup handler */
```

Multiple Cleanup Handlers

More than one cleanup handler can be in effect at once. If a program has set several cleanup handlers and a fault occurs, the most recently established cleanup handler is entered first, followed by the next most recently established cleanup handler, and so on to the first established cleanup handler if necessary.

The Default Cleanup Handler

On Apollo systems, programs invoked by the **pgm_$invoke** call have a default cleanup handler. The default cleanup handler executes only after all other cleanup handlers have executed; it releases any resources still held by the program. On other systems, there is no default cleanup handler.

Portability Considerations

The PFM package uses the C routines **setjmp** and **longjmp** to implement cleanup handlers. If you use local variables in fault handling code, the unusual flow of control introduced by **setjmp** and **longjmp** can lead some optimizing C compilers to generate errant object code. Here, we explain how to circumvent this problem in a portable way.

If a local variable is modified after a cleanup handler is set but before the cleanup handler is invoked, the variable has an indeterminate value when referenced in the "fault handling code path." To ensure that modifications made to the variable in the "normal code path" are visible to the fault handling code, the variable should be declared with the ANSI C **volatile** qualifier.

Since **volatile** is not yet supported by all C compilers, the PFM header file defines a portable **Volatile** macro. This macro translates to **volatile** on systems whose compilers support the qualifier; on other systems it is null. Any program that uses local variables in cleanup handlers should declare those variables **Volatile**.

The following example shows how to portably use a local variable in fault handling code:

```
Volatile boolean flag;
flag = false;
st = pfm_$cleanup(&crec);
if (st.all != pfm_$cleanup_set) {
    if (flag)
        release_pkt(pkt);
    pfm_$signal(st);
}
pkt = allocate_pkt();
flag = true;
more code
if a fault occurs here, the value of flag is indeterminate
more code
pfm_$rls_cleanup(&crec, &st);
```

Without the **Volatile** qualifier, the code in the example would not be portable. If a fault occurred at the point indicated, thereby invoking the cleanup handler, the value of **flag** would be indeterminate, and the cleanup handler would execute incorrectly.

5.3.8 Using the comm_status Parameter Attribute

NIDL supports a **comm_status** parameter attribute which identifies a parameter as a **status parameter**. A status parameter provides a convenient way to check for communications errors in the execution of a remote procedure call. If you specify **comm_status** for an operation parameter, the NIDL Compiler puts a cleanup handler in the client stub routine for the operation. The cleanup handler catches any error with the **rpc_$mod** module code and passes the error to the client in the status parameter.

All **rpc_$** statuses have the **rpc_$mod** module code. The **rpc_$intro** section of Chapter 13 describes the **rpc_$** statuses.

The examples in this subsection are from the **primes** example, which resides online in the directory *examples*/**primes**.

Declaring Status Parameters in Interface Definitions

A status parameter must have the **comm_status** and **out** attributes and must be of type **status_$t**.

The declaration of **primes$gen**, the operation in the **primes** example, identifies a status parameter:

```
[idempotent]
void primes$gen(
    handle_t [in] h,
    int [in, out] *last,
    int [in] max,
    status_$t [comm_status, out] *st,
    int [in, out, last_is(last), max_is(max)] values[]
    );
```

Checking Status Parameters in Client Programs

A client checks status parameters in the same way that it checks statuses returned by **rpc_$** calls or other NCS calls.

The client in the **primes** example checks a status parameter after **primes$gen** returns:

```
primes$gen(h, &last, MAXVALS-1, &st, values);
/* check comm_status value */
if (st.all != status_$ok) {
    fprintf(stderr, "Error in rpc - %s\n", error_text(st));
    exit(1);
}
```

The **primes** client simply prints an error message and exits if the status parameter indicates an error. In other applications, the client might retry the call that failed or try to find another server, depending on the particular status that is returned.

Initializing Status Parameters in Manager Routines

If a remote procedure call executes without error, the value of its status parameter is not set. The manager routine should therefore set the status parameter to **status_$ok** before it returns.

Following is the **primes$gen** manager routine:

```
void primes$gen(h, last, max, status, values)
handle_t h;
status_$t *status;
ndr_$long_int *last, max, values[];
{
    ndr_$long_int n, highest = values[0], index = 0;

    for (n = 2; n <= highest; n++)
        if (is_prime(n)) {
            values[index++] = n;
            if (index > max) break;
        }
    *last = index-1;
    status->all = status_$ok;
    return;
}
```

5.3.9 Using the comm_status Operation Attribute

NIDL also supports a **comm_status** operation attribute which specifies that an operation returns a completion status. The client stub routine for such an operation contains a cleanup handler that catches any error with the **rpc_$mod** module code and returns the error code as its return value.

The manager routine for an operation with **comm_status** should be coded to return **status_$ok** if successful.

5.4 The binopfw Client

The **binopfw** client is the result of compiling four source code modules: **client.c**, **util.c**, **binopfw_cstub.c**, and **binopfw_cswtch.c**. The switch and stub modules, of course, are generated by the NIDL Compiler from the interface definition. The **util.c** module contains a routine to print error messages; both the client and the server use this routine. The **main** routine is in the **client.c** module.

5.4.1 The client.c Module

Figure 5–2 shows the client module **client.c**.

The client module contains directives to include three NCS header files:

- **binopfw.h**, the header file generated from the **binopfw** interface definition

- **socket.h**, the header file for the **socket_** interface

- **ppfm.h**, the header file for the portable PFM interface

The **binopfw.h** header file contains an **include** directive for **rpc.h**, the header file for the **rpc_** interface; the NIDL Compiler automatically puts such a directive in the header file it generates for any remote interface (that is, any interface without the **local** attribute).

The client declares **uuid_$nil**, the nil UUID, as an external variable; **uuid_$nil** will be the object UUID in the handle. We use **globalref** for portability to VAX C; for other C compilers, the *idl*/c/idl_base.h header file, which is included by **rpc.h**, defines **globalref** as a synonym for **extern**.

The client program takes two arguments: the network address of a host where a server is running and the number of passes to execute. After it has processed its arguments, the client calls **pfm_$init** to initialize the PFM package. We recommend that all programs based on NCS call **pfm_$init** before making any NCS calls.

To convert the network address of the server host into a socket address, the client calls **socket_$from_name**. Because the port parameter given to **socket_$from_name** is the predefined constant **socket_$unspec_port**, the resulting socket address identifies a host but not a particular port at that host.

After **socket_$from_name** returns, the client checks the completion status of the call, and if the status is not **status_$ok**, it prints an error message. Both the client and the server check the completion status of any NCS call that returns a status. They use the **error_text** routine, which is defined in **util.c**, to print error messages.

```
#include <stdio.h>
#include "binopfw.h"
#include "socket.h"
#include <ppfm.h>

#define CALLS_PER_PASS 100

globalref uuid_$t uuid_$nil;
extern long time();
extern char *error_text();

main(argc, argv)
int argc;
char *argv[];
{
    handle_t h;
    status_$t st;
    socket_$addr_t loc;
    unsigned long llen;
    socket_$string_t name;
    unsigned long namelen = sizeof(name);
    unsigned long port;
    ndr_$long_int i, n;
    int k, passes;
    long start_time, stop_time;

    if (argc != 3) {
        fprintf(stderr, "usage: client hostname passes\n");
        exit(1);
    }

    passes = atoi(argv[2]);

    pfm_$init((long) pfm_$init_signal_handlers);

    socket_$from_name((long)socket_$unspec, (ndr_$char *)argv[1],
        (long)strlen(argv[1]), (long)socket_$unspec_port, &loc,
        &llen, &st);
    if (st.all != status_$ok) {
        fprintf(stderr, "Can't convert name to sockaddr - %s\n",
                error_text(st));
        exit(1);
    }
```

(continued)

Figure 5-2. The binopfw/client.c Module

```
    h = rpc_$bind(&uuid_$nil, &loc, llen, &st);
    if (st.all != status_$ok) {
        fprintf(stderr, "Can't bind - %s\n", error_text(st));
        exit(1);
    }

    rpc_$inq_binding(h, &loc, &llen, &st);
    if (st.all != status_$ok) {
        fprintf(stderr, "Can't inq binding - %s\n", error_text(st));
        exit(1);
    }
    socket_$to_name(&loc, llen, name, &namelen, &port, &st);
    if (st.all != status_$ok) {
        fprintf(stderr, "Can't convert sockaddr to name - %s\n",
                error_text(st));
        exit(1);
    }
    name[namelen] = 0;
    printf("Bound to port %ld at host %s\n", port, name);

    for (k = 1; k <= passes; k++) {
        start_time = time(NULL);
        for (i = 1; i <= CALLS_PER_PASS; i++) {
            binopfw$add(h, i, i, &n);
            if (n != i+i)
                printf("Two times %ld is NOT %ld\n", i, n);
        }
        stop_time = time(NULL);
        printf("pass %3d; real/call: %2ld ms\n",
            k, ((stop_time - start_time) * 1000) / CALLS_PER_PASS);
    }
}
```

Figure 5–2. The binopfw/client.c Module (continued)

The client supplies the socket address returned by **socket_$from_name** to **rpc_$bind**, which creates an RPC handle and binds it to the socket address. Because the address does not specify a port, **rpc_$bind** generates a bound-to-host handle. The object UUID in the **rpc_$bind** call is **uuid_$nil**, since **binopfw** does not operate on any particular object.

For diagnostic and pedagogic purposes, the client in this example calls **rpc_$inq_binding** and **socket_$to_name**, so that it can print the host and port to which it is bound.

The first time the client calls **binopfw$add**, the call is sent to the LLB forwarding port at the server host, and the LLB forwards the call to the server. On return, the handle is fully bound, so that all subsequent calls are sent directly to the server port. After each pass, the client prints the real elapsed time per call. After the last pass, it exits.

5.4.2 The util.c Module

The **util.c** module, shown in Figure 5-3, contains only one routine, **error_text**. Both the client and the server use this routine to generate error messages.

```
#include "binopfw.h"

char *error_text(st)
status $t st;
{
    static char buff[200];
    extern char *error_$c_text();

    return (error_$c_text(st, buff, sizeof buff));
}
```

Figure 5-3. The binopfw/util.c Module

5.5 Writing Servers

This section explains how to write an NCS server program. Section 5.6 presents the **binopfw** server code.

5.5.1 Server Structure

The source code for a server program consists of the following elements:

- The header file generated from your interface definition by the NIDL Compiler

- The server initialization code, which registers the interface with the RPC runtime library and the Location Broker

- The manager code, which implements the operations in the interface

- The server stub generated from the interface definition by the NIDL Compiler

- Any user-written code that performs data type conversion (see Section 8.2)

If a server exports several interfaces, the server source code must include the header file, manager code, server stub, and any type conversion routines for each interface.

The server in the **binopfw** example is built from the following source files:

- **binopfw.h**, the header file generated from **binopfw.idl** by the NIDL Compiler

- **server.c**, the main program, which contains server initialization code

- **manager.c**, the manager module

- **binopfw_sstub.c**, the server stub generated from **binopfw.idl** by the NIDL Compiler

- **util.c**, a module containing utility routines that are used by both the client and the server.

5.5.2 Writing Server Initialization Code

The server initialization code usually appears in the server main procedure (**main** in C, **PROGRAM** in Pascal). This code typically

1. Processes any arguments supplied on the command line

2. Creates the sockets on which it will listen

3. Registers the server's objects and managers with the RPC runtime library

4. Registers the server's objects and interfaces with the Location Broker

5. Establishes termination and fault handling conditions

6. Begins listening for requests

We discuss each of these activities, using as an example the **binopfw** server program, **server.c**. (We show the complete server module in Figure 5–4.)

Processing Arguments

The **binopfw** server program takes as an argument the textual name of an address family (for example, **ip** or **dds**). It calls **socket_$family_from_name** to convert this name into the integer representation that the **rpc_$** calls use:

```
family = socket_$family_from_name((ndr_$char *)argv[1],
    (long)strlen(argv[1]), &st);
```

The server calls **socket_$valid_family** to check whether the specified address family is valid for the host on which it is running:

```
validfamily = socket_$valid_family(family, &st);
if (!validfamily) {
    printf("Family %s is not valid\n", argv[1]);
    exit(1);
}
```

Creating Sockets

A single server can listen on several sockets at a time. For example, a server could listen on a Domain socket for requests from DDS hosts and listen on an Internet socket for requests from IP hosts. A server that exports several interfaces can listen on one socket for requests for operations in any of those interfaces. Hence, most servers use only one socket per address family.

To get sockets on which to listen, a server calls **rpc_$use_family** or **rpc_$use_family_wk** once for each socket; **rpc_$use_family** dynamically assigns an available opaque port, while **rpc_$use_family_wk** assigns a well-known port specified in the interface definition. We recommend that you avoid using well-known ports; see Subsection 2.2.3.

The **binopfw** server listens on one opaque port. It calls **rpc_$use_family** to obtain its socket:

```
rpc_$use_family(family, &loc, &llen, &st);
```

In this call, **family** is the integer representation of the address family specified on the command line, **loc** is the socket address for the port assigned by the RPC runtime library, and **llen** is the length of **loc**.

Registering with the RPC Runtime Library

As we mentioned in Subsection 2.3.2, a server can export several interfaces and can offer access through these interfaces to several types of objects. Each combination of interface and type requires a separate manager.

When the server RPC runtime library receives a remote procedure call from a client, it determines the correct manager to execute the call, based on the object and the operation requested, and dispatches the call to that manager. Every server must therefore inform the RPC runtime library about its managers and objects. A server calls **rpc_$register_mgr** once for each manager that it implements and calls **rpc_$register_object** once for each object that it supports.

The **binopfw** server program makes the following call to register its manager with the RPC runtime library:

```
rpc_$register_mgr(
    &uuid_$nil,
    &binopfw_v1$if_spec,
    binopfw_v1$server_epv,
    (rpc_$mgr_epv_t)&binopfw_v1$manager_epv,
    &st);
```

To register a manager, a server must supply a type identifier, an interface specifier, a server EPV, and a manager EPV. Since **binopfw** does not involve any particular type, the **binopfw** server specifies **uuid_$nil** as the type identifier. The interface specifier is defined in the header file, and the server EPV is defined in the server stub; both of these files, of course, are generated by the NIDL Compiler from your interface definition. You must define the manager EPV; typically this definition appears in the manager module.

Since **binopfw** does not involve any particular object, the **binopfw** server does not need to call **rpc_$register_object**.

Section 8.5 presents an example that involves more than one object and more than one type.

Registering with the Location Broker

Most servers register their objects and interfaces with the Location Broker; clients can then use **lb_$** lookup calls to locate objects. A server must make a separate **lb_$register** call to register each possible combination of object, interface, and socket address. For example, if a server

- Listens on one DDS socket and one IP socket

- Exports two interfaces

- Manages three objects

the server should make 12 Location Broker registration calls.

As we've mentioned, the **binopfw** application does not involve an object, so its server specifies **uuid_$nil** as the object UUID for its Location Broker registration. Clients locate this server via Location Broker forwarding, so the server should register only with the Local Location Broker and not with the Global Location Broker.

The binopfw server uses the following call to register with the Location Broker:

```
lb_$register(&uuid_$nil, &uuid_$nil, &binopfw_v1$if_spec.id,
    (long)lb_$server_flag_local, (ndr_$char *)"binopfw example",
    &loc, llen, &lb_entry, &st);
```

This call specifies **uuid_$nil** for the object and type identifiers. The interface identifier is the **id** member of the **if_spec** for **binopfw**, defined in the header file. To register only with the Local Location Broker, the server specifies **lb_$server_flag_local**. It supplies the text string "binopfw example" as an annotation for the database entry. The **loc** specified in this call is the socket address that the server obtained via **rpc_$use_family**.

Unregistering and Fault Handling

When a server starts, it should register itself with the RPC runtime library and with the Location Broker, so that clients can locate the server and communicate with it. When a server exits, it should unregister itself, so that clients do not continue trying to use it.

To unregister from the RPC runtime library, a server calls **rpc_$unregister**. To unregister from the Location Broker, a server calls **lb_$unregister**. In servers that export several interfaces or manage several objects, unregistrations should balance registrations: there should be an **rpc_$unregister** for every **rpc_$register_mgr** and an **lb_$unregister** for every **lb_$register**.

The code to unregister a server typically appears in a cleanup handler. The server sets the cleanup handler before it begins listening for requests. If the server receives a signal, it removes its registrations with the RPC runtime library and the Location Broker before exiting.

Following is the cleanup handler in the binopfw server:

```
st = pfm_$cleanup(&crec);
if (st.all != pfm_$cleanup_set) {
    status_$t stat;
    fprintf(stderr, "Server received signal - %s\n",
        error_text(st));
    lb_$unregister(&lb_entry, &stat);
    rpc_$unregister(&binopfw_v1$if_spec, &stat);
    pfm_$signal(st);
}
```

Listening for Requests

To begin listening for requests, a server calls **rpc_$listen**. The first argument specifies the maximum number of requests that the server can process concurrently; the RPC runtime library uses Concurrent Programming Support (CPS) to handle several calls simultaneously. On systems without CPS, this argument has no effect.

The **binopfw** server uses the following call to begin accepting requests from clients:

```
rpc_$listen((long) 5, &st);
```

Normally, **rpc_$listen** does not return.

After a server creates sockets, registers objects and interfaces, and begins listening, it need not make any more calls. However, servers can register or unregister objects and interfaces while running, and they can also shut themselves down. A server can take these actions on its own (in a task, on systems with CPS) or as part of its execution of client requests (in a manager routine).

5.5.3 Writing Manager Code

A manager implements the operations in one interface for objects of one type. In addition to defining a routine for each operation, the manager module defines the EPV through which these routines are called. Manager modules sometimes also require code to identify objects, to identify clients, or to register objects with the Location Broker.

Defining Manager EPVs

A manager EPV names the routines that implement the operations in an interface. The names of manager EPVs and manager routines are arbitrary, since these names appear only in code that you write, not in code that the NIDL Compiler generates. By convention, we choose EPV names similar to those of the client and server EPVs and routine names similar to the operation names in the interface definition.

The **binopfw** manager defines its EPV as follows:

```
globaldef binopfw_v1$epv_t binopfw_v1$manager_epv = {binopfw$add};
```

We show the complete manager module in Figure 5–5.

Sections 8.4 and 8.5 describe examples in which a server contains more than one manager or more than one version of a manager. In these examples, the manager EPVs help to distinguish different implementations of an interface.

Identifying Objects

In some applications, one manager supports several objects, and the manager must be able to identify the particular object on which a client wishes to operate. Clients in such applications typically use explicit handles, so that a handle passes from client to server with each call. If the operation is manually bound, the manager can call **rpc_$inq_object** to extract the object UUID from the RPC handle. If the operation is automatically bound, the generic handle must be either the object UUID itself or some other data type from which the manager can determine the UUID.

Section 8.3 describes automatic binding in the **bank** example, which uses UUIDs as generic handles.

Identifying Clients

A server may wish to identify clients from which it receives requests, for use in diagnostic or logging output.

The RPC runtime library at a server host manipulates the location information in an RPC handle so that on the server side of an application, the handle specifies the location of the client making the call. Thus, just as a client can identify its server by extracting location information from a handle, a server can identify its client.

A manager routine might issue the following calls to report the location from which a server received a request:

```
rpc_$inq_binding(h, &loc, &llen, &st);
socket_$to_name(&loc, llen, name, &namelen, &port, &st);
name[namelen] = 0;
printf("Request from port %ld at host %s\n", port, name);
```

Registering Objects

In most applications, server initialization code registers objects with the RPC runtime library and the Location Broker. However, if a server manages transient objects that it creates and deletes, the manager routine that creates objects should register them, and the manager routine that deletes objects should unregister them.

Initializing Status Parameters

As we mentioned in Subsection 5.3.8, if an operation has a status parameter (a parameter with the **comm_status** attribute), the manager routine that implements the operation should set the status parameter to **status_$ok** before it returns.

5.6 The binopfw Server

The **binopfw** server is the result of compiling four source code modules: **server.c,**
manager.c, util.c, and **binopfw_sstub.c.** The stub module is generated by the NIDL
Compiler from the interface definition. We saw **util.c,** which contains a routine to print
error messages, in Subsection 5.4.2. The manager module, **manager.c,** contains the
binopfw$add routine that executes the actual addition operations. The **server.c** module
performs server initialization.

5.6.1 The server.c Module

Figure 5-4 shows the server module **server.c.**

The **binopfw** server module, like the client module, includes the **binopfw.h, socket.h,** and
ppfm.h header files. In addition, since the server makes Location Broker calls, the server
module includes **lb.h,** the header file for the Location Broker Client Agent interface.

The server declares as an external variable the manager EPV **binopfw_v1$manager_epv.**
The manager module defines this EPV. The server specifies the EPV when it registers its
manager with the RPC runtime library.

Like the client, the server calls **pfm_$init** to initialize the PFM package before it makes
any NCS calls.

The server program takes as an argument the textual name of an address family. It calls
socket_$family_from_name to convert the textual name into the corresponding integer
representation, then calls **socket_$valid_family** to check whether the family is valid.

```
#include <stdio.h>
#include "binopfw.h"
#include "lb.h"
#include "socket.h"
#include <ppfm.h>

globalref uuid_$t uuid_$nil;
globalref binopfw_v1$epv_t binopfw_v1$manager_epv;
extern char *error_text();

main(argc, argv)
int argc;
char *argv[];
{
    status_$t st;
    socket_$addr_t loc;
    unsigned long llen;
    unsigned long family;
    boolean validfamily;
    socket_$string_t name;
    unsigned long namelen = sizeof(name);
    unsigned long port;
    lb_$entry_t lb_entry;
    pfm_$cleanup_rec crec;

    if (argc != 2) {
        fprintf(stderr, "usage: server family\n");
        exit(1);
    }

    pfm_$init((long)pfm_$init_signal_handlers);

    family = socket_$family_from_name((ndr_$char *)argv[1],
        (long)strlen(argv[1]), &st);
    if (st.all != status_$ok) {
        fprintf(stderr, "Can't get family from name - %s\n",
            error_text(st));
        exit(1);
    }
    validfamily = socket_$valid_family(family, &st);
    if (st.all != status_$ok) {
        fprintf(stderr, "Can't check family - %s\n", error_text(st));
        exit(1);
    }
    if (!validfamily) {
        printf("Family %s is not valid\n", argv[1]);
        exit(1);
    }
```

(continued)

Figure 5–4. The binopfw/server.c Module

```
    rpc_$use_family(family, &loc, &llen, &st);
    if (st.all != status_$ok) {
        fprintf(stderr, "Can't use family - %s\n", error_text(st));
        exit(1);
    }

    rpc_$register_mgr(
        &uuid_$nil,
        &binopfw_v1$if_spec,
        binopfw_v1$server_epv,
        (rpc_$mgr_epv_t)&binopfw_v1$manager_epv,
        &st);
    if (st.all != 0) {
        printf("Can't register manager - %s\n", error_text(st));
        exit(1);
    }

    lb_$register(&uuid_$nil, &uuid_$nil, &binopfw_v1$if_spec.id,
        (long)lb_$server_flag_local, (ndr_$char *)"binopfw example",
        &loc, llen, &lb_entry, &st);
    if (st.all != 0) {
        printf("Can't register - %s\n", error_text(st));
        exit(1);
    }

    socket_$to_name(&loc, llen, name, &namelen, &port, &st);
    if (st.all != status_$ok) {
        fprintf(stderr, "Can't convert sockaddr to name - %s\n",
                error_text(st));
        exit(1);
    }
    name[namelen] = 0;
    printf("Registered: name='%s', port=%ld\n", name, port);

    st = pfm_$cleanup(&crec);
    if (st.all != pfm_$cleanup_set) {
        status_$t stat;
        fprintf(stderr, "Server received signal - %s\n",
            error_text(st));
        lb_$unregister(&lb_entry, &stat);
        rpc_$unregister(&binopfw_v1$if_spec, &stat);
        pfm_$signal(st);
    }

    rpc_$listen((long) 5, &st);
}
```

Figure 5-4. The binopfw/server.c Module (continued)

To obtain a socket on which to listen, the server supplies the address family, in its integer representation, to **rpc_$use_family**. The RPC runtime library assigns an available opaque port to the server; the runtime library returns the socket address for this port in the **loc** parameter.

To register its manager with the RPC runtime library, the server supplies the manager EPV to **rpc_$register_mgr**. The first parameter, the type UUID, is **uuid_$nil**, since the **binopfw** application does not involve any particular type.

To register with the Location Broker, the server calls **lb_$register**. It supplies the following information for its entry in the Location Broker database:

- an object UUID, in this case nil

- a type UUID, also nil

- an interface UUID, taken from the **if_spec**

- a flag indicating that the entry should appear only in the Local Location Broker database

- an annotation

- a socket address

The server uses **socket_$to_name** to extract the host name and the port number from its socket address. It prints this information in a message.

Before it begins listening for requests, the server sets a cleanup handler. If the server receives a signal, it removes its registrations with the RPC runtime library and the Location Broker before exiting.

To begin listening for requests, the server calls **rpc_$listen**.

5.6.2 The manager.c Module

Figure 5–5 shows the manager module **manager.c**.

The manager makes no NCS calls, so it includes only **binopfw.h**, which defines **binopfw_v1$epv_t** and declares the **binopfw$add** operation.

The manager module defines **binopfw_v1$manager_epv**, the manager EPV. We use **globaldef** for portability to VAX C; for other C compilers, the *idl*/c/**idl_base.h** header file defines **globaldef** as a macro with no replacement text.

The definition of **binopfw$add** is just as it would be in a local application.

```
#include "binopfw.h"

globaldef binopfw_v1$epv_t binopfw_v1$manager_epv = {binopfw$add};

void binopfw$add(h, a, b, c)
handle_t h;
ndr_$long_int a, b, *c;
{
    *c = a + b;
}
```

Figure 5–5. The binopfw/manager.c Module

5.7 Building Applications

Following are the usual steps in building an NCS application:

1. For each interface, run the NIDL Compiler to generate a header file and to generate source code for the server stub, the client stub, and the client switch.

2. For each interface, use the C compiler to generate object modules for the server stub, the client stub, and the client switch.

3. For each interface, compile any routines that perform automatic binding or data type conversion.

4. Compile the client application code.

5. Compile the server initialization code and the managers.

6. Link the client application object modules, the client switches, the client stubs, any automatic binding routines, and any type conversion routines to make the executable client.

7. Link the server and manager object modules, the server stubs, and any type conversion routines to make the executable server.

For most of the applications in the *examples* directory, we provide scripts named **build.bat, build.com,** and **build.sh** for MS-DOS, VMS, and UNIX systems, respectively.

Chapter 6

NIDL C Syntax

This chapter describes the C syntax of the Network Interface Definition Language (NIDL). The C syntax of NIDL is a subset of ANSI C, with some constructs added to express NCS remote procedure call semantics.

In this book, we present NIDL syntax informally, sacrificing precision for readability. For a more rigorous specification of NIDL syntax, see *Network Computing Architecture*.

Section 6.1 describes the overall structure of an interface definition. Sections 6.2 through 6.6 describe each of the elements in that structure. Section 6.7 is a detailed discussion of NIDL data types.

6.1 Interface Definition Structure

A NIDL interface definition has the following structure:

```
%c
[ interface_attribute_list ] interface identifier
{
import_declarations
constant_declarations
type_declarations
operation_declarations
}
```

6.1.1 Syntax Identifier

The first line of an interface definition file identifies the syntax of NIDL in which the definition is written. For the C syntax of NIDL, this identifier is **%c**.

6.1.2 Heading

The interface definition heading comprises three elements: an interface attribute list, enclosed in brackets; the keyword **interface**; and the interface identifier.

Section 6.2 describes interface attributes in detail.

6.1.3 Body

The interface definition body consists of one or more of these declarations:

import_declaration
constant_declaration
type_declaration
operation_declaration

A semicolon terminates each declaration. Braces enclose the entire body.

We describe the *import_declaration* in Section 6.3, the *constant_declaration* in Section 6.4, the *type_declaration* in Section 6.5, and the *operation_declaration* in Section 6.6.

6.1.4 Comments

As in the C language, **/*** and ***/** delimit comments:

```
/* all natural */
import "potato.idl";  /* no preservatives */
```

6.1.5 C Preprocessor Directives

On Apollo workstations and other UNIX systems, the NIDL Compiler filters interface definitions through a C preprocessor. Definitions to be compiled on UNIX systems therefore can contain C preprocessor directives.

The NIDL Compiler **−confirm**, **−cpp**, **−def**, and **−no_cpp** options relate to this feature. See the **nidl** reference description in Chapter 17 for more information about these options.

Since preprocessing occurs only on UNIX systems, use of this feature makes an interface definition less portable. On other systems, C preprocessor directives will produce errors.

The interface definitions for the examples in this book do not contain C preprocessor directives. We compile the definitions with the **−no_cpp** option.

6.2 Interface Attributes

As we mentioned in Section 6.1, an interface definition heading specifies the name and attributes of the interface, as follows:

[*interface_attribute_list*] **interface** *identifier*

The *interface_attribute_list* includes one or more of the following elements, separated by commas:

uuid (*uuid_string*)
version (*version_number*)
port (*port_identifier_list*)
implicit_handle (*type_specifier identifier*)
local

If an interface definition contains any operation declarations, its heading must specify at least the **local** attribute or the **uuid** attribute.

6.2.1 UUID Attribute

The **uuid** attribute assigns a Universal Unique Identifier (UUID) to the interface. No other object, interface, or type can be assigned this UUID.

The **uuid** attribute has the following syntax:

uuid (*uuid_string*)

The *uuid_string* is the character-string representation of a UUID. (See the description of the **uuid_$string_t** data type in Chapter 16.)

6.2.2 Version Attribute

The **version** attribute helps you to manage multiple versions of an interface. It has the following syntax:

version (*version_number*)

The *version_number* is an integer.

If you were changing the parameters to an operation in the **dblookup** interface, the interface definition heading could look like this:

```
[uuid(338b5f985000.0d.00.00.37.27.00.00.00), version (2)]
interface dblookup
```

6.2.3 Port Attribute

The **port** attribute specifies the well-known port or ports on which servers that export the interface will listen. It has the following syntax:

port (*port_identifier_list*)

Entries in a *port_identifier_list* are separated by commas. Each entry has the following form:

family : [*port_number*]

The *family* is an address family; the *port_number* is a well-known port. Specify at most one port per family. NIDL supports the following values for *family*:

unix	Local to host (UNIX pipes, portals)
ip	Internetwork protocols (TCP, UDP)
implink	ARPANET Interface Message Processor (IMP) addresses
pup	Xerox PARC Universal Packet (PUP) protocols (BSP, for example)
chaos	Massachusetts Institute of Technology (MIT) CHAOS protocols
ns	Xerox Network Systems (XNS) protocols
nbs	National Bureau of Standards (NBS) protocols
ecma	European Computer Manufacturers Association (ECMA)
datakit	Datakit protocols
ccitt	International Telegraph and Telephone Consultative Committee (CCITT) protocols (X.25, for example)
sna	IBM Systems Network Architecture (SNA) protocols
dds	Apollo Domain/Message (DDS) protocol

The NCS runtime software currently supports the **ip** and **dds** address families.

The interface definition for the **binopwk** example, *examples*/**binopwk/binopwk.idl,** specifies well-known ports for the DDS and IP address families:

```
port(dds:[19], ip:[6677])
```

For most applications, you should not use the **port** attribute; instead, you should allow the RPC runtime library to assign opaque ports dynamically. Subsection 2.2.3 discusses well-known and opaque ports.

6.2.4 Implicit Handle Attribute

The **implicit_handle** attribute indicates that an interface uses an implicit global variable rather than explicit operation parameters to represent objects. It has the following syntax:

implicit_handle (*type_specifier identifier*)

The *type_specifier* and *identifier* are the type and name of the global variable to be used as an implicit handle. The *type_specifier* must be either the RPC handle type **handle_t** or a generic handle type for which you have specified the **handle** type attribute.

If you specify an implicit handle for an interface, the client stub uses this handle to represent objects in all remote procedure calls and it passes no handle information to the server. Operations in the interface should not include handle parameters in their signatures.

If you do not specify an implicit handle, the interface uses explicit handles, and each operation must include a handle as the first parameter in its signature.

The interface definition heading for an interface that uses an implicit handle might look like this:

```
[uuid(338b5f985000.0d.00.00.37.27.00.00.00),
        implicit_handle(handle_t h)]
interface array
```

Subsection 2.3.4 discusses implicit and explicit handles.

6.2.5 Local Attribute

The **local** attribute indicates that the interface definition does not declare any remote operations; therefore, the NIDL Compiler should generate only header files and insert files (**.h** and **.ins.pas** files), not stubs.

If you specify the **local** attribute, the NIDL Compiler ignores any other interface attributes.

6.3 Import Declarations

The NIDL *import_declaration* is analogous to the C preprocessor directive **#include**. It specifies an interface definition file that declares constants and types used by the importing interface. It takes the following form:

import *file* ;

The *file* is the pathname, enclosed in double quotation marks, of the interface definition you are importing.

You can import interfaces defined in either of the NIDL syntaxes. Importing an interface many times has the same effect as importing it once.

The NIDL Compiler translates **import** declarations into C **#include** and Pascal **%include** directives to include header files that correspond to the imported interfaces. The Compiler does not generate stub routines for any operations in imported interfaces.

For example, suppose that the interface definition **aioli.idl** contains a declaration to import the definition for the **garlic** interface:

```
import "garlic.idl";
```

The NIDL Compiler will generate a C header file named **aioli.h** that contains the following **#include** directive:

```
#include "garlic.h"
```

and a Pascal insert file named **aioli.ins.pas** that contains the following **%include** directive:

```
%include "garlic.ins.pas";
```

The stub files that the Compiler generates will not contain any code for **garlic** operations.

6.4 Constant Declarations

The NIDL *constant_declaration* takes the following form:

const *type_specifier identifier = integer | string | value* ;

The *type_specifier* is the data type of the constant you are declaring; the *identifier* is the name of the constant; and the *integer, string,* or *value* is the value you are assigning to the constant. A *value* can be any previously defined constant.

The C syntax of NIDL provides only **int** and **char** constants. NIDL currently does not support constant expressions.

Following are examples of constant declarations:

```
const int MAX = 86;
const char DSCH = "Dmitri Shostakovich";
```

6.5 Type Declarations

The NIDL *type_declaration* lets you give a name to a data type. It takes the following form:

typedef [*type_attribute_list*] *type_specifier type_declarator_list* ;

The *type_attribute_list* is optional.

Some of the constructs that appear in type declarations can also appear in the parameter lists of operation declarations. Section 6.6 describes the use of these constructs in operation declarations. Section 6.7 describes NIDL data types in detail.

6.5.1 Type Attributes

The optional *type_attribute_list* includes one or both of the following elements, separated by commas:

handle
transmit_as (*xmit_type*)

These attributes can appear only in **typedef** declarations.

The handle Attribute

The **handle** attribute specifies that a type can serve as a generic handle. You must supply automatic binding routines to convert this type to **handle_t**, the RPC handle type.

The following example declares a generic handle type **filehandle_t**, a structure containing the textual representations of a host and a pathname:

```
typedef [handle] struct {
    socket_$string_t host;
    char path[1024];
    } filehandle_t;
```

Section 8.3 discusses automatic binding, specifies the signatures for autobinding and autounbinding routines, and describes an application that uses UUIDs as generic handles.

The transmit_as Attribute

The **transmit_as** attribute associates a **transmitted type** that stubs pass over the network with a **presented type** that clients and servers manipulate. You must supply routines that perform conversions between the presented and transmitted types.

There are two primary uses for this attribute:

- To pass complex data types for which the NIDL Compiler cannot generate marshalling and unmarshalling code. Such types include trees, linked lists, and structures that contain pointers.

- To pass data more efficiently. An application can provide routines to convert a data type between a sparse representation (presented to the client and server programs) and a compact one (transmitted over the network).

The *xmit_type* in a **transmit_as** attribute must be a named type defined previously in another type declaration; it indicates the transmitted type that the stubs will pass between client and server.

The following **typedef** statements declare presented and transmitted types for a linked list:

```
typedef struct {
    int last;
    int [last_is(last)] values[MAXELEMENTS];
    } trans_t;
```

```
typedef [transmit_as(trans_t)] struct {
    int value;
    list_t *next;
} list_t;
```

Because **list_t** contains a pointer to a **list_t**, the NIDL Compiler cannot generate code to marshall this data type. Instead, it generates code that calls user-written routines to convert between **list_t** and **trans_t**, and the stubs transmit the linked lists as **trans_t** structures.

Section 8.2 discusses type conversion, specifies the signatures for conversion routines, and describes two applications that use type conversion.

6.5.2 Type Specifiers

The *type_specifier* portion of a *type_declaration* can specify any of the following:

- Simple types:
  int
  hyper
  long
  short
  small
  unsigned
  unsigned hyper
  unsigned long
  unsigned short
  unsigned small
  byte
  float
  double
  char
  boolean
  void
  enum
  short enum

- Constructed types:
  bitset
  short bitset
  string0
  struct
  union
  Arrays
  Pointers

- The RPC handle type **handle_t**

- Named types defined via **typedef** declarations

Section 6.7 describes these data types in detail.

6.5.3 Field Attributes

NIDL provides two field attributes that apply only to arrays: **last_is** and **max_is**. These attributes identify *last* and *max* fields that at runtime will supply the stubs with information about the length of an array; **last_is** and **max_is** are typically used for an open array, an array whose declaration does not specify an explicit fixed length.

An array with **last_is** or **max_is** must be either a member of a structure or a parameter of an operation. These attributes therefore can appear either in type declarations or in operation declarations. The attributes precede the array name in a *field_attribute_list*:

type_specifier [*field_attribute_list*] *array_declarator* [*array_length*]

The *field_attribute_list* comprises one or both of the following elements, separated by commas:

last_is (*last*)
max_is (*max*)

The **last_is** attribute identifies another field, *last*, that at runtime will be the index of the last array element to be passed. Client and server programs use this field to dynamically indicate the size of an array.

The **max_is** attribute identifies another field, *max*, that at runtime will be the maximum possible index of the array. Client programs use this field to dynamically indicate the maximum size of an array.

The following type declaration defines a structure that contains an open array, its *max*, and its *last*:

```
typedef struct {
    int pmax;
    int plast;
    int [max is(pmax), last_is(plast)] parray[];
    } pixels;
```

See Subsection 8.1.1 for a detailed discussion of **last_is** and **max_is**.

6.5.4 Type Declarators

The *type_declarator_list* specifies names for a particular type. To include several names in a list, separate the names with commas. For example:

```
typedef long integer32, int32;
```

Pointers

To specify a pointer type, precede the name with an asterisk. For example:

```
typedef int *pointer_to_int;
```

Arrays

To specify an array type, put brackets after the name. Inside the brackets you can supply the array size, an asterisk, or nothing. If you supply an asterisk or you supply nothing, you are declaring an open array (one whose length will not be known until runtime), and you must apply the **last_is** field attribute to the array. Array subscripts start at 0.

The following example of a **struct** includes two arrays:

```
typedef struct {
    char    fixed[32];
    int     last;
    char    [last_is (last)] open[];
    } arrays;
```

In a **struct** that contains an open array, the array must be the last member. A **union** cannot contain an open array. See Section 8.1 for more information about open arrays.

Use consecutive pairs of brackets to declare multidimensional arrays, as in C:

```
typedef int two_by_four [2][4];
```

Only the first dimension of a multidimensional array can be unspecified:

```
typedef int n_by_four [][4];    /* this is valid */
typedef int two_by_n [2][];     /* this is NOT valid */
```

6.6 Operation Declarations

The NIDL *operation_declaration* is analogous to a C function heading. An operation declaration has the following form:

[*operation_attribute_list*] *o_type_specifier operation_declarator* (*parameter_list*) ;

Entries in a *parameter_list* are separated by commas. Each entry has the following form:

p_type_specifier [*field_attribute_list parameter_attribute_list*] *parameter_declarator*

The following subsections discuss the parts of an operation declaration.

6.6.1 Operation Attributes

The optional *operation_attribute_list* includes one or more of the following keywords, separated by commas:

idempotent
broadcast
maybe
comm_status

The idempotent Attribute

By default, the RPC runtime library provides "at most once" call semantics. These semantics ensure that an operation, when called once, is executed not more than once. They require the server to save the results of an operation until the client acknowledges its receipt of those results.

The **idempotent** attribute specifies that an operation can be executed any number of times. If an operation is idempotent, the server does not need to save results and the client does not need to issue acknowledgements, so performance is improved. Use the **idempotent** attribute for any operation that can safely be executed more than once; for instance, an operation that simply reads a value is idempotent, while one that increments a value is not.

The broadcast Attribute

The **broadcast** attribute specifies that the RPC runtime software should always broadcast an operation to all hosts on the local network. The broadcast is to a well-known port if one has been specified, to the Local Location Broker forwarding port if not. When a client calls an operation with the **broadcast** attribute, the runtime software automatically clears any binding from the handle before issuing the remote procedure call.

The RPC runtime library applies idempotent call semantics for all broadcast operations, so it executes any operation with the **broadcast** attribute as though the operation also had the **idempotent** attribute. For clarity, we recommend that you explicitly specify **idempotent** whenever you specify **broadcast**; if you do not, the NIDL Compiler will issue a warning.

You should avoid using the **broadcast** attribute. See the discussion of unbound handles and broadcasting in Subsection 5.3.4.

The maybe Attribute

The **maybe** attribute specifies that the caller of an operation does not expect any response and that the RPC runtime software need not guarantee delivery of the call. Operations with this attribute cannot have any output parameters and cannot return anything. You might use **maybe** for an operation that posts a notification whose receipt is not crucial.

The comm_status Attribute

The **comm_status** attribute specifies that an operation returns a completion status, a status code of type **status_$t**. If a communications error occurs while the operation is executing, a cleanup handler in the client stub will handle the error and return the error code as the return value of the operation. The manager routine for an operation with **comm_status** should be coded to return **status_$ok** if successful.

NIDL also supports a **comm_status** parameter attribute; this attribute identifies an output parameter that will reflect status and hence provides functionality similar to that of the **comm_status** operation attribute. Subsection 5.3.8 describes the use of status parameters.

6.6.2 Operation Type Specifiers

The *o_type_specifier* is the data type that the operation returns. It can be any scalar type or previously named type, but it cannot be a pointer. For example, if the operation returns a short integer, specify **short** as the *o_type_specifier*. Specify **status_$t** if the operation has the **comm_status** operation attribute. Specify **void** if the operation does not return. If you omit the *o_type_specifier*, the operation must return an **int**.

6.6.3 Operation Declarators

The *operation_declarator* is the name of the operation.

6.6.4 Parameter Lists

The parameters of an operation appear in a *parameter_list*. The entry for each parameter takes the following form:

p_type_specifier [*field_attribute_list parameter_attribute_list*] *parameter_declarator*

Use commas to separate the entries in a *parameter_list*.

If an interface uses explicit handles, the first parameter in the *parameter_list* for each operation must be the explicit handle. If an operation uses manual binding, the handle must have the type **handle_t**.

Parameter Type Specifiers

The *p_type_specifier* specifies the data type of the parameter.

Field Attributes and Parameter Attributes

The *field_attribute_list* can include **last_is** and **max_is** and can apply only to array parameters. The associated *last* and *max* must also be parameters in the *parameter_list*. Subsection 6.5.3 describes field attributes; Subsection 8.1.1 discusses them in further detail and presents an example.

The *parameter_attribute_list* can include the following attributes:

in   The parameter is an input. It passes from client to server, that is, from the calling routine (the "caller") to the called routine (the "callee").

out   The parameter is an output. It passes from server to client, that is, from the callee to the caller. Output parameters are passed by reference and must be either pointers or arrays.

comm_status   The parameter is a status parameter. If a communications error occurs, a cleanup handler in the client stub will handle the error and pass the error code to the client in this parameter.

Every parameter must have at least one of the directional attributes **in** and **out**. A list including both **in** and **out** indicates that the parameter passes in both directions.

A parameter with the **comm_status** attribute must be of type **status_$t** and must also have at least the **out** attribute. Subsection 5.3.8 describes the use of status parameters.

Field attributes and parameter attributes can appear in any order. If a parameter has more than one attribute, separate the attributes with commas.

Parameter Declarators

The *parameter_declarator* specifies the name of each parameter.

By default, **in** parameters are passed by value. To denote an **in** parameter that is passed by reference, precede the *parameter_declarator* with an asterisk (*). This construct is typically used when the application software is implemented in Pascal.

All **out** parameters are passed by reference. Unless the parameter is an array, you must precede the *parameter_declarator* with an asterisk (*).

Use brackets to specify arrays. The syntax for array parameters is the same as for array types, which we described in Subsection 6.5.4.

6.6.5 Examples

The following declares an operation named **simple$op** that takes no parameters, returns no value, and need not be executed:

```
[maybe] void simple$op();
```

The interface definition for the **xmitas** example, *examples*/**xmitas/xmitas.idl**, declares the **xmitas$sum** operation. This idempotent operation returns an integer. Its input parameters are an explicit RPC handle and a list structure of the named type **list_t**.

```
[idempotent]
int xmitas$sum(
    handle_t    [in] h,
    list_t      [in] list
    );
```

The interface definition for the **primes** example, *examples*/**primes/primes.idl**, declares the **primes$gen** operation. This operation does not return a value. Its parameters include two pointers and an open array. Its declaration illustrates the use of operation attributes, field attributes, and parameter attributes.

```
[idempotent]
void primes$gen(
    handle_t    [in] h,
    int         [in, out] *last,
    int         [in] max,
    status_$t   [comm_status, out] *st,
    int         [in, out, last_is(last), max_is(max)] values[]
    );
```

6.7 Data Types

This section describes in detail the *type_specifier* expressions that you can use in type declarations and in the parameter lists of operation declarations. These expressions can specify simple types, constructed types, named types, or the RPC handle type **handle_t**.

6.7.1 Simple Types

NIDL supports a variety of simple data types including integers, floating-point numbers, characters, **boolean, byte, void,** and enumerations:

- Integer Types

  int
  hyper
  long
  short
  small
  unsigned
  unsigned hyper
  unsigned long
  unsigned short
  unsigned small

  You can include the keyword **int** after any of the other integer type names; **long** and **long int**, for example, are synonymous. The **int, long, unsigned,** and **unsigned long** types are represented in 32 bits. A **hyper** or **unsigned hyper** is 64 bits. A **short** or **unsigned short** is 16 bits. A **small** or **unsigned small** is 8 bits.

- The **byte** Type

  byte

  The integer types listed above are subject to data conversion when the native data representation formats of client and server hosts differ. The **byte** type is an 8-bit integer whose representation format is guaranteed not to be converted. You can protect data of any type from data conversion by transmitting that type as an array of **byte**; Section 8.2 discusses the use of transmitted types.

- Floating-Point Types

  float
  double

  A **float** is 32 bits. A **double** is 64 bits.

- The Character Type

  char

  A **char** is unsigned. NIDL does not support a signed character.

- The Boolean Type

  boolean

  Following C convention, a value of 0 means "false," and any nonzero value means "true."

- The **void** Type

  void

  This type is used for an operation that does not return a value.

- Enumerations

  enum { *identifier_list* }
  short enum { *identifier_list* }

  The enumerated types provide names for integers. An **enum** is a 32-bit integer; a **short enum** is a 16-bit integer. You can declare these types only in **typedef** statements. The NIDL Compiler assigns integer values, beginning at 0, to **enum** identifiers based on their order in *identifier_list*. For example, in the declaration

  ```
  typedef enum {John, Paul, George, Ringo} beatles;
  ```

  John gets the value 0, **Paul** gets 1, **George** gets 2, and **Ringo** gets 3.

6.7.2 Constructed Types

NIDL also supports constructed data types, including sets, strings, structures, discriminated unions, pointers, and arrays:

- Sets

  bitset enum { *identifier_list* }
  short bitset enum { *identifier_list* }

  A **bitset** is similar to an enumeration, but instead of defining names for integers, it defines names for bits in a single 32-bit integer, starting with the least significant bit. A **short bitset** defines names for bits in a 16-bit integer. For example, in the declaration

  ```
  typedef bitset enum {Steinhardt, Dalley, Tree, Soyer} guarneri;
  ```

  Steinhardt represents the value of bit 0 in an integer, **Dalley** represents bit 1, **Tree** represents bit 2, and **Soyer** represents bit 3.

- Strings

string0 [*length*]

A **string0** is a C-style null-terminated string, that is, a character array whose last element is the null character \0. The *length* indicates the maximum length of the string, including the terminating zero byte. For example, a string specified by

```
string0[7]
```

is long enough to hold "Ligeti".

- Structures

struct *tag* {
    type_specifier [*field_attribute_list*] *declarator* ;
    . . .
    }

A NIDL **struct** cannot contain pointers unless you apply the **transmit_as** type attribute and supply routines to convert the structure to a transmissible type.

The *tag* is optional.

The *field_attribute_list* can apply only to arrays. Subsection 6.5.3 describes field attributes.

An open array can appear in a structure only as the last member. A structure containing an open array must be passed by reference.

- Unions

union switch (*d_type_specifier discriminator*) *tag* {
    case *constant* : *type_specifier declarator* ;
    . . .
    default : *type_specifier declarator* ;
    }

A NIDL **union** must be discriminated and hence differs considerably from its C counterpart. In the union header you specify a discriminator and its type; the discriminator selects a member at the time the union is used. The NIDL **union** is a conflation of C **union** and **switch** syntax.

The *d_type_specifier* and the *discriminator* are the type and the name of the discriminator. The *d_type_specifier* must be one of the simple types described in Subsection 6.7.1. The NIDL Compiler uses the optional *tag* to generate identifiers in source code representations of the union; see Subsection 6.7.5.

A default member, identified by the label **default**, can optionally appear anywhere in the list of cases. At the time the union is used, if the value of *discriminator* does not match any *constant* in the list of cases, the default member applies. In the absence of a default member, failure to match a *discriminator* raises an error.

The NIDL Compiler can generate C source code, but not Pascal source code, to represent a union with a **default** case.

To indicate that several cases take the same declarator, omit the *type_specifier*, the *declarator*, and the semicolon in all but the last **case**. To indicate an empty member, omit the *type_specifier* and the *declarator*. For example:

```
typedef union switch ( int pick ) {
        case 1 :
        case 2 : int fraise;
        case 3 : float framboise;
        case 4 :
        case 5 : ;
        } berries;
```

A **union**, like a **struct**, cannot contain pointers unless you apply the **transmit_as** type attribute and supply routines to convert the union to a transmissible type.

Subsection 6.7.5 discusses how the NIDL Compiler represents discriminated unions in the C and Pascal source code it generates.

● Pointers

*type_specifier *identifier*

To specify a pointer, precede the identifier with an asterisk. For example:

```
int *pointer_to_int
```

A NIDL pointer cannot be null.

The NIDL Compiler generates code that can marshall and unmarshall pointers only "at top level" and not within any constructed types. You can overcome this restriction by applying the **transmit_as** type attribute and supplying routines to convert the constructed type to a transmissible one.

● Arrays

type_specifier identifier [*length*]

To specify an array, follow the name with brackets enclosing the number of elements in the array. If *length* is an asterisk or is omitted, the array is open. Consecutive pairs of brackets specify a multidimensional array. Subsection 6.5.4 describes array syntax in more detail.

6.7.3 The RPC Handle Type

The **handle_t** type denotes an opaque handle type meaningful to the RPC runtime library. If you specify this type for the explicit handles or the implicit handle in an interface, the interface uses manual binding.

6.7.4 Named Types

Named types are types defined via type declarations. For example, the following **typedef** statement defines **integer64** to be a synonym for **hyper**:

```
typedef hyper integer64;
```

Section 6.5 describes type declarations in detail.

6.7.5 Representation of Unions

As we mentioned in Subsection 6.7.2, NIDL unions are discriminated, unlike C unions. Here we explain how the NIDL Compiler represents discriminated unions in the C and Pascal source code it generates.

When the NIDL Compiler generates C code to represent a NIDL union, it embeds the union and the discriminator in a C structure. The name of the NIDL union becomes the name of the C structure. If you assign a tag to the NIDL union in your type declaration, the Compiler uses the tag to name the embedded C union; otherwise, the Compiler uses a generic name.

In our examples of NIDL Compiler output, we've reformatted the code for legibility and we've added comments.

Unions With Tags

In the following declaration, we assign **utag** as the tag for a union named **union_with_tag**:

```
typedef union switch (short i) utag {
    case 1:
    case 2:
        struct { short a, b; } struct1;
    case 3:
    case 4:
        struct { float x, y; } struct2;
    case 5:
        char p;
    case 6:
        char q;
    } union_with_tag;
```

In the C definition that the NIDL Compiler generates, the union name **union_with_tag** becomes the name of the embedding structure, and the tag **utag** becomes the name of the embedded union:

```
typedef struct union_with_tag union_with_tag;
struct union_with_tag {
    ndr_$short_int i;              /* the discriminator */
    union {                        /* the union */
        /* case(s): 1, 2 */
        struct {
            ndr_$short_int a;
            ndr_$short_int b;
            } struct1;
        /* case(s): 3, 4 */
        struct {
            ndr_$short_float x;
            ndr_$short_float y;
            } struct2;
        /* case(s): 5 */
        ndr_$char p;
        /* case(s): 6 */
        ndr_$char q;
        } utag;
    };
```

In the Pascal definition that the NIDL Compiler generates, there is no need to use the union tag:

```
type
union_with_tag = record
    case i : integer of
        1, 2 : (struct1 : record
                    a : integer;
                    b : integer;
                    end;
                );
        3, 4 : (struct2 : record
                    x : real;
                    y : real;
                    end;
                );
        5 :    (p : char;);
        6 :    (q : char;);
        end;
```

The NIDL Compiler cannot generate Pascal source code to represent a union with a **default** case.

Unions Without Tags

The following definition of **union_without_tag** omits the optional union tag:

```
typedef union switch (short i) {
    case 1:
    case 2:
        struct { short a, b; } struct1;
    case 3:
    case 4:
        struct { float x, y; } struct2;
    case 5:
        char p;
    case 6:
        char q;
} union_without_tag;
```

The generated C definition assigns the generic name **tagged_union** to the embedded union:

```
typedef struct union_without_tag union_without_tag;
struct union_without_tag {
    ndr_$short_int i;           /* the discriminator */
    union {                     /* the union */
        /* case(s): 1, 2 */
        struct  {
            ndr_$short_int a;
            ndr_$short_int b;
            } struct1;
        /* case(s): 3, 4 */
        struct  {
            ndr_$short_float x;
            ndr_$short_float y;
            } struct2;
        /* case(s): 5 */
        ndr_$char p;
        /* case(s): 6 */
        ndr_$char q;
        } tagged_union;
    };
```

In a generated Pascal definition, of course, there is no need for the generic name.

Recommendations

It is usually more natural to use the C syntax of NIDL with C applications and the Pascal syntax with Pascal applications. If you use the Pascal syntax of NIDL with a C application, we suggest that you specify the tags rather than allow the NIDL Compiler to assign names.

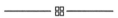

Chapter 7

NIDL Pascal Syntax

This chapter describes the Pascal syntax of the Network Interface Definition Language (NIDL). The Pascal syntax of NIDL is a subset of Domain Pascal, with some constructs added to express NCS remote procedure call semantics.

In this book, we present NIDL syntax informally, sacrificing precision for readability. For a more rigorous specification of NIDL syntax, see *Network Computing Architecture*.

Section 7.1 describes the overall structure of an interface definition. Sections 7.2 through 7.6 describe each of the elements in that structure. Section 7.7 is a detailed discussion of NIDL data types.

7.1 Interface Definition Structure

A NIDL interface definition has the following structure:

%pascal
[*interface_attribute_list*] **interface** *identifier* ;
import_declarations
constant_declarations
type_declarations
operation_declarations
end;

7.1.1 Syntax Identifier

The first line of an interface definition file identifies the syntax of NIDL in which the definition is written. For the Pascal syntax of NIDL, this identifier is **%pascal**.

7.1.2 Heading

The interface definition heading comprises three elements: an interface attribute list, enclosed in brackets; the keyword **interface**; and the interface identifier. A semicolon terminates the heading.

7.1.3 Body

The interface definition body consists of one or more of these declarations:

import_declaration
constant_declaration
type_declaration
operation_declaration

A semicolon terminates each declaration. The keyword **end**, followed by a semicolon, terminates the body.

We describe the *import_declaration* in Section 7.3, the *constant_declaration* in Section 7.4, the *type_declaration* in Section 7.5, and the *operation_declaration* in Section 7.6.

7.1.4 Comments

As in Pascal, braces delimit comments:

```
{ all natural }
import 'potato.idl';   { no preservatives }
```

7.1.5 C Preprocessor Directives

On Apollo workstations and other UNIX systems, the NIDL Compiler filters interface definitions through a C preprocessor. Definitions to be compiled on UNIX systems therefore can contain C preprocessor directives.

The NIDL Compiler **−confirm, −cpp, −def,** and **−no_cpp** options relate to this feature. See the **nidl** reference description in Chapter 17 for more information about these options.

Since preprocessing occurs only on UNIX systems, use of this feature makes an interface definition less portable. On other systems, C preprocessor directives will produce errors.

The interface definitions for the examples in this book do not contain C preprocessor directives. We compile the definitions with the **−no_cpp** option.

7.2 Interface Attributes

As we mentioned in Section 7.1, an interface definition heading specifies the name and attributes of the interface, as follows:

[*interface_attribute_list*] **interface** *identifier* ;

The *interface_attribute_list* includes one or more of the following elements, separated by commas:

uuid (*uuid_string*)
version (*version_number*)
port (*port_identifier_list*)
implicit_handle (*identifier* : *type_specifier*)
local

If an interface definition contains any operation declarations, its heading must specify at least the **local** attribute or the **uuid** attribute.

7.2.1 UUID Attribute

The **uuid** attribute assigns a Universal Unique Identifier (UUID) to the interface. No other object, interface, or type can be assigned this UUID.

The **uuid** attribute has the following syntax:

uuid (*uuid_string*)

The *uuid_string* is the character-string representation of a UUID. (See the description of the **uuid_$string_t** data type in Chapter 16.)

7.2.2 Version Attribute

The **version** attribute helps you to manage multiple versions of an interface. It has the following syntax:

version (*version_number*)

The *version_number* is an integer.

If you were changing the parameters to an operation in the **dblookup** interface, the interface definition heading could look like this:

```
[uuid(338b5f985000.0d.00.00.37.27.00.00.00), version (2)]
interface dblookup;
```

7.2.3 Port Attribute

The **port** attribute specifies the well-known port or ports on which servers that export the interface will listen. It has the following syntax:

port (*port_identifier_list*)

Entries in a *port_identifier_list* are separated by commas. Each entry has the following form:

family : [*port_number*]

The *family* is an address family; the *port_number* is a well-known port. Specify at most one port per family. NIDL supports the following values for *family*:

unix	Local to host (UNIX pipes, portals)
ip	Internetwork protocols (TCP, UDP)
implink	ARPANET Interface Message Processor (IMP) addresses
pup	Xerox PARC Universal Packet (PUP) protocols (BSP, for example)
chaos	Massachusetts Institute of Technology (MIT) CHAOS protocols
ns	Xerox Network Systems (XNS) protocols
nbs	National Bureau of Standards (NBS) protocols
ecma	European Computer Manufacturers Association (ECMA)
datakit	Datakit protocols
ccitt	International Telegraph and Telephone Consultative Committee (CCITT) protocols (X.25, for example)
sna	IBM Systems Network Architecture (SNA) protocols
dds	Apollo Domain/Message (DDS) protocol

The NCS runtime software currently supports the **ip** and **dds** address families.

The following example specifies well-known ports for the DDS and IP address families:

```
port(dds:[19], ip:[6677])
```

For most applications, you should not use the **port** attribute; instead, you should allow the RPC runtime library to assign opaque ports dynamically. Subsection 2.2.3 discusses well-known and opaque ports.

7.2.4 Implicit Handle Attribute

The **implicit_handle** attribute indicates that an interface uses an implicit global variable rather than explicit operation parameters to represent objects. It has the following syntax:

implicit_handle (*identifier* : *type_specifier*)

The *type_specifier* and *identifier* are the type and name of the global variable to be used as an implicit handle. The *type_specifier* must be either the RPC handle type **handle_t** or a generic handle type for which you have specified the **handle** type attribute.

If you specify an implicit handle for an interface, the client stub uses this handle to represent objects in all remote procedure calls and it passes no handle information to the server. Operations in the interface should not include handle parameters in their signatures.

If you do not specify an implicit handle, the interface uses explicit handles, and each operation must include a handle as the first parameter in its signature.

The interface definition heading for an interface that uses an implicit handle might look like this:

```
[uuid(338b5f985000.0d.00.00.37.27.00.00.00),
        implicit_handle(h: handle_t)]
interface array;
```

Subsection 2.3.4 discusses implicit and explicit handles.

7.2.5 Local Attribute

The **local** attribute indicates that the interface definition does not declare any remote operations; therefore, the NIDL Compiler should generate only header files and insert files (**.h** and **.ins.pas** files), not stubs.

If you specify the **local** attribute, the NIDL Compiler ignores any other interface attributes.

7.3 Import Declarations

The NIDL *import_declaration* is analogous to the Pascal **%include** directive. It specifies an interface definition file that declares constants and types used by the importing interface. It takes the following form:

import *file_list* ;

The *file_list* specifies the pathnames of the interface definitions you are importing. Enclose each pathname in single quotation marks and separate the pathnames with commas.

You can import interfaces defined in either of the NIDL syntaxes. Importing an interface many times has the same effect as importing it once.

The NIDL Compiler translates **import** declarations into C **#include** and Pascal **%include** directives to include header files that correspond to the imported interfaces. The Compiler does not generate stub routines for any operations in imported interfaces.

For example, suppose that the interface definition **aioli.idl** contains a declaration to import the definitions for the **garlic** and **oil** interfaces:

```
import 'garlic.idl',
       'oil.idl';
```

The NIDL Compiler will generate a C header file named **aioli.h** that contains the following **#include** directives:

```
#include "garlic.h"
#include "oil.h"
```

and a Pascal insert file named **aioli.ins.pas** that contains the following **%include** directives:

```
%include 'garlic.ins.pas';
%include 'oil.ins.pas';
```

The stub files that the Compiler generates will not contain any code for **garlic** and **oil** operations.

7.4 Constant Declarations

The NIDL *constant_declaration* takes the following form:

const
    identifier = *integer* | *string* | *value* ;
    . . .

The *Identifier* is the name of the constant, *integer*, *string*, or *value* is the value you are assigning to the constant. A *value* can be any previously defined constant. NIDL currently does not support constant expressions. You can declare several constants under one **const** keyword; terminate each declaration with a semicolon.

The following example declares two constants:

```
const
    MAX = 86;
    DSCH = 'Dmitri Shostakovich';
```

7.5 Type Declarations

The NIDL *type_declaration* lets you give a name to a data type. It takes the following form:

type
    type_declarator = [*type_attribute_list*] *type_specifier* ;
    . . .

The *type_attribute_list* is optional. You can declare several types under one **type** keyword; terminate each declaration with a semicolon.

Some of the constructs that appear in type declarations can also appear in the parameter lists of operation declarations. Section 7.6 describes the use of these constructs in operation declarations. Section 7.7 describes NIDL data types in detail.

In ordinary Pascal, you use **type** to define data types and **var** to declare variables of those types. In the Pascal syntax of NIDL, there is no **var** keyword; fields are declared in record declarations, and parameters are declared in operation declarations.

7.5.1 Type Attributes

The optional *type_attribute_list* includes one or both of the following elements, separated by commas:

handle

transmit_as (*xmit_type*)

These attributes can appear only in **type** declarations.

The handle Attribute

The **handle** attribute specifies that a type can serve as a generic handle. You must supply automatic binding routines to convert this type to **handle_t,** the RPC handle type.

The following example declares a generic handle type **filehandle_t,** a record containing the textual representations of a host and a pathname:

```
type filehandle_t = [handle] record
    host:   socket_$string_t;
    path:   array[1..1024] of char;
    end;
```

Section 8.3 discusses automatic binding, specifies the signatures for autobinding and autounbinding routines, and describes an application that uses UUIDs as generic handles.

The transmit_as Attribute

The **transmit_as** attribute associates a **transmitted type** that stubs pass over the network with a **presented type** that clients and servers manipulate. You must supply routines that perform conversions between the presented and transmitted types.

There are two primary uses for this attribute:

- To pass complex data types for which the NIDL Compiler cannot generate marshalling and unmarshalling code. Such types include trees, linked lists, and records that contain pointers.

- To pass data more efficiently. An application can provide routines to convert a data type between a sparse representation (presented to the client and server programs) and a compact one (transmitted over the network).

The *xmit_type* in a **transmit_as** attribute must be a named type defined previously in another type declaration; it indicates the transmitted type that the stubs will pass between client and server.

The following **type** statement declares presented and transmitted types for a linked list:

```
type
    trans_t = record
        last : integer32;
        [last_is(last)] values : array [1..MAXELEMENTS] of integer32;
        end;
    list_t = [transmit_as(trans_t)] record
        value : integer32;
        next : ^list_t;
        end;
```

Because **list_t** contains a pointer to a **list_t**, the NIDL Compiler cannot generate code to marshall this data type. Instead, it generates code that calls user-written routines to convert between **list_t** and **trans_t**, and the stubs transmit the linked lists as **trans_t** structures.

Section 8.2 discusses type conversion, specifies the signatures for conversion routines, and describes two applications that use type conversion.

7.5.2 Type Specifiers

The *type_specifier* portion of a *type_declaration* can specify any of the following:

- Simple types:
  integer
  integer64
  integer32
  integer8
  unsigned
  unsigned64
  unsigned32
  unsigned8
  real
  double
  char
  boolean
  byte
  Enumerations
  Subranges

- Constructed types:
  array
  string0
  set
  record
  Pointers

- The RPC handle type **handle_t**

- Named types defined via **type** declarations

Section 7.7 describes these data types in detail.

7.5.3 Field Attributes

NIDL provides two field attributes that apply only to arrays: **last_is** and **max_is**. These attributes identify *last* and *max* fields that at runtime will supply the stubs with information about the length of an array; **last_is** and **max_is** are typically used for an open array, an array whose declaration does not specify an explicit fixed length.

An array with **last_is** or **max_is** must be either a member of a record or a parameter of an operation. These attributes therefore can appear either in type declarations or in operation declarations. The attributes precede the array name in a *field_attribute_list*:

[*field_attribute_list*] *array_declarator* : **array** [*range_list*] **of** *type_specifier*

The *field_attribute_list* comprises one or both of the following elements, separated by commas:

last_is (*last*)
max_is (*max*)

The **last_is** attribute identifies another field, *last*, that at runtime will be the index of the last array element to be passed. Client and server programs use this field to dynamically indicate the size of an array.

The **max_is** attribute identifies another field, *max*, that at runtime will be the maximum possible index of the array. Client programs use this field to dynamically indicate the maximum size of an array.

The following type declaration defines a record that contains an open array, its *max*, and its *last*:

```
type pixels = record
    pmax, plast : integer;
    [max_is(pmax), last_is(plast)] parray : array[1..*] of integer32;
    end;
```

See Subsection 8.1.1 for a detailed discussion of **last_is** and **max_is**.

7.6 Operation Declarations

The NIDL *operation_declaration* is analogous to a procedure or function heading in Pascal. It can take two forms:

[*operation_attribute_list*]
procedure *operation_declarator* (*parameter_list*) ;

[*operation_attribute_list*]
function *operation_declarator* (*parameter_list*) : *o_type_specifier* ;

Entries in a *parameter_list* are separated by semicolons. Each entry has the following form:

[*field_attribute_list parameter_attribute_list*] *parameter_declarator_list* : *p_type_specifier*

The following subsections discuss the parts of an operation declaration.

7.6.1 Operation Attributes

The optional *operation_attribute_list* includes one or more of the following keywords, separated by commas:

idempotent
broadcast
maybe
comm_status

The idempotent Attribute

By default, the RPC runtime library provides "at most once" calling semantics. These semantics ensure that an operation, when called once, is executed not more than once. They require the server to save the results of an operation until the client acknowledges its receipt of those results.

The **idempotent** attribute specifies that an operation can be executed any number of times. If an operation is idempotent, the server does not need to save results and the client does not need to issue acknowledgements, so performance is improved. Use the **idempotent** attribute for any operation that can safely be executed more than once; for instance, an operation that simply reads a value is idempotent, while one that increments a value is not.

The broadcast Attribute

The **broadcast** attribute specifies that the RPC runtime software should always broadcast an operation to all hosts on the local network. The broadcast is to a well-known port if one has been specified, to the Local Location Broker forwarding port if not. When a client calls an operation with the **broadcast** attribute, the runtime software automatically clears any binding from the handle before issuing the remote procedure call.

The RPC runtime library applies idempotent call semantics for all broadcast operations, so it executes any operation with the **broadcast** attribute as though the operation also had the **idempotent** attribute. For clarity, we recommend that you explicitly specify **idempotent** whenever you specify **broadcast**; if you do not, the NIDL Compiler will issue a warning.

You should avoid using the **broadcast** attribute. See the discussion of unbound handles and broadcasting in Subsection 5.3.4.

The maybe Attribute

The **maybe** attribute specifies that the caller of an operation does not expect any response and that the RPC runtime software need not guarantee delivery of the call. Operations with this attribute cannot have any output parameters and cannot return anything. You might use **maybe** for an operation that posts a notification whose receipt is not crucial.

The comm_status Attribute

The **comm_status** attribute specifies that an operation returns a completion status, a status code of type **status_$t**. If a communications error occurs while the operation is executing, a cleanup handler in the client stub will handle the error and return the error code as the return value of the operation. The manager routine for an operation with **comm_status** should be coded to return **status_$ok** if successful.

NIDL also supports a **comm_status** parameter attribute; this attribute identifies an output parameter that will reflect status and hence provides functionality similar to that of the **comm_status** operation attribute. Subsection 5.3.8 describes the use of status parameters.

7.6.2 Operation Type Specifiers

An operation is a **function** if it returns a value and a **procedure** if it does not.

The *o_type_specifier* is the data type that a function returns. It can be any scalar type or previously named type, but it cannot be a pointer. For example, if the function returns a 32-bit integer, specify **integer32** as the *o_type_specifier*. The *o_type_specifier* for an operation with the **comm_status** operation attribute must be **status_$t**.

7.6.3 Operation Declarators

The *operation_declarator* is the name of the operation.

7.6.4 Parameter Lists

The parameters of an operation appear in a *parameter_list*. The entry for each parameter takes the following form:

| *field_attribute_list parameter_attribute_list* | *parameter_declarator_list* : *p_type_specifier*

Use semicolons to separate the entries in a *parameter_list*.

If an interface uses explicit handles, the first parameter in the *parameter_list* for each operation must be the explicit handle. If an operation uses manual binding, the handle must have the type **handle_t**.

Parameter Type Specifiers

The *p_type_specifier* specifies the data type of the parameter.

Field Attributes and Parameter Attributes

The *field_attribute_list* can include **last_is** and **max_is** and can apply only to array parameters. The associated *last* and *max* must also be parameters in the *parameter_list*. Subsection 7.5.3 describes field attributes; Subsection 8.1.1 discusses them in further detail and presents an example.

The *parameter_attribute_list* can include the following attributes:

in   The parameter is an input. It passes from client to server, that is, from the calling routine (the "caller") to the called routine (the "callee").

out   The parameter is an output. It passes from server to client, that is, from the callee to the caller.

ref   The parameter is passed by reference.

comm_status   The parameter is a status parameter. If a communications error occurs, a cleanup handler in the client stub will handle the error and pass the error code to the client in this parameter.

Every parameter must have at least one of the directional attributes **in** and **out**. A list including both **in** and **out** indicates that the parameter passes in both directions.

The **ref** attribute, applicable only in combination with **in**, specifies that an input is to be passed by reference. Users of Domain Pascal should note that values larger than 32 bits must be passed by reference and therefore must have **ref** specified.

A parameter with the **comm_status** attribute must be of type **status_$t** and must also have at least the **out** attribute. Subsection 5.3.8 describes the use of status parameters.

Field attributes and parameter attributes can appear in any order. If a parameter has more than one attribute, separate the attributes with commas.

Parameter Declarator Lists

A *parameter_declarator_list* contains one or more parameter declarators, all of which have the same type and attributes. Separate the declarators with commas.

7.6.5 Examples

The following declares an operation named **sample$proc** that has no parameters, returns no value, and need not be executed:

```
[maybe] procedure sample$proc();
```

The following declares an operation named **sample$func** that has two input parameters and a status parameter and returns a **real**:

```
function sample$func (
    [in, ref] h : handle_t;
    [in, ref] inputs : array [0..12] of
        record
            a : integer32;
            x : real;
        end;
    [out, comm_status] st : status_$t
    ) : real ;
```

7.7 Data Types

This section describes in detail the *type_specifier* expressions that you can use in type declarations and in the parameter lists of operation declarations. These expressions can specify simple types, constructed types, named types, or the RPC handle type **handle_t**.

7.7.1 Simple Types

NIDL supports a variety of simple data types including integers, floating-point numbers, characters, **boolean**, **byte**, enumerations, and subranges:

- Integer Types

  integer
  integer64
  integer32
  integer8
  unsigned
  unsigned64
  unsigned32
  unsigned8

  The **integer** and **unsigned** types are represented in 16 bits. An **integer64** or **unsigned64** is 64 bits. An **integer32** or **unsigned32** is 32 bits. An **integer8** or **unsigned8** is 8 bits.

- The **byte** Type

  byte

  The integer types listed above are subject to data conversion when the native data representation formats of client and server hosts differ. The **byte** type is an 8-bit integer whose representation format is guaranteed not to be converted. You can protect data of any type from data conversion by transmitting that type as an array of **byte**; Section 8.2 discusses the use of transmitted types.

- Floating-Point Types

  real
  double

  The **real** type is represented in 32 bits. A **double** is 64 bits.

- The Character Type

  char

  A **char** is unsigned. NIDL does not support a signed character.

- The Boolean Type

  boolean

  A value of 0 means "false," and any nonzero value means "true."

- Enumerations

  (*identifier_list*)

  An enumeration provides names for integers. To specify an enumeration, make a list of identifiers separated by commas, and enclose the list in parentheses. The NIDL Compiler assigns 16-bit integer values, beginning at 0, to the identifiers based on their order in the list. For example, in the declaration

  ```
  type
        beatles = (John, Paul, George, Ringo);
  ```

  John gets the value 0, **Paul** gets 1, **George** gets 2, and **Ringo** gets 3.

- Subranges

  lower .. upper

  To specify a subrange of integers or of any previously defined enumeration, supply the lower and upper limits of the subrange, and separate these limits with two periods. For example, the subrange

  ```
  93..104
  ```

  specifies integers ranging from 93 through 104.

7.7.2 Constructed Types

NIDL also supports constructed data types, including sets, strings, records, pointers, and arrays:

- Sets

  set of *enumeration* | (*identifier_list*)

  A set is similar to an enumeration, but instead of defining names for integers, it defines names for bits in a single 16-bit integer, starting with the least significant bit. The following example declares an enumeration called **beatles** and a set called **beatles_set**:

  ```
  type
        beatles = (John, Paul, George, Ringo);
        beatles_set = set of beatles;
  ```

  In this set, **John** represents the value of bit 0 in an integer, **Paul** represents bit 1, **George** represents bit 2, and **Ringo** represents bit 3.

You can declare an enumerated type and a set in one step. For example:

```
type
    guarneri_set = set of (Steinhardt, Dalley, Tree, Soyer);
```

- Strings

string0 [*length*]

A **string0** is a C-style null-terminated string, that is, a character array whose last element is the null character \0. The *length* indicates the maximum length of the string, including the terminating zero byte. For example, a string specified by

```
string0[7]
```

is long enough to hold "Ligeti".

- Records

record
    [*field_attribute_list*] *field_declarator_list* : *type_specifier* ;
    . . .
end

The *field_declarator_list* consists of one or more identifiers, separated by commas.

The *field_attribute_list* can apply only to arrays. Subsection 7.5.3 describes field attributes.

An open array can appear in a record only as the last field. A record containing an open array must be passed by reference.

- Variant Records

record
    [*field_attribute_list*] *field_declarator_list* : *type_specifier* ;
    . . .
    rectag : **case** *vartag* : *v_type_specifier* **of**
        constant, . . . : *ctag* (*field_declaration* ; . . .) ;
        . . .
        otherwise *ctag* (*field_declaration* ; . . .) ;
end

A NIDL variant record consists of a fixed part and a variant part. The optional fixed part is identical to the body of an ordinary record. The variant part specifies several field lists, one of which is selected according to the *vartag* at the time the variant record is used.

The *vartag* is analogous to the tag field in the **case** portion of a Pascal variant record. The *v_type_specifier* specifies the type of *vartag*; it must be one of the simple types described in Subsection 7.7.1.

Each *constant* can be an integer, an enumeration value, or a previously defined constant. Each *field_declaration* has the same form as a field declaration in an ordinary record:

[*field_attribute_list*] *field_declarator_list* : *type_specifier*

A default field list, preceded by the label **otherwise**, can optionally appear as the last case. At the time the variant record is used, if the value of *vartag* does not match any *constant*, the default field list applies. In the absence of a default field list, failure to match a *vartag* raises an error.

The NIDL Compiler can generate C source code, but not Pascal source code, to represent a variant record with an **otherwise** case.

To indicate an empty field list, omit the list of field declarations and supply only the parentheses.

The NIDL Compiler uses the optional *rectag* and *ctag* to generate identifiers in source code representations of the record. Subsection 7.7.5 explains how the NIDL Compiler represents variant records in the C and Pascal source code it generates.

A variant record cannot contain an open array.

- Pointers

  ^type_expression

  To specify a pointer, precede the type expression with a circumflex. For example:

  type
      pointer_to_integer = ^integer;

  The NIDL Compiler generates code that can marshall and unmarshall pointers only "at top level" and not within any constructed types. You can overcome this restriction by applying the **transmit_as** type attribute and supplying routines to convert the constructed type to a transmissible one.

  A NIDL pointer cannot be null.

- Arrays

  array [*range_list*] **of** *type_specifier*

  The *range_list* is a list of data types, each of which indicates the index values allowed for a dimension of the array. A data type in the *range_list* can be a subrange, an enumeration, or a named type that resolves to a subrange or an enumeration.

The following array has two dimensions:

```
type
    ten_by_five = array[1..10, 1..5] of integer;
```

To specify an open array (one whose length will not be known until runtime), supply an asterisk as the upper limit of the index value. You must apply the **last_is** field attribute to any open array.

An open array can appear in a record only as the last field. A variant record cannot contain an open array.

Only the first dimension of a multidimensional array can be open:

```
type
    n_by_four = array[1..*, 1..4] of real;   { this is valid }
    two_by_n = array[1..2, 1..*] of real;   { this is NOT valid }
```

See Section 8.1 for more information about open arrays and use of **last_is**.

7.7.3 The RPC Handle Type

The **handle_t** type denotes an opaque handle type meaningful to the RPC runtime library. If you specify this type for the explicit handles or the implicit handle in an interface, the interface uses manual binding.

7.7.4 Named Types

Named types are types defined via type declarations. For example, the following **type** statement defines **hyper** to be a synonym for **integer64**:

```
type hyper = integer64;
```

Section 7.5 describes type declarations in detail.

7.7.5 Representation of Variant Records

Here we explain how the NIDL Compiler represents variant records in the C and Pascal source code it generates.

In our examples of NIDL Compiler output, we've reformatted the code for legibility and we've added comments.

Representing Variant Records in C

When the NIDL Compiler generates C code to represent a NIDL variant record, it creates C structures to contain the variant part of the NIDL record and to contain field lists.

The NIDL Compiler embeds a variant record and its discriminating tag in a C structure. The name of the NIDL record becomes the name of the C structure. If you assign a tag to the record in your type declaration, the Compiler uses the tag to name the embedded C union; otherwise, the Compiler uses a generic name.

The NIDL Compiler embeds a field list in a C structure if the list contains more than one field. If you assign a tag to such a field list in your type declaration, the Compiler uses the tag to name the embedding C structure; otherwise, the Compiler derives a name from the label for that case.

Variant Records With Tags

In the following declaration, we assign **vtag** as the tag for a variant record, and we assign **ctag1** and **ctag6** as tags for two of the cases.

```
type
variant_with_tags = record
    vtag: case i: integer of
        1,2:  ctag1: (a,b : integer);
        3,4:         (x,y : real);
        5:           (p: char);
        6:    ctag6: (q: char);
        end;
```

In the C definition that the NIDL Compiler generates, the tags are used where C requires explicit names for constructs:

```
typedef struct variant_with_tags variant_with_tags;
struct variant_with_tags {
    ndr_$short_int i;               /* the discriminator */
    union {                         /* the union */
        /* case(s): 1, 2 */
        struct {
            ndr_$short_int a;
            ndr_$short_int b;
            } ctag1;
        /* case(s): 3, 4 */
        struct {
            ndr_$short_float x;
            ndr_$short_float y;
            } case_3;
        /* case(s): 5 */
        ndr_$char p;
        /* case(s): 6 */
        ndr_$char q;
        } vtag;
};
```

The record name **variant_with_tags** becomes the name of the overall structure. The tag **vtag** becomes the name of the embedded union.

To name the structure that embeds the first field list, the Compiler uses the tag **ctag1**. For the second field list, which has no tag, the Compiler derives a name from the first label for that case. The other cases do not require structures; the tag in the fourth case is ignored.

If a variant record contains an **otherwise** case with no tag and several fields, the Compiler assigns the name **default_case** to the C structure it generates to embed the field list.

In the Pascal definition that the NIDL Compiler generates, there is no need to use any of the optional tags:

```
type
variant_with_tags = record
    case i : integer of
        1, 2 : (a : integer; b : integer;));
        3, 4 : (x : real; y : real;));
        5 :    (p : char;);
        6 :    (q : char;);
        end;
```

The NIDL Compiler cannot generate Pascal source code to represent a variant record with an **otherwise** case.

Variant Records Without Tags

The following definition of **variant_without_tags** omits all optional tags:

```
type
variant_without_tags = record
    case i: integer of
        1,2:          (a,b : integer);
        3,4:          (x,y : real);
        5:            (p: char);
        6:            (q: char);
        end;
```

The generated C definition assigns the generic name **tagged_union** to the embedded union and assigns derived names to the structures that contain field lists:

```
typedef struct variant_without_tags variant_without_tags;
struct variant_without_tags {
    ndr_$short_int i;          /* the discriminator */
    union {                    /* the union */
        /* case(s): 1, 2 */
        struct {
            ndr_$short_int a;
            ndr_$short_int b;
            } case_1;
        /* case(s): 3, 4 */
        struct {
            ndr_$short_float x;
            ndr_$short_float y;
            } case_3;
        /* case(s): 5. */
        ndr_$char p;
        /* case(s): 6 */
        ndr_$char q;
        } tagged_union;
    };
```

In a generated Pascal definition, of course, there is no need for generic or derived names.

Recommendations

It is usually more natural to use the C syntax of NIDL with C applications and the Pascal syntax with Pascal applications. If you use the Pascal syntax of NIDL with a C application, we suggest that you specify the tags rather than allow the NIDL Compiler to assign names.

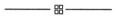

Chapter 8

Special Topics

This chapter covers the following special topics:

- Open arrays

- Data type conversion

- Automatic binding

- Servers that export multiple interface versions

- Servers that contain multiple managers

For each topic, we describe a simple illustrative application. The figures in this chapter show portions of the source code for these applications. In the figures, we omit most error-handling code, and we use ellipsis points (. . .) to indicate substantial omissions. See the *examples* directory for complete source code.

8.1 Open Arrays

NCS supports both fixed arrays, which have an explicitly declared length, and open arrays, which have no explicitly declared length. Since the length of an open array is not known until runtime, special treatment is required to dynamically inform stubs about the array length.

In this section, we describe the NIDL constructs associated with open arrays and discuss the interface definition, client module, and manager module for the **primes** example, a simple application that generates prime numbers and passes an open array as input and output. Complete source code for the example resides in the directory *examples*/**primes**.

8.1.1 NIDL Attributes for Arrays

NIDL provides two field attributes that apply only to arrays: **last_is** and **max_is**. These attributes identify *last* and *max* fields that at runtime will contain information about the length of an array. The client stub and server stub use the *last* and *max* information to marshall, unmarshall, and store the array.

An array with **last_is** or **max_is** must be either a member of a structure or a parameter of an operation. The attributes precede the array name in a *field_attribute_list*:

type_specifier [*field_attribute_list*] *array_declarator* [*array_length*]

The *array_length* is optional. To specify an open array, supply an asterisk (*) as the *array_length* or omit the *array_length* altogether.

The *field_attribute_list* comprises one or both of the following elements, separated by commas:

last_is (*last*)
max_is (*max*)

The last_is Attribute

The **last_is** attribute enables client and server programs to indicate dynamically the size of an array. This attribute informs the NIDL Compiler that *last* will at runtime be the index of the last array element to be passed. When an array passes from client to server, the client program assigns a value for *last*, and the client stub uses this value to marshall the array. Likewise, when an array passes from server to client, the server manager code assigns a value for *last*, and the server stub uses this value to marshall the array.

Note that *last* is an index, not a count.

The **last_is** attribute is required for open arrays. For a fixed array, **last_is** is not required, but you can use it to increase efficiency when you intend to pass only part of the array; the stubs will not marshall any element with an index greater than *last*. Section 8.2 describes two examples that apply **last_is** to fixed arrays.

An array with **last_is** can appear either in the parameter list of an operation declaration or in the declaration of a structure. In an operation declaration, the array and its *last* are parameters of the operation; in a structure declaration, the array and its *last* are members of the structure, and the array must be the last member.

The following declaration specifies that **nlast** will at runtime be the index of the last element to be passed in the array **narray**:

```
typedef struct {
    int nlast;
    char [last_is (nlast)] narray[];
    } name;
```

If an array has a *last*, the stub that sends the array uses the *last* to determine how many elements to marshall, and it embeds the element count in the transmitted representation of the array. The stub that receives the array uses this embedded count to determine how many elements it should unmarshall. Therefore, the *last*, whether a structure member or a parameter, must be available to the sending stub but need not be available to the receiving stub. If the array and its *last* are members of a structure, this condition is automatically met because the array and the *last* are always sent together. However, if the array and its *last* are parameters of an operation, you must ensure that the *last* parameter travels with or before the array parameter: an **in** array requires an **in** *last*, but an **out** array can have either an **in** or an **out** *last*.

It is possible for a *last* to serve as both *last* and *max* for an array. We discuss this case in the description of **max_is**, which follows.

The max_is Attribute

The **max_is** attribute enables a client program to indicate dynamically the maximum possible size of an array. This attribute informs the NIDL Compiler that *max* will at runtime be the maximum possible index of the array. The client program assigns the value of *max*; the server stub uses this value when it allocates storage for the "surrogate" copy of the array on the server side.

Like *last*, *max* is an index, not a count.

You typically apply **max_is** to open arrays that are returned by the server, but you can always omit it. If you omit **max_is** for an open array, the NIDL Compiler uses the *last* of the array as its *max*, as though you had declared **max_is** (*last*).

Like **last_is**, **max_is** can appear in an operation declaration or in a structure declaration. In an operation declaration, the array and its *max* are parameters of the operation; in a structure declaration, the array and its *max* are members of the structure, and the array must be the last member.

The following declaration specifies both **max_is** and **last_is** attributes for the array **parray**:

```
typedef struct {
    int pmax;
    int plast;
    int [max is(pmax), last_is(plast)] parray[];
    } pixels;
```

Since the client program supplies *max* for use by the server stub, *max* must always pass from client to server and therefore must have at least the **in** attribute. If you omit the **max_is** attribute and allow a *last* to serve as a *max*, this directional requirement applies to the *last*.

One implication of the preceding paragraph is that a structure containing an open array can never be simply an **out**. If you intend the array to pass in the **out** direction only, the interface definition should declare the structure as both **in** and **out**, and the client program should set the input value of *last* to prevent the client stub from marshalling data; in the C syntax of NIDL, arrays are zero-based, so the input value of *last* should be −1.

8.1.2 The primes Interface Definition

Figure 8–1 shows the NIDL definition for the **primes** interface. This definition contains only one declaration, that of the **primes$gen** operation. The operation passes input and output in the array **values**.

```
%c
[uuid(443d5a1a4000.0d.00.00.fe.da.00.00.00), version(1)]
interface primes
{
[idempotent]
void primes$gen(
    handle_t    [in] h,
    int         [in, out] *last,
    int         [in] max,
    status_$t   [comm_status, out] *st,
    int         [in, out, last_is(last), max_is(max)] values[]
    );
    /* the first element of values[] will be used
        to hold an input parameter */
}
```

Figure 8–1. The primes/primes.idl Interface Definition

The empty brackets indicate that **values** is an open array. The array, its *last*, and its *max* are all parameters of the **primes$gen** operation.

This interface definition also illustrates use of the **comm_status** parameter attribute. If a communications error occurs during a **primes$gen** call, a cleanup handler inserted by the NIDL Compiler in the client stub will handle the error and pass the error code to the client in the **st** status parameter. Subsection 5.3.8 discusses status parameters.

8.1.3 The primes Client Module

Figure 8-2 shows excerpts from the client module, **client.c**.

The client initializes **values** to a length of 1000 elements. It asks the user to specify the integer up to which prime numbers will be generated, and it assigns this integer to the first element of **values**.

The client sets **last** to 0, so that only one element will pass as input to the server. When it calls **primes$gen**, the client supplies 999 as the **max** parameter, to ensure that on return the array will not exceed the space allocated for it.

When **primes$gen** returns, the client prints the array elements whose indexes range from 0 to **last**.

```
...
#define MAXVALS 1000
...
main()
{
    handle_t h;
    status_$t st;
...
    ndr_$long_int values[MAXVALS], last;
    char buf[100];
    int i;
...
    printf("Generate primes up to what integer: ");
    gets(buf);
    values[0] = (ndr_$long_int)atoi(buf);

    last = 0;    /* marshall only the first element of the array */

    primes$gen(h, &last, MAXVALS-1, &st, values);
...
    printf("Primes are:\n");
    for (i = 0; i <= last; i++) printf("%d ", values[i]);

    printf("\n");
}
```

Figure 8-2. Excerpts from the primes/client.c Module

8.1.4 The primes Manager Module

Figure 8–3 shows the manager module, **manager.c**.

The manager routine **primes$gen** checks integers for primeness and assigns prime numbers to elements of values. It quits when it reaches the limit specified on input by the client or when it reaches the array element with index **max**. Before it returns, **primes$gen** sets **last** to the index of the last element in **value**.

```
#include "primes.h"

globaldef primes_v1$epv_t primes_v1$manager_epv = {primes$gen};

void primes$gen(h, last, max, status, values)
handle_t h;
status_$t *status;
ndr_$long_int *last, max, values[];
{
    ndr_$long_int n, highest = values[0], index = 0;

    for (n = 2; n <= highest; n++)
        if (is_prime(n)) {
            values[index++] = n;
            if (index > max) break;
        }
    *last = index-1;
    status->all = status_$ok;
    return;
}

static int is_prime(n)
ndr_$long_int n;
{
    int i;

    for (i = n/2; i > 1; i--)
        if (i*(n/i) == n) return 0;
    return 1;
}
```

Figure 8–3. The primes/manager.c Module

8.1.5 Related Examples

The **xmitas** and **sparse** examples, which we describe in Section 8.2, apply **last_is** to fixed arrays; these examples also show how to pass an array as a member of a structure.

8.2 Data Type Conversion

The NIDL **transmit_as** attribute lets you associate a **transmitted type** that stubs pass over the network with a **presented type** that clients and servers manipulate. You write routines to convert between the presented and transmitted types, and you link those routines with the stubs.

Subsections 6.5.1 and 7.5.1 describe the use of **transmit_as** in NIDL definitions. Here, we specify the requirements for the conversion routines and present two examples: one that uses type conversion to pass a complex data type and one that uses type conversion for efficiency.

8.2.1 Type Conversion Routines

When you associate a transmitted type with a presented type, you must write four routines to perform conversion and to manage storage for the types. Here, we specify C prototypes for these routines; in the prototypes, *PRES* is the name of the presented type and *TRANS* is the name of the transmitted type.

The *PRES*_to_xmit_rep routine allocates storage for the transmitted type and converts from the presented type to the transmitted type:

        void *PRES*_to_xmit_rep (
            PRES presented,
            *TRANS **transmitted*)

The *PRES*_from_xmit_rep routine allocates storage for the presented type and converts from the transmitted type to the presented type:

        void *PRES*_from_xmit_rep (
            *TRANS *transmitted*,
            *PRES *presented*)

The *PRES*_free routine frees any storage that has been allocated for the presented type by *PRES*_from_xmit_rep:

        void *PRES*_free (
            PRES presented)

The *PRES*_free_xmit_rep routine frees any storage that has been allocated for the transmitted type by *PRES*_to_xmit_rep:

        void *PRES*_free_xmit_rep (
            *TRANS *transmitted*)

8.2.2 Using Type Conversion to Pass Complex Types

The NIDL Compiler cannot generate stub code to marshall and unmarshall complex types such as trees, linked lists, and structures that contain pointers. Any data type containing a pointer not "at top level" is complex.

The **xmitas** example uses type conversion to pass a linked list as an open array. The client and server manipulate the linked list type. The client and server stubs transmit arrays over the network.

This subsection discusses the interface definition and **util.c** module for **xmitas**. Complete source code for the example resides in the directory *examples*/**xmitas**.

The xmitas Interface Definition

Figure 8-4 shows the NIDL definition for the **xmitas** interface.

```
%c
[uuid(441f8a28a000.0d.00.00.fe.da.00.00.00), version(1)]
interface xmitas
{
    const int MAXELEMENTS = 100;     /* maximum size of list */

    typedef struct {
        int last;
        int [last_is(last)] values[MAXELEMENTS];
    } trans_t;

    typedef [transmit_as(trans_t)] struct {
        int value;
        list_t *next;
    } list_t;

    [idempotent]
        int xmitas$sum(handle_t [in] h, list_t [in] list);
}
```

Figure 8-4. The xmitas/xmitas.idl Interface Definition

The transmitted type, **trans_t**, is a structure whose members are the integer **last** and the integer array **values**. Though **values** has a declared length, we give it the **last_is** attribute so that no more elements are passed than necessary.

The presented type, **list_t**, is a linked list structure whose members are the integer **value** and the pointer **next**, which points to the next **list_t**.

There is one operation in the **xmitas** interface, **xmitas$sum**. Its inputs are **h** (a handle) and **list** (a linked list). The operation returns an integer which is the sum of the values in **list**.

The xmitas util.c Module

Figure 8-5 shows the **util.c** module, which contains routines to convert between the **list_t** and **trans_t** types and to allocate and free storage for those types.

The first routine, **list_t_to_xmit_rep**, allocates storage for the structure to be transmitted, then copies values from the linked list into the array. It sets **(*xmit_struct)->last** to the index of the last element that it copied to **(*xmit_struct)->values**.

The second routine, **list_t_from_xmit_rep**, copies values from the transmitted array into the linked list, allocating additional storage as it builds the list, until it reaches the array element with index **last**.

Any storage allocated by **list_t_from_xmit_rep** for the linked list is freed by **list_t_free**. Likewise, any storage allocated by **list_t_to_xmit_rep** is freed by **list_t_free_xmit_rep**.

```
#include <stdio.h>
#include "xmitas.h"

static void free_list_recursively();    /* auxiliary function */

void list_t_to_xmit_rep(list, xmit_struct)
list_t list;
trans_t **xmit_struct;
{
    int count = 0;
    list_t *l = &list;

    /* allocate the structure */
    *xmit_struct = (trans_t *)malloc(sizeof(trans_t));

    /* copy the values from the list to the array */
    while (1) {
        (*xmit_struct)->values[count++] = l->value;
        l = l->next;
    }
    (*xmit_struct)->last = (ndr_$long_int)(count-1);
}
```

(continued)

Figure 8-5. The xmitas/util.c Module

```
void list_t_from_xmit_rep(xmit_struct, list)
trans_t *xmit_struct;
list_t *list;
{
    int index = 0;

    /* reconstruct the linked list from the array */
    do {
        list->value = xmit_struct->values[index++];

        if (index <= xmit_struct->last)
            list->next = (list_t *)malloc(sizeof(list_t));
        else list->next = NULL;

        list = list->next;
    } while (index <= xmit_struct->last);
}

void list_t_free(list)
list_t list;
{
    free_list_recursively(list.next);
}

void list_t_free_xmit_rep(xmit_struct)
trans_t *xmit_struct;
{
    free(xmit_struct);
}

static void free_list_recursively(l)
list_t *l;
{
    if (l->next) free_list_recursively(l->next);
    free(l);
}

char *error_text(st)
status_$t st;
{
    static char buff[200];
    extern char *error_$c_text();

    return (error_$c_text(st, buff, sizeof buff));
}
```

Figure 8-5. The xmitas/util.c Module (continued)

8.2.3 Using Type Conversion for Efficiency

The **sparse** example uses type conversion to transmit arrays in a run-length-encoded format. We supply routines to encode and decode the arrays. The stubs present sparse arrays to the client and server but pass compact arrays over the network.

This subsection discusses the interface definition and **util.c** module for **sparse**. Complete source code for the example resides in the directory *examples*/**sparse**.

The sparse Interface Definition

Figure 8–6 shows the NIDL definition for the **sparse** interface.

```
%c
[uuid(442548088000.0d.00.00.fe.da.00.00.00), version(1)]
interface sparse
{
    const int ARRAY_SIZE = 1000;
    const int CARRAY_SIZE = 2000;
    /* worst case: twice the original size */

    /* a run-length-encoded representation of an array */
    typedef struct {
        int last;
        int [last_is(last)] data[CARRAY_SIZE];
    } compress_t;

    /* this type will be transmitted as a more compact type */
    typedef [transmit_as(compress_t)] int compress_array[ARRAY_SIZE];

    /* this type will be transmitted as is */
    typedef int nocompress_array[ARRAY_SIZE];

    [idempotent]
        int sparse$compress_sum(
            handle_t [in] h,
            compress_array [in] array
            );
    [idempotent]
        int sparse$nocompress_sum(
            handle_t [in] h,
            nocompress_array [in] array
            );
}
```

Figure 8–6. The sparse/sparse.idl Interface Definition

In the worst case, encoding doubles the length of an array, so the declared length of the compact array is twice that of the sparse array. Of course, we expect the compact array to be shorter, so we give it the **last_is** attribute and embed it in the **compress_t** structure with a **last**.

We declare two sparse array types: **compress_array** has **compress_t** as its transmitted form; **nocompress_array** is transmitted unchanged.

Both of the operations in the **sparse** interface take a sparse array as input and return the sum of its elements; **sparse$compress_sum** passes its inputs in a compact array, while **sparse$nocompress_sum** passes a sparse array.

The sparse util.c Module

Figure 8-7 shows the **util.c** module, which contains the conversion routines for the **sparse** example. These routines are similar to those for the **xmitas** example.

```
#include <stdio.h>
#include "sparse.h"

void compress_array_to_xmit_rep(array, xmit_struct)
compress_array array;
compress_t **xmit_struct;
{
    int rep, val, index = 0, pos = 0;

    /* allocate the structure */
    *xmit_struct = (compress_t *)malloc(sizeof(struct compress_t));

    /* run-length encode the array */
    do {
        rep = 0;
        val = array[pos];
        while (pos < ARRAY_SIZE && array[pos] == val) {
            pos++;
            rep++;
        }
        (*xmit_struct)->data[index] = rep;
        (*xmit_struct)->data[index+1] = val;
        index += 2;
    } while (pos < ARRAY_SIZE);

    (*xmit_struct)->last = index-1;
}
```

(continued)

Figure 8-7. The sparse/util.c Module

```
void compress_array_from_xmit_rep(xmit_struct, array)
compress_t *xmit_struct;
compress_array *array;
{
    int index, rep, count = 0;

    for (index = 0; index < xmit_struct->last; index+=2)
        for (rep = 0; rep < xmit_struct->data[index]; rep++)
            (*array)[count++] = xmit_struct->data[index+1];
}

void compress_array_free(object)
compress_array object;
{
    /* no freeing is appropriate here */
}

void compress_array_free_xmit_rep(xmit_struct)
compress_t *xmit_struct;
{
    free(xmit_struct);
}

char *error_text(st)
status_$t st;
{
    static char buff[200];
    extern char *error_$c_text();

    return (error_$c_text(st, buff, sizeof buff));
}
```

Figure 8-7. The sparse/util.c Module (continued)

The **compress_array_to_xmit_rep** routine allocates storage for the compact array, then encodes the sparse array. The routine sets **(*xmit_struct)->last** to the index of the last element that it copied to **(*xmit_struct)->data** so that no more elements are passed than necessary.

The **compress_array_from_xmit_rep** routine decodes the compact array, reconstructing the sparse array. Storage for the sparse array has already been allocated, so this routine does not perform any allocation.

Since **compress_array_from_xmit_rep** did not allocate any storage, **compress_array_free** does not need to free any and thus is defined as a null operation. Storage allocated by **compress_array_to_xmit_rep** is freed by **compress_array_free_xmit_rep**.

8.2.4 Restrictions

You cannot use a data type with the **transmit_as** attribute as an element of an array or as a member of a structure or union. In effect, you can use a type with **transmit_as** only as an operation parameter.

A data type with the **transmit_as** attribute cannot serve as the transmitted type for another type.

8.3 Automatic Binding

Automatic binding allows a client to represent objects with generic handles rather than RPC handles. The data type of a generic handle must have the **handle** type attribute. The generic handle can be either a first parameter in each operation (an explicit handle) or a global variable in the client (an implicit handle).

Since the RPC runtime library uses only RPC handles, you must supply an autobinding routine that generates RPC handles from generic handles. The client stub invokes the autobinding routine each time the client makes a remote procedure call. In addition, you supply an autounbinding routine that performs any necessary cleanup (for instance, freeing the RPC handle) after the remote call returns.

8.3.1 Automatic Binding Activity

If an application uses automatic binding, the following occurs when the client makes a remote procedure call:

1. The client makes a remote procedure call, through the client switch, to the stub.

2. The stub calls the autobinding procedure, passing to it the generic handle.

3. The autobinding procedure returns an RPC handle to the stub.

4. The stub uses the RPC handle as a parameter to the **rpc_$sar** library call.

5. The **rpc_$sar** call returns the server response to the stub.

6. The stub calls the autounbinding procedure, passing to it the RPC handle.

7. The autounbinding procedure frees the RPC handle and any unneeded resources associated with the generic handle.

8. The stub returns to the client.

8.3.2 Autobinding and Autounbinding Routines

When you use a generic handle type, you must write autobinding and autounbinding routines. Here, we specify C prototypes for these routines; in the prototypes, *GENERIC* is the name of the generic handle type.

The autobinding routine *GENERIC*_bind generates an RPC handle from a generic handle and returns the RPC handle:

    handle_t GENERIC_bind (
        GENERIC g-handle)

The autounbinding routine *GENERIC*_unbind takes two inputs, a generic handle and the RPC handle that was generated from it, and has no outputs:

    void GENERIC_unbind (
        GENERIC g-handle,
        handle_t rpc-handle)

An autounbinding routine typically frees the RPC handle and any unneeded resources associated with the generic handle, but it is not required to do anything.

8.3.3 Automatic Binding in the bank Example

Figure 8–8 and Figure 8–9 show the autobinding and autounbinding routines from the application in *examples*/**bank**. These routines, defined in the **uuidbind.c** module, enable the **bank** example to use UUIDs as generic handles. They maintain a cache of handles to save the expense of invoking **lb_$lookup_object** and **rpc_$bind** every time the client makes a remote procedure call; this approach is particularly useful in applications where the client tends to make several calls to access the same object.

The file *idl*/**nbase.idl** defines the UUID data type, **uuid_$t**, and assigns to this type the **handle** type attribute.

The bank Autobinding Routine

The autobinding routine, **uuid_$t_bind**, searches the cache for an RPC handle that matches the generic handle (the object UUID). If there is no matching handle in the cache, it calls **lb_$lookup_object** to get the location of the object and calls **rpc_$bind** to create a new handle. It uses **rpc_$dup_handle** to return a copy of the handle.

Each handle in the cache has an associated reference count. When all copies of a handle have been freed, meaning that its binding is not in use, the "original" handle is kept available but is considered "collectible"; if its entry in the cache is needed for a new handle, it can be freed.

```
/*
 * Table mapping UUIDs into RPC handles.
 */

static struct db_entry {
    boolean  valid;           /* Is this entry valid? */
    uuid_$t  obj;             /* Object UUID */
    handle_t handle;          /* RPC handle for the object */
    unsigned short refcnt;    /* # of references on this entry */
} uuid_db[MAX_ENTRIES];

/*
 * Autobinding procedure for type "uuid_$t".
 */

handle_t uuid_$t_bind(object)
uuid_$t object;
{
    short i, invalid_i = -1, collectible_i = -1;
    lb_$entry_t lb_entry;
    unsigned long n_results;
    status_$t st;
    lb_$lookup_handle_t ehandle = lb_$default_lookup_handle;

    /*
     * Scan the table for an entry that has a matching UUID.  If
     * we find one, return the handle that's stored there.  While
     * scanning, keep note of the last invalid entry (i.e. one that
     * is unused) and the last collectible entry (i.e. one that has
     * an object and handle but isn't being referenced by anyone).
     */
    for (i = 0; i < MAX_ENTRIES; i++) {
        struct db_entry *db = &uuid_db[i];
        if (! db->valid)
            invalid_i = i;
        else {
            if (bcmp(&db->obj, &object, sizeof object) == 0) {
                db->refcnt++;
                return (rpc_$dup_handle(db->handle, &st));
            }
            if (db->refcnt == 0)
                collectible_i = i;
        }
    }
```

(continued)

Figure 8-8. An Autobinding Routine for UUIDs

```
        /*
         * Didn't find a match in the table.
         * Ask the LB for the location.
         */
        lb_$lookup_object(&object, &ehandle, 1L, &n_results,
                &lb_entry, &st);
        if (st.all != status_$ok || n_results <= 0) {
            fprintf(stderr,
                    "(uuid_$t_bind) Lookup failed, n_results=%ld\n",
                    n_results);
            pfm_$signal(st);
        }

        /*
         * Decide whether we have an entry to use.
         * Free the current handle if we're collecting the entry.
         */
        if (invalid_i != -1)
            i = invalid_i;
        else if (collectible_i != -1) {
            i = collectible_i;
            rpc_$free_handle(uuid_db[i].handle, &st);
        }
        else {
            fprintf(stderr, "(uuid_$t_bind) No space in cache\n");
            abort();
        }

        /*
         * Fill in the entry with our values.
         */
        uuid_db[i].obj    = object;
        uuid_db[i].valid  = true;
        uuid_db[i].refcnt = 1;

        /*
         * Make an RPC handle for the object and location and return it.
         */
        uuid_db[i].handle = rpc_$bind(&object, &lb_entry.saddr,
                lb_entry.saddr_len, &st);
        if (st.all != status_$ok)
            pfm_$signal(st);
        return (rpc_$dup_handle(uuid_db[i].handle, &st));
}
```

Figure 8–8. An Autobinding Routine for UUIDs (continued)

The bank Autounbinding Routine

The autounbinding routine, **uuid_$t_unbind,** uses **rpc_$free_handle** to free a copy of the
RPC handle that matches the generic handle, then decrements the reference count of the
generic handle.

```
/*
 * Autounbinding procedure for type "uuid_$t".
 */

void uuid_$t_unbind(object, handle)
uuid_$t object;
handle_t handle;
{
    unsigned short i;
    status_$t st;

    /*
     * Scan the table looking for the handle.
     */
    for (i = 0; i < MAX_ENTRIES; i++) {
        struct db_entry *db = &uuid_db[i];

        if (db->valid && db->handle == handle) {
            rpc_$free_handle(handle, &st);
            db->refcnt--;
            return;
        }
    }

    fprintf(stderr,
        "(uuid_$t_bind) tried to free a handle we didn't return\n");
    abort();
}
```

Figure 8-9. An Autounbinding Routine for UUIDs

8.4 Multiple Interface Versions

NCS allows a single server to simultaneously export several versions of an interface.

The **binopmv** example—an extension of the **binoplu** example, which we described in Section 2.7—illustrates this feature. There are two versions of the **binopmv** interface. The first version is essentially identical to the **binoplu** interface; the second version has one additional operation.

The **binopmv** example actually does not require a server that exports both versions of the interface. Section 5.3.6 describes a way to add operations to interfaces while maintaining backward compatibility. However, **binopmv** illustrates the most general way to compatibly modify an interface.

In this section, we discuss the interface definitions, the client modules, the server module, and the manager module for **binopmv**. Complete source code for the example resides in the directory *examples*/**binopmv**.

8.4.1 The binopmv Interface Definitions

The **binopmv** example has two interface definition files, which we name **vers1.idl** and **vers2.idl**.

The vers1.idl Interface Definition

Figure 8–10 shows **vers1.idl**, the NIDL definition for version 1 of the **binopmv** interface. This interface definition declares one operation, **binopmv$add**.

```
%c
[uuid(4433af7ed000.0d.00.00.fe.da.00.00.00), version(1)]
interface binopmv
{
[idempotent]
    void binopmv$add(
        handle_t [in] h,
        long [in] a,
        long [in] b,
        long [out] *c
        );
}
```

Figure 8–10. The binopmv/vers1.idl Interface Definition

The vers2.idl Interface Definition

Figure 8–11 shows **vers2.idl**, the NIDL definition for version 2 of the **binopmv** interface. The definitions for the two versions of **binopmv** specify the same interface UUID and the same interface name, but different version numbers. The definition for version 2 declares two operations, **binopmv$add** and **binopmv$sub**.

```
%c
[uuid(4433af7ed000.0d.00.00.fe.da.00.00.00), version(2)]
interface binopmv
{
[idempotent]
    void binopmv$add(
        handle_t [in] h,
        long [in] a,
        long [in] b,
        long [out] *c
        );

[idempotent]
    void binopmv$sub(
        handle_t [in] h,
        long [in] a,
        long [in] b,
        long [out] *c
        );
}
```

Figure 8–11. The binopmv/vers2.idl Interface Definition

Compiling the Interface Definitions

When you compile interface definitions for an application whose server will export multiple interface versions, you must specify the NIDL Compiler option **–m**. The build scripts for **binopmv** (and for most of our other examples) specify this option.

If invoked with **–m**, the NIDL Compiler appends the version number to the interface name when it generates identifiers in the stub and header files. In effect, different versions of an interface have different names.

The **nidl** reference description in Chapter 17 describes all of the NIDL Compiler options.

Table 8-1 lists the identifiers that the NIDL Compiler generates for the **binopmv** example. These identifiers are all generated from the interface name and the version number.

Table 8-1. Identifiers in the binopmv Example

	Identifier for Version 1	**Identifier for Version 2**
EPV Type	**binopmv_v1$epv_t**	**binopmv_v2$epv_t**
Client EPV	**binopmv_v1$client_epv**	**binopmv_v2$client_epv**
Server EPV	**binopmv_v1$server_epv**	**binopmv_v2$server_epv**
Interface Specifier	**binopmv_v1$if_spec**	**binopmv_v2$if_spec**

8.4.2 The binopmv Client Modules

There are two client programs. The first, **client1.c,** uses version 1 of the interface and calls **binopmv$add**. The second, **client2.c,** uses version 2 of the interface and calls both **binopmv$add** and **binopmv$sub**.

In most respects, the **client1.c** and **client2.c** programs are similar to the **binoplu** client, which we described in Subsection 2.7.2. Here we discuss aspects of the client programs that pertain to their use of multiple interface versions.

Header Files

Each client includes the header file for its version of the interface:

client1.c:
```
#include "vers1.h"
```

client2.c:
```
#include "vers2.h"
```

Location Broker Lookup Criteria

The clients perform Location Broker lookups by interface. Each client supplies to **lb_$lookup_interface** the **id** member of the **if_spec** for its version of the interface:

client1.c:
```
lb_$lookup_interface(&binopmv_v1$if_spec.id, &ehandle, 1L,
    &nresults, &entry, &st);
```

client2.c:
```
lb_$lookup_interface(&binopmv_v2$if_spec.id, &ehandle, 1L,
    &nresults, &entry, &st);
```

Although these lookup calls appear to be different, they are in effect identical because versions 1 and 2 of the interface have the same UUID. Hence, the lookup calls will return information about all servers for **binopmv**, regardless of version. Each client must either check that a server exports the correct version or deal with possible version mismatches.

Subsection 5.3.6 discusses version mismatches. Here, we show how to check versions.

Checking Interface Versions

After a **binopmv** client has obtained the Location Broker entry for a **binopmv** server, the client binds its handle to the location of the server, then checks that the server exports a matching version of the interface.

Figure 8–12 shows the version checking code in **client1.c**; **client2.c** contains essentially identical code. The client calls **rrpc_$inq_interfaces** to obtain an **rrpc_$interface_vec_t**, an array of interface specifiers for the interfaces exported by the server. It checks the **vers** member of each interface specifier against its own version until it finds a match.

If you are using the **rrpc_** interface on Apollo systems, see the discussion in Appendix B.

```
...
#include "vers1.h"
...
#define VERSION 1     /* version of interface requested */
...
    handle_t h;
    status_$t st;
    rrpc_$interface_vec_t ifs;
    unsigned long lastif;
    int k, passes, found_version;
...

    /* check for appropriate version */

    rrpc_$inq_interfaces(h, 2L, ifs, (ndr_$long_int *)&lastif, &st);

    for (k = 0, found_version = 0; k <= lastif; k++)
        if (ifs[k].vers == VERSION) found_version = 1;
    if (!found_version) {
        fprintf(stderr, "Couldn't get version %d\n", VERSION);
        exit(1);
    }
    else printf("Found version %d\n", VERSION);
...
```

Figure 8–12. Version Checking Code in the binopmv/client1.c Module

8.4.3 The binopmv Server Module

The server module, **server.c**, largely resembles the **binoplu** server, which we described in Subsection 2.7.3, but does all of its registrations and unregistrations twice, once for each interface version.

Header Files

The server includes the header files for both versions of the interface:

```
#include "vers1.h"
#include "vers2.h"
```

Manager EPVs

The server declares two manager EPVs as external variables:

```
globalref binopmv_v1$epv_t binopmv_v1$manager_epv;
globalref binopmv_v2$epv_t binopmv_v2$manager_epv;
```

These EPVs are defined in the manager module. Their names resemble those of the client and server EPVs, but this is merely by convention. Manager EPV names are arbitrary, since they appear only in server and manager code that you write, not in code that the NIDL Compiler generates.

Registrations and Unregistrations

Figure 8-13 shows the registration and unregistration code in **server.c**.

Since it exports several interface versions, the **binopmv** server must register each of its manager versions with the RPC runtime library at its host. These registrations enable the runtime library to dispatch incoming requests to the correct version of the manager.

The server also registers twice with the Location Broker. These registrations supply the same UUID to the Location Broker, and hence are indistinguishable to a client performing lookups. We provide different annotations for the two entries.

Before it calls **rpc_$listen** to begin accepting requests, the server sets a cleanup handler. If it is signaled, the server removes all of its registrations before it exits.

```
...
#include "vers1.h"
#include "vers2.h"

globalref uuid_$t uuid_$nil;
globalref binopmv_v1$epv_t binopmv_v1$manager_epv;
globalref binopmv_v2$epv_t binopmv_v2$manager_epv;
...
    status_$t st;
    socket_$addr_t loc;
    unsigned long llen;
    lb_$entry_t lb_entry[2];
    pfm_$cleanup_rec crec;
...
    /* register version 1... */
    rpc_$register_mgr(&uuid_$nil, &binopmv_v1$if_spec,
        binopmv_v1$server_epv,
        (rpc_$mgr_epv_t)&binopmv_v1$manager_epv, &st);

    /* ...and version 2 with the runtime library */
    rpc_$register_mgr(&uuid_$nil, &binopmv_v2$if_spec,
        binopmv_v2$server_epv,
        (rpc_$mgr_epv_t)&binopmv_v2$manager_epv, &st);

    /* register version 1... */
    lb_$register(&uuid_$nil, &uuid_$nil, &binopmv_v1$if_spec.id, OL,
        (ndr_$char *)"binopmv example (v1)", &loc, llen,
        &lb_entry[0], &st);

    /* ...and version 2 with the lb */
    lb_$register(&uuid_$nil, &uuid_$nil, &binopmv_v2$if_spec.id, OL,
        (ndr_$char *)"binopmv example (v2)", &loc, llen,
        &lb_entry[1], &st);

    st = pfm_$cleanup(&crec);
    if (st.all != pfm_$cleanup_set) {
        status_$t stat;
        fprintf(stderr, "Server received signal - %s\n",
            error_text(st));
        lb_$unregister(&lb_entry[0], &stat);
        lb_$unregister(&lb_entry[1], &stat);
        rpc_$unregister(&binopmv_v1$if_spec, &stat);
        rpc_$unregister(&binopmv_v2$if_spec, &stat);
        pfm_$signal(st);
    }
...
```

Figure 8-13. Registrations and Unregistrations in the binopmv/server.c Module

8.4.4 The binopmv Manager Module

Figure 8–14 shows **manager.c**, the manager module for **binopmv**. This module contains all the code to implement both versions of **binopmv**.

```
#include "vers1.h"
#include "vers2.h"

globaldef binopmv_v1$epv_t binopmv_v1$manager_epv =
    {binopmv0add};
globaldef binopmv_v2$epv_t binopmv_v2$manager_epv =
    {binopmv$add, binopmv$sub};

void binopmv$add(h, a, b, c)
handle_t h;
ndr_$long_int a, b, *c;
{
    *c = a + b;
}

void binopmv$sub(h, a, b, c)
handle_t h;
ndr_$long_int a, b, *c;
{
    *c = a - b;
}
```

Figure 8-14. The binopmv/manager.c Module

The manager includes both versions of the header file and defines both manager EPVs. The EPV for version 1 lists only one operation. The EPV for version 2 lists two.

8.4.5 Changing Operations in Interfaces with Multiple Versions

In the **binopmv** example, version 1 and version 2 can share the manager routine for **binopmv$add** because the operation is identical in the two versions. If an operation has different signatures or implementations in two versions of the interface, you must write two manager routines for the operation.

Suppose you are changing the implementation of **binopmv$add** between versions 1 and 2, and you are building a server that exports both versions. You must give distinct names such as **binopmv_v1$add** and **binopmv_v2$add** to the two versions of the manager routine. Since these names are not declared in the **vers1.h** and **vers2.h** header files that the NIDL Compiler generates, you must declare them in the manager module.

Figure 8–15 shows what a **binopmv** manager with two versions of **binopmv$add** might look like.

```
#include "vers1.h"
#include "vers2.h"

void binopmv_v1$add();
void binopmv_v2$add();

globaldef binopmv_v1$epv_t binopmv_v1$manager_epv =
    {binopmv_v1$add};
globaldef binopmv_v2$epv_t binopmv_v2$manager_epv =
    {binopmv_v2$add, binopmv$sub};

void binopmv_v1$add(h, a, b, c)      /* "old implementation" */
handle_t h;
ndr_$long_int a, b, *c;
{
    *c = a + b;
}

void binopmv_v2$add(h, a, b, c)      /* "new implementation" */
handle_t h;
ndr_$long_int a, b, *c;
{
    *c = b + a;
}

void binopmv$sub(h, a, b, c)
handle_t h;
ndr_$long_int a, b, *c;
{
    *c = a - b;
}
```

Figure 8-15. A Manager Module with Two Versions of an Operation

In this manager, the two versions of the add operation have different names and trivially different implementations. Clients of either interface version continue to invoke the operation by its name in the interface definition, **binopmv$add**.

Of course, if an operation has a different signature as well as a different implementation in two versions of an interface, the manager routines and the interface definitions must reflect this difference.

8.4.6 Constants and Types in Interfaces with Multiple Versions

When you define a manager EPV, you can declare either that two versions of an interface will share a manager routine (as in Figure 8–14) or that they will use different manager routines (as in Figure 8–15). Thus, the names of the manager routines in a server will not conflict. The names of constants and types, however, can conflict.

If you declare the same type in two versions of an interface definition, the NIDL Compiler emits a C **typedef** declaration for the type in both of the C header files it generates. When you build a server program that exports both interface versions, the server includes both header files, and hence the type declarations are duplicated. Most C compilers reject such duplicate type declarations.

To avoid conflicts of type names, extract type declarations that are shared by the two versions of the interface and put these declarations in a "version-independent" interface definition that is imported by the two "version-specific" interface definitions. When you compile the definitions, the NIDL Compiler emits directives in the version-specific header files to include the version-independent header file. In effect, a server that exports both versions of the interface includes this file twice, but every header file generated by the NIDL Compiler contains conditional statements to ensure that its contents are read only once, and therefore no declarations are duplicated.

If you declare a constant in two versions of an interface definition, the NIDL Compiler emits a C preprocessor **#define** directive for the constant in both of the C header files it generates. Though most C preprocessors accept the resulting duplication, it is better practice to define each constant only once, so we recommend that you keep shared constants together with shared types in a separate interface definition file.

Figure 8–16 shows what an interface definition file for shared types and constants might look like. The "interface" requires a name but no attributes.

```
%c
interface sharedstuff
{
const VSIZE 1024;

typedef struct {
    int vlast;
    float [last_is(vlast)] varray [VSIZE];
    } values;
}
```

Figure 8–16. An Interface Definition File for Shared Types and Constants

8.5 Multiple Managers

NCS allows one server to implement an interface for several object types. A separate manager implements each combination of interface and type. The server registers its objects and their types with the RPC runtime library and the Location Broker; it registers its managers with the RPC runtime library.

This section describes the **stacks** example, in which a server manages two types of stacks, one based on lists and one based on arrays. Complete source code for the example resides in the directory *examples/***stacks**.

8.5.1 The stacks Interface Definition

Figure 8–17 shows **stacks.idl,** the NIDL definition for the **stacks** interface. There are operations to initialize a stack, to push a value onto a stack, and to pop a value off of a stack. Since the interface definition is purely syntactic, it does not indicate in any way the existence of two types of stacks. Different object types require different implementations of operations, but not different signatures.

When you compile **stacks.idl,** specify the NIDL Compiler option **–m**. The **nidl** reference description in Chapter 17 describes the NIDL Compiler options.

```
%c
[uuid(4438675bf000.0d.00.00.fe.da.00.00.00), version(1)]
interface stacks
{
[idempotent]
    void stacks$init(
        handle_t [in] h
        );

/* stack functions return non-zero on error, zero otherwise */

int stacks$push(
    handle_t [in] h,
    int [in] value
    );

int stacks$pop(
    handle_t [in] h,
    int [out] *value
    );
}
```

Figure 8–17. The stacks/stacks.idl Interface Definition

8.5.2 The stacksdf.h Header File

Most of the examples in this book do not involve a particular object and hence specify **uuid_$nil** as the object identifier. The **bank** example, which we introduced to illustrate automatic binding, accesses two bank databases that are objects of the same type. The **stacks** example accesses two stacks that are objects of different types.

The **stacksdf.h** header file, shown in Figure 8–18, defines symbolic constants to represent UUIDs for the two stacks and their types. The replacement texts for these constants are C representations of UUIDs, which we generated by invoking **uuid_gen** with the   **C** option.

```
/* the two stack objects and their types */

/* the array-based object */
#define ASTACK      {0x44349d2c, 0x2000, 0x0000, 0x0d, \
                        {0x00, 0x00, 0xfe, 0xda, 0x00, 0x00, 0x00}}

#define ASTACKT     {0x44349e25, 0x0000, 0x0000, 0x0d, \
                        {0x00, 0x00, 0xfe, 0xda, 0x00, 0x00, 0x00}}

/* the list-based object */
#define LSTACK      {0x44349e48, 0x2000, 0x0000, 0x0d, \
                        {0x00, 0x00, 0xfe, 0xda, 0x00, 0x00, 0x00}}

#define LSTACKT     {0x44349eed, 0x6000, 0x0000, 0x0d, \
                        {0x00, 0x00, 0xfe, 0xda, 0x00, 0x00, 0x00}}
```

Figure 8–18. The stacks/stacksdf.h Header File

8.5.3 The stacks Client Module

Figure 8–19 shows excerpts from the client module **client.c**.

The client program lets the user access both types of stacks within one session; it maintains a separate handle for each stack. (Other clients we have seen maintain only one handle.) The handles are kept in an array, as are the UUIDs for the stack types.

For each type, the client

1. Performs a Location Broker lookup by type

2. Scans the entries returned for one with the desired interface and address family

3. Binds a handle to represent the object and the location registered in the entry

When the client program calls **stacks$push** or **stacks$pop**, the object UUID in the handle determines the stack to be accessed.

```
...
#include "stacks.h"
#include "stackdf.h"
...
#define MAXENTRIES 5      /* how many L.B. entries we can handle */
...
main()
{
    handle_t handle[2];
    status_$t st;
    lb_$entry_t entries[MAXENTRIES];
...
    static uuid_$t types[2] = {ASTACKT, LSTACKT};
    int s, t, k, found_if;
    ndr_$long_int val;
    char command[100], which[100], value[100];
...
    /* bind handles for each object type */
    for (t = 0; t < 2; t++) {
        /* find lb entries for the type */
        lb_$lookup_type(&types[t], &ehandle, MAXENTRIES, &nresults,
                entries, &st);
        if (nresults < 1) {
            fprintf(stderr,
                    "Couldn't find interfaces for type[%d]\n", t);
            exit(1);
        }

        /* check for appropriate interface for the type */
        for (k = 0, found_if = 0; k < nresults; k++)
            if (uuid_$equal(&entries[k].obj_interface,
                    &stacks_v1$if_spec.id) &&
                socket_$valid_family(entries[k].saddr.family,&st)) {
                found_if = 1; /* found appropriate interface */
                break;
            }
        if (!found_if) {
            fprintf(stderr, "Couldn't find appropriate interface\n");
            exit(1);
        }

        /* bind handle */
        handle[t] = rpc_$bind(&entries[k].object,
            &entries[k].saddr, entries[k].saddr_len, &st);
    }
```

(continued)

Figure 8–19. Excerpts from the stacks/client.c Module

```
    printf("Initialize stack objects (y/n)? ");
    gets(command);
    if (*command != 'n' && *command != 'N') {
        stacks$init(handle[0]);
        stacks$init(handle[1]);
    }

    do {
        printf("push, pop, or quit: ");
        gets(command);

        if (!strcmp(command, "quit")) break;

        printf("astack or lstack: ");
        gets(which);

        if (!strcmp(which, "astack")) s = 0;
        else s = 1;

        if (!strcmp(command, "push")) {
            printf("value: ");
            gets(value);
            val = (ndr_$long_int)atoi(value);
            printf("Pushing %d onto %s...",
                val, s?"lstack":"astack");
            if (stacks$push(handle[s], val)) printf("stack full!\n");
            else printf("successful\n");
        }
        else if (!strcmp(command, "pop")) {
            printf("Popping off of %s...", s?"lstack":"astack");
            if (stacks$pop(handle[s], &val))
                printf("nothing on stack!\n");
            else printf("value is %d\n", val);
        }
    } while (strcmp(command, "quit"));
}
```

Figure 8-19. Excerpts from the stacks/client.c Module (continued)

8.5.4 The stacks Server Module

The **server.c** module is linked together with two manager modules to form the **stacks** server program.

Manager EPVs

The server module declares two manager EPVs as external variables:

```
globalref stacks_v1$epv_t stacks_v1$amanager_epv;
globalref stacks_v1$epv_t stacks_v1$lmanager_epv;
```

Each EPV is defined in its own manager module.

Registrations and Unregistrations

Figure 8–20 shows the registration and unregistration code in **server.c**.

The **stacks** server offers access to both types of stacks. It registers the stack objects and types with the RPC runtime library and the Location Broker, and it registers its managers with the RPC runtime library.

The Location Broker registrations enable clients to look up the objects, types, and interfaces that the server supports, along with the location of the server.

The object registrations (**rpc_$register_object** calls) tell the RPC runtime library what objects the server supports and what the type of each object is. The manager registrations (**rpc_$register_mgr** calls) tell the RPC runtime library what combination of interface and type each manager implements. When the server receives a remote procedure call from a client, the runtime library dispatches the call to the correct manager.

Before it calls **rpc_$listen** to begin accepting requests, the server sets a cleanup handler. If it is signaled, the server removes all of its registrations before it exits.

```
...
#include "stackdf.h"
#include "stacks.h"
...
globalref stacks_v1$epv_t stacks_v1$amanager_epv;
globalref stacks_v1$epv_t stacks_v1$lmanager_epv;
...
    status_$t st;
    lb_$entry_t lb_entry[2];
    pfm_$cleanup_rec crec,
    static uuid_$t astack = ASTACK, astackt = ASTACKT;
    static uuid_$t lstack = LSTACK, lstackt = LSTACKT;
...
    /* register manager and object for array-based stack object... */
    rpc_$register_mgr(&astackt, &stacks_v1$if_spec,
        stacks_v1$server_epv,
        (rpc_$mgr_epv_t)&stacks_v1$amanager_epv, &st);

    rpc_$register_object(&astack, &astackt, &st);

    /* ...and list-based stack object with the runtime library */
    rpc_$register_mgr(&lstackt, &stacks_v1$if_spec,
        stacks_v1$server_epv,
        (rpc_$mgr_epv_t)&stacks_v1$lmanager_epv, &st);

    rpc_$register_object(&lstack, &lstackt, &st);

    /* register array-based stack object/interface... */
    lb_$register(&astack, &astackt, &stacks_v1$if_spec.id, 0L,
        (ndr_$char *)"astack example", &loc, llen, &lb_entry[0], &st);

    /* ...and list-based stack object/interface with the lb*/
    lb_$register(&lstack, &lstackt, &stacks_v1$if_spec.id, 0L,
        (ndr_$char *)"lstack example", &loc, llen, &lb_entry[1], &st);

    st = pfm_$cleanup(&crec);
    if (st.all != pfm_$cleanup_set) {
        status_$t stat;
        fprintf(stderr, "Server received signal - %s\n",
            error_text(st));
        lb_$unregister(&lb_entry[0], &stat);
        lb_$unregister(&lb_entry[1], &stat);
        rpc_$unregister(&stacks_v1$if_spec, &stat); /* once for each */
        rpc_$unregister(&stacks_v1$if_spec, &stat); /*     manager   */
        pfm_$signal(st);
    }
...
```

Figure 8-20. Registrations and Unregistrations in the stacks/server.c Module

8.5.5 The stacks Manager Modules

A separate manager module implements the **stacks** interface for each type of stack:
lmanager.c (Figure 8–21) manages stacks based on linked lists, and **amanager.c**
(Figure 8–22) manages stacks based on arrays.

Each manager module defines a manager EPV. The EPV specifies the names under which
the **stacks** operations are implemented. Since we are linking both managers together in one
server, the two implementations of each operation have different names.

```
#include "stacks.h"

void stacks$lstack_init();
ndr_$long_int stacks$lstack_push(), stacks$lstack_pop();

globaldef stacks_v1$epv_t stacks_v1$lmanager_epv =
    {stacks$lstack_init, stacks$lstack_push, stacks$lstack_pop};

#define NULL (struct node *)0
extern struct node *malloc();

static struct node {
    ndr_$long_int value;
    struct node *next;
} the_stack;

void stacks$lstack_init(h)
handle_t h;
{
    the_stack.next = NULL;
}

ndr_$long_int stacks$lstack_push(h, value)
handle_t h;
ndr_$long_int value;
{
    struct node *head = malloc(sizeof(struct node));
    if (head == NULL) return -1;              /* stack is full */

    head->value = value;
    head->next = the_stack.next;
    the_stack.next = head;
    return 0;
}

ndr_$long_int stacks$lstack_pop(h, value)
handle_t h;
ndr_$long_int *value;
{
    struct node *head = the_stack.next;
    if (head == NULL) return -1;              /* stack is empty */

    *value = head->value;
    the_stack.next = head->next;
    free(head);
    return 0;
}
```

Figure 8-21. The stacks/lmanager.c Manager Module

```
#include "stacks.h"

void stacks$astack_init();
ndr_$long_int stacks$astack_push(), stacks$astack_pop();

globaldef stacks_v1$epv_t stacks_v1$amanager_epv =
    {stacks$astack_init, stacks$astack_push, stacks$astack_pop};

#define STACKSIZE    1000

static struct {
    int head;
    ndr_$long_int values[STACKSIZE];
} the_stack;

void stacks$astack_init(h)
handle_t h;
{
    the_stack.head = STACKSIZE;
}

ndr_$long_int stacks$astack_push(h, value)
handle_t h;
ndr_$long_int value;
{
    if (the_stack.head == 0) return -1;          /* stack is full */

    the_stack.values[--the_stack.head] = value;

    return 0;
}

ndr_$long_int stacks$astack_pop(h, value)
handle_t h;
ndr_$long_int *value;
{
    if (the_stack.head == STACKSIZE) return -1; /* stack is empty */

    *value = the_stack.values[the_stack.head++];

    return 0;
}
```

Figure 8-22. The stacks/amanager.c Manager Module

————— ⊞ —————

Chapter 9

crror_$ Calls

Contents

NAME
>
> error_$intro – error text database operations

DESCRIPTION

> The **error_$** calls convert status codes into textual error messages.
>
> There is no header file for the **error_$** calls. They can be declared as follows:

```
extern void error_$c_get_text();
extern char *error_$c_text();
```

> The **error_$** calls use the **status_$t** data type, which is defined in **<idl/c/nbase.h>**.

DATA TYPES

> The **error_$** calls take as input a status code in **status_$t** format.
>
> **status_$t** A status code. Most of the NCS calls supply their completion status in this format. The **status_$t** type is defined as a structure containing a long integer:

```
struct status_$t {
    long all;
    }
```

> However, the calls can also use **status_$t** as a set of bit fields. To access the fields in a returned status code, you can assign the value of the status code to a union defined as follows:

```
typedef union {
    struct {
        unsigned fail : 1,
                 subsys : 7,
                 modc : 8;
        short    code;
    } s;
    long all;
} status_u;
```

> **all** All 32 bits in the status code. If **all** is equal to **status_$ok**, the call that supplied the status was successful.
>
> **fail** If this bit is set, the error was not within the scope of the module invoked, but occurred within a lower-level module.
>
> **subsys** This indicates the subsystem that encountered the error.
>
> **modc** This indicates the module that encountered the error.
>
> **code** This is a signed number that identifies the type of error that occurred.

NAME
>   **error_$c_get_text** – return subsystem, module, and error texts for a status code

SYNOPSIS (C)
>   **void error_$c_get_text(**
>>   **status_$t** *status,*
>>   **char ****subsys,*
>>   **long** *subsysmax,*
>>   **char ****module,*
>>   **long** *modulemax,*
>>   **char ****error,*
>>   **long** *errormax)*

SYNOPSIS (PASCAL)
>   **procedure error_$c_get_text(**
>>   **in** *status:* **status_$t;**
>>   **out** *subsys:* **univ char;**
>>   **in** *subsysmax:* **integer32;**
>>   **out** *module:* **univ char;**
>>   **in** *modulemax:* **integer32;**
>>   **out** *error:* **univ char;**
>>   **in** *errormax:* **integer32);**

DESCRIPTION
>   The **error_$c_get_text** call returns predefined text strings that describe the subsystem, the module, and the error represented by a status code. The strings are null terminated.

>   *status*   A status code in **status_$t** format.

>   *subsys*   A character string. The subsystem represented by the status code.

>   *subsysmax*
>>   The maximum number of bytes to be returned in *subsys*.

>   *module*   A character string. The module represented by the status code.

>   *modulemax*
>>   The maximum number of bytes to be returned in *module*.

>   *error*   A character string. The error represented by the status code.

>   *errormax* The maximum number of bytes to be returned in *error*.

EXAMPLE
>   The following statement returns text strings for the subsystem, module, and error represented by the status code **st**:

```
error_$c_get_text (st, subsys, MAX, module, MAX, error, MAX);
```

SEE ALSO
>   error_$c_text

NAME

>   **error_$c_text** – return an error message for a status code

SYNOPSIS (C)

>   **char *error_$c_text(**
>>   **status_$t** *status,*
>>   **char ***message,*
>>   **int** *messagemax)*

SYNOPSIS (PASCAL)

>   **procedure error_$c_text(**
>>   **in** *status*: **status_$t;**
>>   **out** *message*: **univ char;**
>>   **in** *messagemax*: **integer32);**

DESCRIPTION

>   The **error_$c_text** call returns a null-terminated error message for reporting the completion status of a call. The error message is composed from predefined text strings that describe the subsystem, the module, and the error represented by the status code.

>   *status*   A status code in **status_$t** format.

>   *message*   A character string. The error message represented by the status code.

>   *messagemax*
>>   The maximum number of bytes to be returned in *message*.

EXAMPLE

>   The following statement returns an error message for reporting the status code **st**:

```
error_$c_text (st, message, MAX);
```

SEE ALSO

>   error_$c_get_text

Chapter 10

lb_$ Calls

Contents

NAME

lb_$intro – interface to the Location Broker

SYNOPSIS (C)

#include <idl/c/lb.h>

SYNOPSIS (PASCAL)

%include '/sys/ins/lb.ins.pas';

DESCRIPTION

The **lb_$** calls constitute the programmatic interface to the Location Broker Client Agent. This interface is defined by the file *idl*/**lb.idl**, where the symbol *idl* denotes the system **idl** directory. On Apollo workstations and other UNIX systems, *idl* is **/usr/include/idl**.

EXTERNAL VARIABLES

The following external variable is used in **lb_$** lookup calls:

uuid_$nil

An external **uuid_$t** variable that is preassigned the value of the nil UUID. Do not change the value of this variable.

CONSTANTS

The following constants are used in **lb_$** calls:

lb_$default_lookup_handle

A value for **lb_$lookup_handle_t**. On input, it specifies that a lookup is to start searching at the beginning of the database. On output, it indicates that a lookup reached the end of the database.

lb_$mod A module code indicating the Location Broker module. See the description of the **status_$t** type.

lb_$server_flag_local

Used in the **flags** field of an **lb_$entry_t** variable. Specifies that an entry is to be registered only in the Local Location Broker (LLB) database. See the description of **lb_$server_flag_t** in the "DATA TYPES" section.

DATA TYPES

This section describes data types used in **lb_$** calls.

lb_$entry_t

An identifier for an object, a type, an interface, and the socket address used to access a server exporting the interface to the object. The **lb_$entry_t** type is defined as follows:

```
typedef struct lb_$entry_t lb_$entry_t;
struct lb_$entry_t {
    uuid_$t object;
    uuid_$t obj_type;
    uuid_$t obj_interface;
    lb_$server_flag_t flags;
    ndr_$char annotation[64];
    ndr_$ulong_int saddr_len;
    socket_$addr_t saddr;
};
```

object   A **uuid_$t**. The UUID for the object. Can be **uuid_$nil**.

obj_type   A **uuid_$t**. The UUID for the type of the object. Can be **uuid_$nil**.

obj_interface

A **uuid_$t**. The UUID for the interface. Can be **uuid_$nil**.

flags   An **lb_$server_flag_t**. Must be 0 or **lb_$server_flag_local**. A value of 0 specifies that the entry is to be registered in both the Local Location Broker (LLB) and Global Location Broker (GLB) databases. A value of **lb_$server_flag_local** specifies registration only in the LLB database.

annotation

A 64-character array. User-defined textual annotation.

saddr_len

A 32-bit integer. The length of the **saddr** field.

saddr   A **socket_$addr_t**. The socket address of the server.

lb_$lookup_handle_t

A 32-bit integer used to specify the point in the database at which a Location Broker lookup operation will start.

lb_$server_flag_t

A 32-bit integer used to specify the Location Broker databases in which an entry is to be registered. A value of 0 specifies registration in both the LLB and GLB databases. A value of **lb_$server_flag_local** specifies registration only in the LLB database.

socket_$addr_t

A socket address record that uniquely identifies a socket. See the **socket_$intro** section of Chapter 15 for a full description of this type.

status_$t A status code. Most of the NCS calls supply their completion status in this format. The **status_$t** type is defined as a structure containing a long integer:

```
struct status_$t {
    long all;
    }
```

However, the calls can also use **status_$t** as a set of bit fields. To access the fields in a returned status code, you can assign the value of the status code to a union defined as follows:

```
typedef union {
    struct {
        unsigned fail : 1,
                 subsys : 7,
                 modc : 8;
        short    code;
    } s;
    long all;
} status_u;
```

all All 32 bits in the status code. If **all** is equal to **status_$ok**, the call that supplied the status was successful.

fail If this bit is set, the error was not within the scope of the module invoked, but occurred within a lower-level module.

subsys This indicates the subsystem that encountered the error.

modc This indicates the module that encountered the error.

code This is a signed number that identifies the type of error that occurred.

uuid_$t A 128-bit value that uniquely identifies an object, type, or interface for all time. See the **uuid_$intro** section of Chapter 16 for a full description of this type.

STATUS CODES
The following are status codes returned by **lb_$** calls:

lb_$cant_access
The Location Broker cannot access the database. Among the possible reasons: (1) the database does not exist, and the Location Broker cannot create it; (2) the database exists, but the Location Broker cannot access it; (3) the GLB entry table or the GLB propagation queue is full.

lb_$database_busy
The Location Broker database is currently in use in an incompatible manner.

lb_$database_invalid
The format of the Location Broker database is out of date. The database may have been created by an old version of the Location Broker; in this case, delete the out-of-date database and reregister any entries that it contained. The LLB or GLB that was accessed may be running out-of-date software; in this case, update all Location Brokers to the current software version.

lb_$not_registered
The Location Broker does not have any entries that match the criteria specified in the lookup or unregister call. The requested object, type, interface, or combination thereof is not registered in the specified database. If you are using an **lb_$lookup_object_local** or **lb_$lookup_range call** specifying an LLB, check that you have specified the correct LLB.

lb_$server_unavailable
The Location Broker Client Agent cannot reach the requested GLB or LLB. A communications failure occurred or the broker was not running.

lb_$update_failed
The Location Broker was unable to register or unregister the entry (for example, because the broker ran out of disk space).

status_$ok
The call was successful.

FILES
idl/**lb.idl**

NAME

> lb_$lookup_interface – look up information about an interface in the GLB database

SYNOPSIS (C)

> #include <idl/c/lb.h>
>
> void lb_$lookup_interface(
>   uuid_$t *obj_interface,
>   lb_$lookup_handle_t *lookup_handle,
>   unsigned long max_results,
>   unsigned long *num_results,
>   lb_$entry_t results[],
>   status_$t *status)

SYNOPSIS (PASCAL)

> %include '/usr/include/idl/pas/lb.ins.pas'
>
> procedure lb_$lookup_interface(
>   in obj_interface: uuid_$t;
>   in out lookup_handle: lb_$lookup_handle_t;
>   in max_results: unsigned32;
>   out num_results: unsigned32;
>   out results: array [1..*] of lb_$entry_t;
>   out status: status_$t);

DESCRIPTION

> The **lb_$lookup_interface** call returns GLB database entries whose **obj_interface** fields match the specified interface. It returns information about all replicas of all objects that can be accessed through that interface.
>
> The **lb_$lookup_interface** call cannot return more than *max_results* matching entries at a time. The *lookup_handle* parameter enables you to find all matching entries by doing sequential lookups.
>
> If you use a sequence of lookup calls to find entries in the database, it is possible that the returned results will skip or duplicate entries. This is because the Location Broker does not prevent modification of the database between lookups, and such modification can change the positions of entries relative to a *lookup_handle* value.
>
> It is also possible that the results of a single lookup call will skip or duplicate entries.
>
> *obj_interface*
>> The UUID of the interface being looked up.
>
> *lookup_handle*
>> A position in the database.
>>
>> On input, the *lookup_handle* indicates the position in the database where the search begins. An input value of **lb_$default_lookup_handle** specifies that the search will start at the beginning of the database.

On return, the *lookup_handle* indicates the next unsearched part of the database (that is, the point at which the next search should begin). A return value of **lb_$default_lookup_handle** indicates that the search reached the end of the database; any other return value indicates that the search found *max_results* matching entries before it reached the end of the database.

max_results
The maximum number of entries that can be returned by a single call. This should be the number of elements in the *results* array.

num_results
The number of entries that were returned in the *results* array.

results   An array that contains the matching GLB database entries, up to the number specified by the *max_results* parameter. If the array contains any entries for servers on the local network, those entries appear first.

status   The completion status.

EXAMPLE
The following statement looks up information in the GLB database about the directory interface identified by **dirid**:

```
lb_$lookup_interface (&dirid, &lookup_handle, max_results,
    &num_results, results, &st);
```

FILES
idl/**lb.idl**

SEE ALSO
lb_$lookup_object, lb_$lookup_range, lb_$lookup_type

NAME

   lb_$lookup_object – look up information about an object in the GLB database

SYNOPSIS (C)

   #include <idl/c/lb.h>

   void lb_$lookup_object(
           uuid_$t **object,*
           lb_$lookup_handle_t **lookup_handle,*
           unsigned long *max_results,*
           unsigned long **num_results,*
           lb_$entry_t *results[],*
           status_$t **status*)

SYNOPSIS (PASCAL)

   %include '/usr/include/idl/pas/lb.ins.pas'

   procedure lb_$lookup_object(
           in *object*: **uuid_$t;**
           in out *lookup_handle*: **lb_$lookup_handle_t;**
           in *max_results*: **unsigned32;**
           out *num_results*: **unsigned32;**
           out *results*: **array [1..*] of lb_$entry_t;**
           out *status*: **status_$t);**

DESCRIPTION

   The **lb_$lookup_object** call returns GLB database entries whose **object** fields match the specified type. It returns information about all replicas of an object and about all interfaces to the object.

   The **lb_$lookup_object** call cannot return more than *max_results* matching entries at a time. The *lookup_handle* parameter enables you to find all matching entries by doing sequential lookups.

   If you use a sequence of lookup calls to find entries in the database, it is possible that the returned results will skip or duplicate entries. This is because the Location Broker does not prevent modification of the database between lookups, and such modification can change the positions of entries relative to a *lookup_handle* value.

   It is also possible that the results of a single lookup call will skip or duplicate entries.

   object   The UUID of the object being looked up.

   lookup_handle

           A position in the database.

           On input, the *lookup_handle* indicates the position in the database where the search begins. An input value of **lb_$default_lookup_handle** specifies that the search will start at the beginning of the database.

           On return, the *lookup_handle* indicates the next unsearched part of the database (that is, the point at which the next search should begin). A return value of **lb_$default_lookup_handle** indicates that the search reached the end of the database; any other return value indicates that the search found *max_results* matching entries before it reached the end of the database.

max_results

The maximum number of entries that can be returned by a single call. This should be the number of elements in the *results* array.

num_results

The number of entries that were returned in the *results* array.

results   An array that contains the matching GLB database entries, up to the number specified by the *max_results* parameter. If the array contains any entries for servers on the local network, those entries appear first.

status   The completion status.

EXAMPLE

The following statement looks up GLB database entries for the object identified by **objid**:

```
lb_$lookup_object (&objid, &lookup_handle, max_results,
    &num_results, results, &st);
```

FILES

idl/**lb.idl**

SEE ALSO

lb_$lookup_interface, lb_$lookup_object_local, lb_$lookup_range, lb_$lookup_type

NAME

   lb_$lookup_object_local – look up information about an object in an LLB database

SYNOPSIS (C)

   #include <idl/c/lb.h>

   void lb_$lookup_object_local(
           uuid_$t *****object,
           socket_$addr_t *****location,
           unsigned long *location_length,*
           **lb_$lookup_handle_t *****lookup_handle,*
           unsigned long *max_results,*
           **unsigned long *****num_results,*
           lb_$entry_t *results[],*
           **status_$t *****status)*

SYNOPSIS (PASCAL)

   %include '/usr/include/idl/pas/lb.ins.pas'

   procedure lb_$lookup_object_local(
           in *object*: **uuid_$t;**
           in *location*: **socket_$addr_t;**
           in *location_length*: **unsigned32;**
           in out *lookup_handle*: **lb_$lookup_handle_t;**
           in *max_results*: **unsigned32;**
           out *num_results*: **unsigned32;**
           out *results*: **array [1..*] of lb_$entry_t;**
           out *status*: **status_$t);**

DESCRIPTION

   The **lb_$lookup_object_local** call searches the specified LLB database and returns all entries whose **object** fields match the specified object. It returns information about all replicas of an object and all interfaces to the object that are located on the specified host.

   The **lb_$lookup_object_local** call cannot return more than *max_results* matching entries at a time. The *lookup_handle* parameter enables you to find all matching entries by doing sequential lookups.

   If you use a sequence of lookup calls to find entries in the database, it is possible that the returned results will skip or duplicate entries. This is because the Location Broker does not prevent modification of the database between lookups, and such modification can change the positions of entries relative to a *lookup_handle* value.

   It is also possible that the results of a single lookup call will skip or duplicate entries.

   object   The UUID of the object being looked up.

   location The location of the LLB database to be searched. The socket address must specify the network address of a host. However, the port number in the socket address is ignored, and the lookup request is always sent to the LLB port.

   location_length
           The length, in bytes, of the socket address specified by the location field.

lookup_handle
> A position in the database.
>
> On input, the *lookup_handle* indicates the position in the database where the search begins. An input value of **lb_$default_lookup_handle** specifies that the search will start at the beginning of the database.
>
> On return, the *lookup_handle* indicates the next unsearched part of the database (that is, the point at which the next search should begin). A return value of **lb_$default_lookup_handle** indicates that the search reached the end of the database; any other return value indicates that the search found *max_results* matching entries before it reached the end of the database.

max_results
> The maximum number of entries that can be returned by a single call. This should be the number of elements in the *results* array.

num_results
> The number of entries that were returned in the *results* array.

results
> An array that contains the matching GLB database entries, up to the number specified by the *max_results* parameter. If the array contains any entries for servers on the local network, those entries appear first.

status
> The completion status.

EXAMPLE
> The following statement looks up the replicated object identified by **repobjid** in the LLB database at the host specified by **loc**. Though this object is replicated, only one replica is located on any host, so the call will return at most one result.
>
> ```
> lb_$lookup_object_local (&repobjid, &loc, loc_len, &lookup_handle,
>     1, &num_results, results, &st);
> ```

FILES
> *idl*/**lb.idl**

SEE ALSO
> lb_$lookup_range

NAME

  lb_$lookup_range – look up information in a GLB or LLB database

SYNOPSIS (C)

  #include <idl/c/lb.h>

  void lb_$lookup_range(
        uuid_$t **object,*
        uuid_$t **obj_type,*
        uuid_$t **obj_interface,*
        socket_$addr_t **location,*
        unsigned long *location_length,*
        lb_$lookup_handle_t **lookup_handle,*
        unsigned long *max_results,*
        unsigned long **num_results,*
        lb_$entry_t *results*[],
        status_$t **status*)

SYNOPSIS (PASCAL)

  %include '/usr/include/idl/pas/lb.ins.pas'

  procedure lb_$lookup_range(
        in *object*: **uuid_$t;**
        in *obj_type*: **uuid_$t;**
        in *obj_interface*: **uuid_$t;**
        in *location*: **socket_$addr_t;**
        in *location_length*: **unsigned32;**
        in out *lookup_handle*: **lb_$lookup_handle_t;**
        in *max_results*: **unsigned32;**
        out *num_results*: **unsigned32;**
        out *results*: **array [1..*] of lb_$entry_t;**
        out *status*: **status_$t);**

DESCRIPTION

  The **lb_$lookup_range** call returns database entries whose **object**, **obj_type**, and **obj_interface** fields
  match the specified values. A value of **uuid_$nil** in any of these input parameters acts as a wildcard and
  will match any value in the corresponding entry field. You can specify wildcards in any combination of
  these parameters.

  The **lb_$lookup_range** call cannot return more than *max_results* matching entries at a time. The
  lookup_handle parameter enables you to find all matching entries by doing sequential lookups.

  If you use a sequence of lookup calls to find entries in the database, it is possible that the returned results
  will skip or duplicate entries. This is because the Location Broker does not prevent modification of the
  database between lookups, and such modification can change the positions of entries relative to a
  lookup_handle value.

  It is also possible that the results of a single lookup call will skip or duplicate entries.

object   The UUID of the object being looked up.

obj_type   The UUID of the type being looked up.

obj_interface
             The UUID of the interface being looked up.

location   The location of the database to be searched. If the value of *location_length* is 0, the GLB data-
             base is searched. Otherwise, the LLD database at the host specified by the socket address is
             searched; in this case, the port number in the socket address is ignored, and the lookup request is
             sent to the LLB port.

location_length
             The length, in bytes, of the socket address specified by the *location* field. A value of 0 indicates
             that the GLB database is to be searched.

lookup_handle
             A position in the database.

             On input, the *lookup_handle* indicates the position in the database where the search begins. An
             input value of **lb_$default_lookup_handle** specifies that the search will start at the beginning of
             the database.

             On return, the *lookup_handle* indicates the next unsearched part of the database (that is, the
             point at which the next search should begin). A return value of **lb_$default_lookup_handle**
             indicates that the search reached the end of the database; any other return value indicates that the
             search found *max_results* matching entries before it reached the end of the database.

max_results
             The maximum number of entries that can be returned by a single call. This should be the
             number of elements in the *results* array.

num_results
             The number of entries that were returned in the *results* array.

results   An array that contains the matching GLB database entries, up to the number specified by the
             max_results parameter. If the array contains any entries for servers on the local network, those
             entries appear first.

status   The completion status.

EXAMPLE
     The following statement looks up information in the GLB database about servers that export the interface
     identified by **matrix_id** for any objects of the type identified by **array_id**. The variable **glb** is defined else-
     where as a null pointer.

```
lb_$lookup_range (&uuid_$nil, &array_id, &matrix_id, glb, 0,
    &lookup_handle, max_results, &num_results, results, &st);
```

FILES
     *idl/***lb.idl**

SEE ALSO
     lb_$lookup_interface, lb_$lookup_object, lb_$lookup_object_local, lb_$lookup_type

NAME

> **lb_$lookup_type** – look up information about a type in the GLB database

SYNOPSIS (C)

> **#include <idl/c/lb.h>**
>
> **void lb_$lookup_type(**
> > **uuid_$t ***_obj_type_**,**
> > **lb_$lookup_handle_t ***_lookup_handle_**,**
> > **unsigned long** _max_results_**,**
> > **unsigned long ***_num_results_**,**
> > **lb_$entry_t** _results_**[],**
> > **status_$t ***_status_**)**

SYNOPSIS (PASCAL)

> **%include '/usr/include/idl/pas/lb.ins.pas'**
>
> **procedure lb_$lookup_type(**
> > **in** _obj_type_**: uuid_$t;**
> > **in out** _lookup_handle_**: lb_$lookup_handle_t;**
> > **in** _max_results_**: unsigned32;**
> > **out** _num_results_**: unsigned32;**
> > **out** _results_**: array [1..*] of lb_$entry_t;**
> > **out** _status_**: status_$t);**

DESCRIPTION

> The **lb_$lookup_type** call returns GLB database entries whose **obj_type** fields match the specified type. It returns information about all replicas of all objects of that type and about all interfaces to each of these objects.
>
> The **lb_$lookup_type** call cannot return more than _max_results_ matching entries at a time. The _lookup_handle_ parameter enables you to find all matching entries by doing sequential lookups.
>
> If you use a sequence of lookup calls to find entries in the database, it is possible that the returned results will skip or duplicate entries. This is because the Location Broker does not prevent modification of the database between lookups, and such modification can change the positions of entries relative to a _lookup_handle_ value.
>
> It is also possible that the results of a single lookup call will skip or duplicate entries.
>
> _obj_type_   The UUID of the type being looked up.
>
> _lookup_handle_
> > A position in the database.
> >
> > On input, the _lookup_handle_ indicates the position in the database where the search begins. An input value of **lb_$default_lookup_handle** specifies that the search will start at the beginning of the database.

On return, the *lookup_handle* indicates the next unsearched part of the database (that is, the point at which the next search should begin). A return value of **lb_$default_lookup_handle** indicates that the search reached the end of the database; any other return value indicates that the search found *max_results* matching entries before it reached the end of the database.

max_results
> The maximum number of entries that can be returned by a single call. This should be the number of elements in the *results* array.

num_results
> The number of entries that were returned in the *results* array.

results
> An array that contains the matching GLB database entries, up to the number specified by the *max_results* parameter. If the array contains any entries for servers on the local network, those entries appear first.

status   The completion status.

EXAMPLE
> The following statement looks up information in the GLB database about the type identified by **array_id**:

```
lb_$lookup_type (&array_id, &lookup_handle, max_results,
    &num_results, results, &st);
```

FILES
> *idl*/**lb.idl**

SEE ALSO
> lb_$lookup_interface, lb_$lookup_object, lb_$lookup_range

NAME

lb_$register – register an object and an interface with the Location Broker

SYNOPSIS (C)

#include <idl/c/lb.h>

void lb_$register(
        uuid_$t *object,
        uuid_$t *obj_type,
        uuid_$t *obj_interface,
        lb_$server_flag_t flags,
        unsigned char annotation[64],
        socket_$addr_t *location,
        unsigned long location_length,
        lb_$entry_t *entry,
        status_$t *status)

SYNOPSIS (PASCAL)

%include '/usr/include/idl/pas/lb.ins.pas'

procedure lb_$register(
        in object: uuid_$t;
        in obj_type: uuid_$t;
        in obj_interface: uuid_$t;
        in flags: lb_$server_flag_t;
        in annotation: array [0..63] of char;
        in location: socket_$addr_t;
        in location_length: unsigned32;
        out entry: lb_$entry_t;
        out status: status_$t);

DESCRIPTION

The **lb_$register** call registers with the Location Broker an interface to an object and the location of a server that exports that interface. This call replaces any existing entry in the Location Broker database that matches *object*, *obj_type*, *obj_interface*, and both the address family and host in *location*; if no such entry exists, the call adds a new entry to the database.

If the *flags* parameter is **lb_$server_flag_local**, the entry is registered only in the LLB database at the host where the call is issued. Otherwise, the entry is registered in both the LLB and the GLB databases.

object   The UUID of the object being registered.

obj_type   The UUID of the type of the object being registered.

obj_interface

        The UUID of the interface being registered.

flags   Must be either **lb_$server_flag_local** (specifying registration with only the LLB at the local host) or 0 (specifying registration with both the LLB and the GLB).

annotation
> A character array used only for informational purposes. This field can contain a textual descrip-
> tion of the object and the interface. For proper display by the **lb_admin** tool, the *annotation*
> should be terminated by a null character.

location   The socket address of the server.

location_length
> The length, in bytes, of the socket address specified by the *location* field.

entry   A copy of the entry that was entered in the Location Broker database.

status   The completion status.

EXAMPLE
> The following statement from *examples*/**stacks/server.c**, the server for the **stacks** example, registers an
> object and an interface for array-based stacks with the Location Broker:

```
lb_$register(&astack, &astackt, &stacks_v1$if_spec.id, 0L,
    (ndr_$char *)"astack example", &loc, llen, &lb_entry[0], &st);
```

FILES
> *idl*/**lb.idl**

SEE ALSO
> lb_$unregister

NAME

lb_$unregister – remove an entry from the Location Broker database

SYNOPSIS (C)

```
#include <idl/c/lb.h>

void lb_$unregister(
        lb_$entry_t *entry,
        status_$t *status)
```

SYNOPSIS (PASCAL)

```
%include '/usr/include/idl/pas/lb.ins.pas'

procedure lb_$unregister(
        out entry: lb_$entry_t;
        out status: status_$t);
```

DESCRIPTION

The **lb_$unregister** call removes from the Location Broker database the entry that matches *entry*. The value of *entry* should be identical to that returned by the **lb_$register** call when the database entry was created. However, **lb_$unregister** does not compare all of the fields in *entry*; it ignores the **flags** field, the **annotation** field, and the port number in the **saddr** field.

This call removes the specified entry from the LLB database on the local host (the host that issues the call). If the **flags** field of the entry is not **lb_$server_flag_local**, the call also removes the entry from the GLB database.

entry   The entry being removed from the Location Broker database.

status   The completion status.

EXAMPLE

The following statement from *examples*/**stacks**/**server.c**, the server for the **stacks** example, unregisters the first entry in the **lb_entry** array with the Location Broker:

```
lb_$unregister(&lb_entry[0], &stat);
```

FILES

idl/**lb.idl**

SEE ALSO

lb_$register

Chapter 11

pfm_$ Calls

Contents

NAME

   pfm_$intro – fault management

SYNOPSIS (C)

   #include <idl/c/base.h>
   #include <ppfm.h>

SYNOPSIS (PASCAL)

   %include '/sys/ins/base.ins.pas';
   %include '/sys/ins/ppfm.ins.pas';

DESCRIPTION

   The **pfm_$** calls allow programs to manage signals, faults, and exceptions by establishing cleanup handlers.

   We supply with the NCS software products a portable subset of the Apollo Domain/OS **pfm_$** calls.

Cleanup Handlers

   A cleanup handler is a piece of code that allows a program to terminate gracefully when it receives an error. A cleanup handler begins with a **pfm_$cleanup** call and usually ends with a call to **pfm_$signal** or **pgm_$exit**, though it can also simply continue back into the program after the cleanup code.

Include Files in NCS Software

   This section describes the include files for the **pfm_** interface that we provide with NCS software.

   In Version 1.1 of NCK and NIDL, we supplied a **pfm.h** include file that supports the **std_$call** calling convention of Apollo SR9 system software, whereby all parameters of a call are passed by reference rather than by value. For example, a call in C source code to **pfm_$reset_cleanup** looks like

   ```
   pfm_$reset_cleanup (crec, st)
   ```

   even though both **crec** and **st** are passed by reference to the implementation of **pfm_$reset_cleanup**. On Apollo SR9 systems, the C compiler treats these parameters as though each were preceded by the address operator **&**. On SunOS, ULTRIX, and VMS systems with Version 1.1 of NCK or NIDL, the **pfm.h** that we supplied defines macros that convert these parameters to **&crec** and **&st**.

   In Version 1.5.1 of NCK and NIDL, we supply a new include file for the **pfm_$** calls, **ppfm.h**. This is the include file for the "portable PFM" interface, an interface in the style of ANSI C. When an application invokes a call through this interface, all output parameters must be preceded by an explicit **&**. For example, a call to **pfm_$reset_cleanup** looks like

   ```
   pfm_$reset_cleanup (&crec, &st)
   ```

   since **crec** and **st** are output parameters passed by reference. This calling convention is more natural to most C programmers.

   The previous include file, **pfm.h**, is still available, providing backward compatibility for programs coded according to the **std_$call** convention. However, we recommend that new programs include **ppfm.h**.

Include Files in Apollo SR10 Domain/OS Software

   In Apollo SR10 system software, we supply the include file **<apollo/pfm.h>**, which defines the **pfm_** interface in the style of ANSI C.

   Beginning at SR10.2, we also supply the file **<apollo/ppfm.h>**, which includes **<apollo/pfm.h>**; **/usr/include/ppfm.h** is a symbolic link pointing to **/usr/include/apollo/ppfm.h**.

Thus, you can use the directive

```
#include <ppfm.h>
```

both on Apollo SR10.2 systems and on other systems with Version 1.5.1 of NCK or NIDL.

The signatures for **pfm_$reset_cleanup** and **pfm_$rls_cleanup** in the SR10.0 and SR10.1 versions of **<apollo/pfm.h>** are incorrect. They have been corrected at SR10.2. These corrections may require you to modify an application developed on SR10.0 and SR10.1 Apollo systems in order to compile it on an SR10.2 Apollo system. See the reference descriptions of these calls for details.

CONSTANTS

    pfm_$init_signal_handlers

        A constant used as the *flags* parameter to **pfm_$init**, causing C signals to be intercepted and converted to PFM signals.

DATA TYPES

    pfm_$cleanup_rec

        An opaque data type for passing process context among cleanup handler calls.

  status_$t A status code. Most of the NCS calls supply their completion status in this format. The **status_$t** type is defined as a structure containing a long integer:

```
struct status_$t {
    long all;
    }
```

However, the calls can also use **status_$t** as a set of bit fields. To access the fields in a returned status code, you can assign the value of the status code to a union defined as follows:

```
typedef union {
    struct {
        unsigned fail : 1,
                 subsys : 7,
                 modc : 8;
        short    code;
    } s;
    long all;
} status_u;
```

  all   All 32 bits in the status code. If **all** is equal to **status_$ok**, the call that supplied the status was successful.

  fail   If this bit is set, the error was not within the scope of the module invoked, but occurred within a lower-level module.

  subsys This indicates the subsystem that encountered the error.

  modc   This indicates the module that encountered the error.

  code   This is a signed number that identifies the type of error that occurred.

STATUS CODES

pfm_$bad_rls_order
Attempted to release a cleanup handler out of order.

pfm_$cleanup_not_found
There is no pending cleanup handler.

pfm_$cleanup_set
A cleanup handler was established successfully.

pfm_$cleanup_set_signalled
Attempted to use **pfm_$cleanup_set** as a signal.

pfm_$invalid_cleanup_rec
Passed an invalid cleanup record to a call.

pfm_$no_space
Cannot allocate storage for a cleanup handler.

status_$ok
The call was successful.

NAME

>   **pfm_$cleanup** – establish a cleanup handler

SYNOPSIS (C)

>   **#include <idl/c/base.h>**
>   **#include <ppfm.h>**
>
>   **status_$t pfm_$cleanup(**
>   **pfm_$cleanup_rec *cleanup_record)**

SYNOPSIS (PASCAL)

>   **%include '/sys/ins/base.ins.pas';**
>   **%include '/sys/ins/ppfm.ins.pas';**
>
>   **function pfm_$cleanup(**
>   **out** *cleanup_record*: **pfm_$cleanup_rec): status_$t;**

DESCRIPTION

>   The **pfm_$cleanup** call establishes a cleanup handler that is executed when a fault occurs. A cleanup
>   handler is a piece of code executed before a program exits when a signal is received by the process. The
>   cleanup handler begins where **pfm_$cleanup** is called; the **pfm_$cleanup** call registers an entry point with
>   the system where program execution resumes when a fault occurs. When a fault occurs, execution resumes
>   after the most recent call to **pfm_$cleanup**.
>
>   There can be more than one cleanup handler in a program. Multiple cleanup handlers are executed con-
>   secutively on a last-in/first-out basis, starting with the most recently established cleanup handler and ending
>   with the first cleanup handler.
>
>   On Apollo systems, a default cleanup handler is established at program invocation. The default cleanup
>   handler is always called last, just before a program exits, and releases any system resources still held before
>   returning control to the process that invoked the program.
>
>   On other systems, there is no default cleanup handler.
>
>   When called to establish a cleanup handler, **pfm_$cleanup** returns the status **pfm_$cleanup_set** to indicate
>   that the cleanup handler was successfully established. When the cleanup handler is entered in response to a
>   fault signal, **pfm_$cleanup** effectively returns the value of the fault that triggered the cleanup handler.
>
>   See the reference description of **pfm_$init** for a list of the C signals that the PFM package intercepts.
>
>   *cleanup_record*
>
> >   A record of the context when **pfm_$cleanup** is called. A program should treat this as an opaque
> >   data structure and not try to alter or copy its contents. It is needed by **pfm_$rls_cleanup** and
> >   **pfm_$reset_cleanup** to restore the context of the calling process at the cleanup handler entry
> >   point.

NOTE

The **pfm_$cleanup** call implicitly performs a **pfm_$inhibit**. Cleanup handler code hence runs with asynchronous faults inhibited. When **pfm_$cleanup** returns something other than **pfm_$cleanup_set**, indicating that a fault has occurred, there are four possible ways to leave the cleanup code:

- The program can call **pfm_$signal** to start the next cleanup handler with a fault signal you specify.

- The program can call **pgm_$exit** to start the next cleanup handler with a status of **status_$ok**.

- The program can continue with the code following the cleanup handler. It should generally call **pfm_$enable** to re-enable asynchronous faults. Execution continues from the end of the cleanup handler code; it does not resume where the fault signal was received.

- The program can re-establish the cleanup handler by calling **pfm_$reset_cleanup** (which implicitly performs a **pfm_$enable**) before proceeding.

SEE ALSO

pfm_$init, pfm_$signal

NAME
        pfm_$enable – enable asynchronous faults

SYNOPSIS (C)
        #include <idl/c/base.h>
        #include <ppfm.h>

        void pfm_$enable(void)

SYNOPSIS (PASCAL)
        %include '/sys/ins/base.ins.pas';
        %include '/sys/ins/pfm.ins.pas';

        procedure pfm_$enable;

DESCRIPTION
        The **pfm_$enable** call enables asynchronous faults after they have been inhibited by a call to
        pfm_$inhibit; **pfm_$enable** causes the operating system to pass asynchronous faults on to the calling pro-
        cess.

        While faults are inhibited, the operating system holds at most one asynchronous fault. Consequently, when
        pfm_$enable returns, there can be at most one fault waiting on the process. If more than one fault was
        received between calls to **pfm_$inhibit** and **pfm_$enable**, the process receives the first asynchronous fault
        received while faults were inhibited.

SEE ALSO
        pfm_$enable_faults, pfm_$inhibit

NAME
> **pfm_$enable_faults** – enable asynchronous faults

SYNOPSIS (C)
> **#include <idl/c/base.h>**
> **#include <ppfm.h>**
>
> **void pfm_$enable_faults(void)**

SYNOPSIS (PASCAL)
> **%include '/sys/ins/base.ins.pas';**
> **%include '/sys/ins/pfm.ins.pas';**
>
> **procedure pfm_$enable_faults;**

DESCRIPTION
> The **pfm_$enable_faults** call enables asynchronous faults after they have been inhibited by a call to **pfm_$inhibit_faults**; **pfm_$enable_faults** causes the operating system to pass asynchronous faults on to the calling process.
>
> While faults are inhibited, the operating system holds at most one asynchronous fault. Consequently, when **pfm_$enable_faults** returns, there can be at most one fault waiting on the process. If more than one fault was received between calls to **pfm_$inhibit_faults** and **pfm_$enable_faults**, the process receives the first asynchronous fault received while faults were inhibited.

SEE ALSO
> pfm_$enable, pfm_$inhibit_faults

NAME

   pfm_$inhibit – inhibit asynchronous faults

SYNOPSIS (C)

   #include <idl/c/base.h>
   #include <ppfm.h>

   void pfm_$inhibit(void);

SYNOPSIS (PASCAL)

   %include '/sys/ins/base.ins.pas';
   %include '/sys/ins/pfm.ins.pas';

   procedure pfm_$inhibit;

DESCRIPTION

   The **pfm_$inhibit** call prevents asynchronous faults from being passed to the calling process. While faults
   are inhibited, the operating system holds at most one asynchronous fault. Consequently, a call to
   pfm_$inhibit can result in the loss of some signals. For that and other reasons, it is good practice to inhibit
   faults only when absolutely necessary.

   On systems with Concurrent Programming Support (CPS), **pfm_$inhibit** also disables time-sliced task
   switching. It does not prevent task switching due to voluntary task yielding, either explicitly via
   task_$yield or implicitly via other functions that yield. You should not use **pfm_$inhibit** for critical
   region concurrency control; use the **mutex_** facility instead.

   See the reference description of **pfm_$init** for a list of the C signals that the PFM package intercepts.

NOTE

   This call has no effect on the processing of synchronous faults such as floating-point and overflow exceptions, access violations, and so on.

SEE ALSO

   pfm_$enable, pfm_$inhibit_faults, pfm_$init
   Concurrent Programming Support Reference

NAME
  pfm_$inhibit_faults – inhibit asynchronous faults but allow time-sliced task switching

SYNOPSIS (C)
  #include <idl/c/base.h>
  #include <ppfm.h>

  void pfm_$inhibit_faults(void);

SYNOPSIS (PASCAL)
  %include '/sys/ins/base.ins.pas';
  %include '/sys/ins/pfm.ins.pas';

  procedure pfm_$inhibit_faults;

DESCRIPTION
  The **pfm_$inhibit_faults** call prevents asynchronous faults, except for time-sliced task switching, from being passed to the calling process. While faults are inhibited, the operating system holds at most one asynchronous fault. Consequently, a call to **pfm_$inhibit_faults** can result in the loss of some signals. For that and other reasons, it is good practice to inhibit faults only when absolutely necessary.

  See the reference description of **pfm_$init** for a list of the C signals that the PFM package intercepts.

NOTE
  This call has no effect on the processing of synchronous faults such as floating-point and overflow exceptions, access violations, and so on.

SEE ALSO
  pfm_$enable_faults, pfm_$inhibit, pfm_$init

NAME
>   **pfm_$init** – initialize the PFM package

SYNOPSIS (C)
>   **#include <idl/c/base.h>**
>   **#include <ppfm.h>**
>
>   **void pfm_$init(**
>   **unsigned long** *flags*)

DESCRIPTION
>   The **pfm_$init** call initializes the PFM package. The *flags* parameter indicates which initialization activities to perform.
>
>   *flags*   Currently, only one value is valid:
>
>   **pfm_$init_signal_handlers**
>   This causes C signals to be intercepted and converted to PFM signals. On UNIX and VMS systems, the signals intercepted are SIGINT, SIGILL, SIGFPE, SIGTERM, SIGHUP, SIGQUIT, SIGTRAP, SIGBUS, SIGSEGV, and SIGSYS. On MS-DOS systems, the first four of these, plus SIGABRT, are intercepted.
>
>   On Apollo systems, the PFM package does not require initialization, and **pfm_$init** is a no-op. On all other systems, applications that use the PFM package should invoke **pfm_$init** before invoking any other NCS calls.

NAME
     pfm_$reset_cleanup – reset a cleanup handler

SYNOPSIS (C)
     #include <idl/c/base.h>
     #include <ppfm.h>

     void pfm_$reset_cleanup(
          pfm_$cleanup_rec *cleanup_record,
          status_$t *status)

SYNOPSIS (PASCAL)
     %include '/sys/ins/base.ins.pas';
     %include '/sys/ins/pfm.ins.pas';

     procedure pfm_$reset_cleanup(
          in cleanup_record: pfm_$cleanup_rec;
          out status: status_$t);

DESCRIPTION
     The **pfm_$reset_cleanup** call re-establishes the cleanup handler last entered so that any subsequent errors enter it first. This procedure should only be used within cleanup handler code.

     A **pfm_$reset_cleanup** implicitly performs a **pfm_$enable**, thereby undoing the implicit **pfm_$inhibit** that **pfm_$cleanup** performs.

     cleanup_record
          A record of the context at the cleanup handler entry point. It is supplied by **pfm_$cleanup** when the cleanup handler is first established.

     status   The completion status.

NOTE
     This note concerns use of **pfm_$reset_cleanup** on Apollo systems.

     In the SR10.0 and SR10.1 versions of **<apollo/pfm.h>**, the first argument of **pfm_$reset_cleanup** is incorrectly preceded by an ampersand (**&**). In the SR10.2 version, the first argument is correctly preceded by an asterisk (*).

     Programs compiled under SR10.0 or SR10.1 will continue to run correctly, since the implementation of **pfm_$reset_cleanup** has not changed, but you may need to modify these programs in order to compile them under SR10.2. Invocations of **pfm_$reset_cleanup** that looked like

     pfm_$reset_cleanup(crec, &st)

     when compiled under SR10.0 and SR10.1 must be modified to

     pfm_$reset_cleanup(&crec, &st)

     when compiled under SR10.2.

NAME
        pfm_$rls_cleanup – release a cleanup handler

SYNOPSIS (C)
        #include <idl/c/base.h>
        #include <ppfm.h>

        void pfm_$rls_cleanup(
                pfm_$cleanup_rec **cleanup_record,*
                status_$t **status)*

SYNOPSIS (PASCAL)
        %include '/sys/ins/base.ins.pas';
        %include '/sys/ins/pfm.ins.pas';

        procedure pfm_$rls_cleanup(
                in *cleanup_record*: **pfm_$cleanup_rec;**
                out *status*: **status_$t);**

DESCRIPTION
        The **pfm_$rls_cleanup** call releases the cleanup handler associated with *cleanup_record*.

        On Apollo systems, this call releases the specified cleanup handler and all cleanup handlers established after it.

        On other systems, this call releases only the specified cleanup handler, and only the most recently established cleanup handler can be released.

        If you are concerned about portability, use **pfm_$rls_cleanup** only to release the most recent cleanup handler.

        cleanup_record
                The cleanup record for the cleanup handler to release.

        status   The completion status.

ERRORS
        pfm_$bad_rls_order
                The caller attempted to release a cleanup handler other than the one most recently established. On Apollo systems, this status is only a warning; the specified cleanup handler is released, along with any established after it. On other systems, this status probably indicates a user programming error; no cleanup handlers are released, and continued execution may result in more serious errors.

NOTE

This note concerns use of **pfm_$rls_cleanup** on Apollo systems.

In the SR10.0 and SR10.1 versions of **<apollo/pfm.h>**, the first argument of **pfm_$rls_cleanup** is incorrectly preceded by an ampersand (**&**). In the SR10.2 version, the first argument is correctly preceded by an asterisk (*****).

Programs compiled under SR10.0 or SR10.1 will continue to run correctly, since the implementation of **pfm_$rls_cleanup** has not changed, but you may need to modify these programs in order to compile them under SR10.2. Invocations of **pfm_$rls_cleanup** that looked like

```
pfm_$rls_cleanup(crec, &st)
```

when compiled under SR10.0 and SR10.1 must be modified to

```
pfm_$rls_cleanup(&crec, &st)
```

when compiled under SR10.2.

NAME

    pfm_$signal – signal the calling process

SYNOPSIS (C)

    #include <idl/c/base.h>
    #include <ppfm.h>

    void pfm_$signal(status_$t *fault_signal***)**

SYNOPSIS (PASCAL)

    %include '/sys/ins/base.ins.pas';
    %include '/sys/ins/pfm.ins.pas';

    procedure pfm_$signal(in *fault_signal*: **status_$t);**

DESCRIPTION

    The **pfm_$signal** call signals the fault specified by *fault_signal* to the calling process. It is usually called to leave cleanup handlers.

    fault_signal
        A fault code.

NOTE

    This call does not return when successful.

Chapter 12

pgm_$ Calls

Contents

NAME

pgm_$intro – program management

SYNOPSIS (C)

#include <idl/c/base.h>
#include <ppfm.h>

SYNOPSIS (PASCAL)

%include '/sys/ins/base.ins.pas';
%include '/sys/ins/pgm.ins.pas';

DESCRIPTION

We supply with the NCS software products a portable version of the Apollo Domain/OS **pgm_$exit** call. The include file for the "portable PFM" interface (see Chapter 11) contains a declaration for this call.

NAME
>   **pgm_$exit** – exit a program

SYNOPSIS (C)
>   **#include <idl/c/base.h>**
>   **#include <ppfm.h>**
>
>   **void pgm_$exit(void)**

SYNOPSIS (PASCAL)
>   **%include '/sys/ins/base.ins.pas';**
>   **%include '/sys/ins/pgm.ins.pas';**
>
>   **procedure pgm_$exit;**

DESCRIPTION
>   The **pgm_$exit** call exits from the calling program.
>
>   Any cleanup handlers that have been established are executed in order from the most recently established to the first.
>
>   On Apollo systems, this call invokes **pfm_$signal** with a fault code equal to the last severity level set by **pgm_$set_severity**, or **pgm_$ok** if **pgm_$set_severity** was not called.
>
>   On other systems, this call invokes **pfm_$signal** with a fault code of **status_$ok**.

SEE ALSO
>   pfm_$cleanup, pfm_$signal

Chapter 13

rpc_$ Calls

Contents

NAME
>   rpc_$intro – interface to the Remote Procedure Call runtime library

SYNOPSIS (C)
>   **#include <idl/c/rpc.h>**

SYNOPSIS (PASCAL)
>   **%include '/sys/ins/rpc.ins.pas';**

DESCRIPTION
>   The **rpc_$** calls implement the NCS Remote Procedure Call (RPC) mechanism.
>
>   The **rpc_** interface is defined by the file *idl/***rpc.idl**, where the symbol *idl* denotes the system **idl** directory. On Apollo workstations and other UNIX systems, *idl* is **/usr/include/idl**.
>
>   Most of the **rpc_$** calls can be used only by clients or only by servers. We indicate this aspect of their usage at the beginning of each call description, in the "NAME" section.

EXTERNAL VARIABLES
>   The following external variable is used in **rpc_$** calls:
>
>   **uuid_$nil**
>   >   An external **uuid_$t** variable that is preassigned the value of the nil UUID. Do not change the value of this variable.

CONSTANTS
>   The following constants are used in **rpc_$** calls:
>
>   **rpc_$mod**
>   >   A module code indicating the RPC module. See the description of the **status_$t** type.
>
>   **rpc_$unbound_port**
>   >   A port number indicating that no port is specified. This constant is obsolete; use instead **socket_$unspec_port**.
>
>   The following 16-bit-integer constants are used to specify the address families in **socket_$addr_t** structures. Note that several of the **rpc_$** and **socket_$** calls use the 32-bit-integer equivalents of these values.
>
>   >   **socket_$unspec**
>   >   >   Address family is unspecified.
>   >
>   >   **socket_$internet**
>   >   >   Internet Protocols (IP).
>   >
>   >   **socket_$dds**
>   >   >   Domain protocols (DDS).

DATA TYPES
>   The following data types are used in **rpc_$** calls:
>
>   **handle_t**   An RPC handle.
>
>   **rpc_$epv_t**
>   >   An entry point vector (EPV). An array of pointers to server stub routines.
>
>   **rpc_$generic_epv_t**
>   >   An entry point vector. An array of pointers to generic server stub routines.

rpc_$if_spec_t
> An RPC interface specifier. An opaque structure containing information about an interface, including the UUID, the version number, the number of operations in the interface, and any well-known ports used by servers that export the interface. Applications may need to access two members of **rpc_$if_spec_t**:
>
> **id**   A **uuid_$t** indicating the interface UUID.
>
> **vers**   An unsigned 32-bit integer indicating the interface version.

rpc_$mgr_epv_t
> An entry point vector. An array of pointers to manager routines.

rpc_$shut_check_fn_t
> A pointer to a function. If a server supplies this pointer to **rpc_$allow_remote_shutdown**, the function will be called when a remote shutdown request arrives, and if the function returns true, the shutdown is allowed. The following C definition for **rpc_$shut_check_fn_t** illustrates the syntax for this function:

```
typedef boolean (*rpc_$shut_check_fn_t) (
    handle_t h,
    status_$t *st);
```

> The handle argument can be used to determine information about the remote caller.

socket_$addr_t
> A socket address record that uniquely identifies a socket. See the **socket_$intro** section of Chapter 15 for a full description of this type.

status_$t A status code. Most of the NCS calls supply their completion status in this format. The **status_$t** type is defined as a structure containing a long integer:

```
struct status_$t {
    long all;
    }
```

However, the calls can also use **status_$t** as a set of bit fields. To access the fields in a returned status code, you can assign the value of the status code to a union defined as follows:

```
typedef union {
    struct {
        unsigned fail : 1,
                 subsys : 7,
                 modc : 8;
        short    code;
    } s;
    long all;
} status_u;
```

all   All 32 bits in the status code. If **all** is equal to **status_$ok**, the call that supplied the status was successful.

fail   If this bit is set, the error was not within the scope of the module invoked, but occurred within a lower-level module.

subsys This indicates the subsystem that encountered the error.

modc This indicates the module that encountered the error.

code This is a signed number that identifies the type of error that occurred.

uuid_$t A 128-bit value that uniquely identifies an object, type, or interface for all time. See the **uuid_$intro** section of Chapter 16 for a full description of this type.

STATUS CODES

The following are status codes returned by **rpc_$** calls:

rpc_$addr_in_use
The address and port specified in an **rpc_$use_family_wk** call are already in use. This is caused by multiple calls to **rpc_$use_family_wk** with the same well-known port.

rpc_$bad_pkt
The server or client has received an ill-formed packet.

rpc_$cant_bind_sock
The RPC runtime library created a socket but was unable to bind it to a socket address.

rpc_$cant_create_sock
The RPC runtime library was unable to create a socket.

rpc_$comm_failure
The client was unable to get a response from the server.

rpc_$illegal_register
You are trying to register an interface that is already registered, and you are using an EPV (with the **rpc_$register** call) or a generic EPV (with the **rpc_$register_mgr** call) different from the one used when the interface was first registered.

rpc_$not_in_call
An internal error.

rpc_$op_rng_error
The requested operation does not correspond to a valid operation in the requested interface.

rpc_$proto_error
An internal protocol error.

rpc_$too_many_ifs
The maximum number of interfaces is already registered with the RPC runtime library; the server must unregister some interface before it registers an additional interface.

rpc_$too_many_sockets
The server is trying to use more than the maximum number of sockets that is allowed; it has called **rpc_$use_family** or **rpc_$use_family_wk** too many times.

rpc_$unbound_handle

The handle is not bound and does not represent a particular host address. Returned by **rpc_$inq_binding**.

rpc_$unk_if

The requested interface is not known. The server has not registered the interface with the RPC runtime library, the version number in the request does not match the version number of the registered interface, or the UUID in the request does not match the UUID of the registered interface.

rpc_$wrong_boot_time

The server boot time value maintained by the client does not correspond to the current server boot time. The server program was probably restarted while the client program was running.

rpc_$you_crashed

This error can occur if a server has crashed and restarted. The RPC runtime library at a client host sends the error to the server if the client makes a remote procedure call before the server crashes, then receives a response after the server restarts.

status_$ok

The call was successful.

FILES

idl/**rpc.idl**

NAME

   rpc_$alloc_handle – create an RPC handle (CLIENT ONLY)

SYNOPSIS (C)

   #include <idl/c/rpc.h>

   handle_t rpc_$alloc_handle(
       uuid_$t **object**,
       unsigned long *family*,
       status_$t **status**)

SYNOPSIS (PASCAL)

   %include '/usr/include/idl/pas/rpc.ins.pas'

   function rpc_$alloc_handle(
       in *object*: **uuid_$t;**
       in *family*: **unsigned32;**
       out *status*: **status_$t): handle_t;**

DESCRIPTION

   The **rpc_$alloc_handle** call creates an unbound RPC handle, a handle that identifies a particular object but not a particular server or host.

   When a client uses an unbound handle to make a remote procedure call, the RPC runtime library broadcasts the call on the local network. If a well-known port was specified in the definition of the requested interface, the call is broadcast to that port. Otherwise, the call is broadcast to the Local Location Broker (LLB) forwarding port. The client RPC runtime library returns the first response that it receives and binds the handle to the server.

   Because broadcasting is inefficient, we discourage use of unbound handles.

   object   The UUID of the object to be accessed. If there is no specific object, specify **uuid_$nil**.

   family   The address family to use in communications to access the object. The **rpc_$intro** section describes possible values.

   status   The completion status.

EXAMPLE

   The following statement allocates a handle that identifies a print queue object:

```
h = rpc_$alloc_handle (&printq_id, (unsigned long) socket_$dds, &st);
```

FILES

   idl/**rpc.idl**

SEE ALSO

   rpc_$dup_handle, rpc_$free_handle, rpc_$set_binding

NAME
   rpc_$allow_remote_shutdown – allow or disallow remote shutdown of a server (SERVER ONLY)

SYNOPSIS (C)
   #include <idl/c/rpc.h>

   void rpc_$allow_remote_shutdown(
         unsigned long *allow*,
         rpc_$shut_check_fn_t *checkproc*,
         status_$t *status)

SYNOPSIS (PASCAL)
   %include '/usr/include/idl/pas/rpc.ins.pas'

   procedure rpc_$allow_remote_shutdown(
         in *allow*: **unsigned32;**
         in *checkproc*: **rpc_$shut_check_fn_t;**
         out *status*: **status_$t);**

DESCRIPTION
   The **rpc_$allow_remote_shutdown** call allows or disallows remote callers to shut down a server via **rrpc_$shutdown**.

   By default, servers do not allow remote shutdown. If a server calls **rpc_$allow_remote_shutdown** with *allow* "true" (nonzero) and *checkproc* nil, then remote shutdown will be allowed. If *allow* is "true" and *checkproc* is not nil, then when a remote shutdown request arrives, the function referenced by *checkproc* is called and the shutdown is allowed if the function returns true. If *allow* is "false" (zero), remote shutdown is disallowed.

   allow   A value indicating "false" if zero, "true" otherwise.

   checkproc
               A pointer to a Boolean function. See the **rpc_$intro** section for a full description of **rpc_$shut_check_fn_t**.

   status   The completion status.

FILES
   idl/**rpc.idl**

SEE ALSO
   rpc_$shutdown, rrpc_$shutdown

NAME

> rpc_$bind – allocate an RPC handle and set its binding to a server (CLIENT ONLY)

SYNOPSIS (C)

> #include <idl/c/rpc.h>
>
> handle_t rpc_$bind(
>   uuid_$t *object,
>   socket_$addr_t *sockaddr,
>   unsigned long slength,
>   status_$t *status)

SYNOPSIS (PASCAL)

> %include '/usr/include/idl/pas/rpc.ins.pas'
>
> function rpc_$bind(
>   in object: uuid_$t;
>   in sockaddr: socket_$addr_t;
>   in slength: unsigned32;
>   out status: status_$t): handle_t;

DESCRIPTION

> The **rpc_$bind** function creates an RPC handle that represents the object identified by *object*. This call is equivalent to an **rpc_$alloc_handle** call followed by an **rpc_$set_binding** call.
>
> If you supply a fully specified *sockaddr*, **rpc_$bind** creates a fully bound handle, one whose location information identifies a particular port at a particular host. When a client uses a fully bound handle to make a remote procedure call, the RPC runtime library delivers the call directly to the host and port identified in the handle.
>
> If the port number in *sockaddr* is **socket_$unspec_port**, **rpc_$bind** creates a bound-to-host handle, one whose location information identifies a host, but not a port. When a client uses a bound-to-host handle to make a remote procedure call, the RPC runtime library sends the call to the host identified in the handle; unless the requested interface specifies a well-known port, the call is sent to the Local Location Broker (LLB) forwarding port, and the LLB forwards the call to the server.
>
> *object*   The UUID of the object to be accessed. If there is no specific object, specify **uuid_$nil**.
>
> *sockaddr* The socket address of the server.
>
> *slength*   The length, in bytes, of *sockaddr*.
>
> *status*   The completion status.

EXAMPLE

> The following statement from *examples*/**binoplu/client.c**, the **binoplu** example client program, binds the client to the specified object and socket address. The **entry** is from the results of a previous Location Broker lookup call.
>
> ```
> h = rpc_$bind (&uuid_$nil, &entry.saddr, entry.saddr_len, &st);
> ```

FILES

   idl/**rpc.idl**

SEE ALSO

   rpc_$clear_binding, rpc_$clear_server_binding, rpc_$set_binding

NAME

rpc_$clear_binding – unset the binding of an RPC handle (CLIENT ONLY)

SYNOPSIS (C)

#include <idl/c/rpc.h>

void rpc_$clear_binding(
       handle_t *handle*,
       status_$t **status*)

SYNOPSIS (PASCAL)

%include '/usr/include/idl/pas/rpc.ins.pas'

procedure rpc_$clear_binding(
       in *handle*: handle_t;
       out *status*: status_$t);

DESCRIPTION

The **rpc_$clear_binding call** clears the binding of an RPC handle to a particular server and host. The handle continues to represent an object but is unbound. It can be reused to access the object, either by broadcasting or after resetting the binding to another server.

When a client uses an unbound handle to make a remote procedure call, the RPC runtime library broadcasts the call on the local network. If a well-known port was specified in the definition of the requested interface, the call is broadcast to that port. Otherwise, the call is broadcast to the Local Location Broker (LLB) forwarding port. The client RPC runtime library returns the first response that it receives and binds the handle to the server.

Because broadcasting is inefficient, we discourage use of unbound handles.

The **rpc_$clear_binding** call is the inverse of the **rpc_$set_binding** call.

handle   The RPC handle whose binding is being cleared.

status   The completion status.

EXAMPLE

The following statement clears the binding represented in **handle**:

```
rpc_$clear_binding (handle, &st);
```

FILES

idl/**rpc.idl**

SEE ALSO

rpc_$bind, rpc_$clear_server_binding, rpc_$set_binding

NAME
>   rpc_$clear_server_binding – unset the binding of an RPC handle to a server (CLIENT ONLY)

SYNOPSIS (C)
>   #include <idl/c/rpc.h>
>
>   void rpc_$clear_server_binding(
>   handle_t *handle*,
>   status_$t **status*)

SYNOPSIS (PASCAL)
>   %include '/usr/include/idl/pas/rpc.ins.pas'
>
>   procedure rpc_$clear_server_binding(
>   in *handle*: handle_t;
>   out *status*: status_$t);

DESCRIPTION
>   The **rpc_$clear_server_binding** call clears the binding of an RPC handle to a particular server (that is, a particular port number), but does not clear the binding to a host (that is, a network address). The handle continues to represent an object.
>
>   This call replaces a fully bound handle with a bound-to-host handle. A bound-to-host handle identifies an object and a host but does not identify a server at that host.
>
>   When a client uses a bound-to-host handle to make a remote procedure call, the RPC runtime library sends the call to the host identified in the handle. If a well-known port was specified in the definition of the requested interface, the call is delivered to that port. Otherwise, the call is delivered to the Local Location Broker (LLB) forwarding port. The LLB, provided a server for the requested object and interface has registered with it, forwards the call to the port on which the server is listening. When the remote procedure call returns, the RPC runtime library at the client host binds the handle to that port, and any subsequent calls are sent directly to the server.
>
>   The **rpc_$clear_server_binding** call is useful for client error recovery when a server that listens on opaque ports dies and restarts; the restarted server may be listening on a different port. This call enables the client to unbind from the old port while retaining the binding to the host, so that when the client sends its next request, the call is forwarded to the new port.
>
>   *handle*   The RPC handle whose server binding is being cleared.
>
>   *status*   The completion status.

EXAMPLE
>   The following statement clears the server binding represented in **handle**:
>
>       ```
>       rpc_$clear_server_binding (handle, &st);
>       ```

FILES
>   *idl/*rpc.idl

SEE ALSO
>   rpc_$bind, rpc_$clear_binding, rpc_$set_binding

NAME

>**rpc_$dup_handle** – make a copy of an RPC handle (CLIENT ONLY)

SYNOPSIS (C)

>#include <idl/c/rpc.h>

>**handle_t rpc_$dup_handle(**
>>**handle_t** *handle*,
>>**status_$t** **status*)

SYNOPSIS (PASCAL)

>%include '/usr/include/idl/pas/rpc.ins.pas'

>**function rpc_$dup_handle(**
>>in *handle*: **handle_t**;
>>out *status*: **status_$t**): **handle_t**;

DESCRIPTION

>The **rpc_$dup_handle** call returns a copy of an existing RPC handle. Both handles can then be used in the client program for concurrent multiple accesses to a binding. Because all duplicates of a handle reference the same data, an **rpc_$set_binding**, **rpc_$clear_binding**, or **rpc_$clear_server_binding** call made on any one duplicate affects all duplicates. However, an RPC handle is not freed until **rpc_$free_handle** is called on all copies of the handle.

>The **rpc_$dup_handle** call is designed to support programs that use Concurrent Programming Support (CPS). It allows multiple threads of execution within a process to use separate copies of the handle but to share the resources that are identified by the handle.

>*handle*   The RPC handle to be copied.

>*status*   The completion status.

EXAMPLE

>The following statement creates as **handle2** a copy of **handle1**:

>```
>handle2 = rpc_$dup_handle (handle1, &st);
>```

FILES

>*idl*/**rpc.idl**

SEE ALSO

>rpc_$alloc_handle, rpc_$free_handle

NAME
    rpc_$free_handle – free an RPC handle (CLIENT ONLY)

SYNOPSIS (C)
    #include <idl/c/rpc.h>

    void rpc_$free_handle(
        handle_t *handle*,
        **status_$t ***status*)

SYNOPSIS (PASCAL)
    %include '/usr/include/idl/pas/rpc.ins.pas'

    procedure rpc_$free_handle(
        in *handle*: **handle_t;**
        out *status*: **status_$t);**

DESCRIPTION
    The **rpc_$free_handle** call frees an RPC handle. This call releases the resources identified by the RPC handle. The client program cannot use a handle after it is freed.

    If you make several remote procedure calls that access the same object but at different locations, it is more efficient to use **rpc_$set_binding** (replacing the binding in an existing handle) than to use **rpc_$free_handle** and **rpc_$bind** (creating a new handle).

    If you create copies of an RPC handle by using the **rpc_$dup_handle** call, the handles are not freed until **rpc_$free_handle** is called once for each copy of the handle. However, the RPC runtime library does not differentiate between calling **rpc_$free_handle** several times on one copy of a handle and calling it one time for each of several copies of a handle. Therefore, if you use duplicate handles, you must ensure that no thread inadvertently makes multiple **rpc_$free_handle** calls on a single handle.

    handle   The RPC handle to be freed.

    status   The completion status.

EXAMPLE
    The following statements free two copies of a handle:

```
rpc_$free_handle (handle1, &st);
rpc_$free_handle (handle2, &st);
```

FILES
    idl/**rpc.idl**

SEE ALSO
    rpc_$alloc_handle, rpc_$dup_handle

NAME

rpc_$inq_binding – return the socket address represented by an RPC handle (CLIENT OR SERVER)

SYNOPSIS (C)

#include <idl/c/rpc.h>

void rpc_$inq_binding(
        handle_t *handle,*
        socket_$addr_t **sockaddr,*
        unsigned long **slength,*
        status_$t **status*)

SYNOPSIS (PASCAL)

%include '/usr/include/idl/pas/rpc.ins.pas'

procedure rpc_$inq_binding(
        in *handle*: **handle_t;**
        out *sockaddr*: **socket_$addr_t;**
        out *slength*: **unsigned32;**
        out *status*: **status_$t);**

DESCRIPTION

The **rpc_$inq_binding** call enables a client or server to determine the socket address identified by an RPC handle.

A client might invoke **rpc_$inq_binding** if it has used an unbound handle to make a remote procedure call and it wants to determine the particular server that responded to the call.

Conversely, a server might use **rpc_$inq_binding** to identify its clients. The RPC runtime library manipulates the location information in an RPC handle so that on the server side of an application, the handle specifies the location of the client making the call.

handle   An RPC handle.

sockaddr The socket address represented by *handle*.

slength   The length, in bytes, of *sockaddr*.

status   The completion status.

ERRORS

rpc_$unbound_handle
        The handle is not bound and does not represent a specific host address.

EXAMPLE

The Location Broker administrative tool, **lb_admin,** uses the following statement to determine the particular Global Location Broker (GLB) that responded to a lookup request:

```
rpc_$inq_binding (glb_$handle, &global_broker_addr,
    &global_broker_addr_len, &status);
```

FILES

idl/**rpc.idl**

SEE ALSO

rpc_$bind, rpc_$set_binding

NAME
>   rpc_$inq_object – return the object UUID represented by an RPC handle (CLIENT OR SERVER)

SYNOPSIS (C)
>   #include <idl/c/rpc.h>
>
>   void rpc_$inq_object(
>   handle_t *handle*,
>   uuid_$t **object*,
>   status_$t **status*)

SYNOPSIS (PASCAL)
>   %include '/usr/include/idl/pas/rpc.ins.pas'
>
>   procedure rpc_$inq_object(
>   in *handle*: handle_t;
>   out *object*: uuid_$t;
>   out *status*: status_$t);

DESCRIPTION
>   The **rpc_$inq_object** call enables a client or server to determine the particular object that a handle
>   represents.
>
>   If a server exports an interface through which clients can access several objects, it can use
>   **rpc_$inq_object** to determine the object requested in a call. This call requires an RPC handle as input, so
>   the server can make the call only if the interface uses explicit handles, that is, if each operation in the inter-
>   face has a handle parameter.
>
>   *handle*   An RPC handle.
>
>   *object*   The UUID of the object identified by *handle*.
>
>   *status*   The completion status.

EXAMPLE
>   A database server that manages several databases must determine the particular database to be accessed
>   when it receives a remote procedure call. Each manager routine therefore makes the following call; the
>   routine then uses the returned UUID to identify the database to be accessed.
>
>    ```
>    rpc_$inq_object (handle, &db_uuid, &st);
>    ```

FILES
>   *idl*/**rpc.idl**

NAME
>   **rpc_$listen** – listen for and handle remote procedure call packets (SERVER ONLY)

SYNOPSIS (C)
>   **#include <idl/c/rpc.h>**
>
>   **void rpc_$listen(**
>   unsigned long *max_calls,*
>   **status_$t ****status*)

SYNOPSIS (PASCAL)
>   **%include '/usr/include/idl/pas/rpc.ins.pas'**
>
>   **procedure rpc_$listen(**
>   in *max_calls*: **unsigned32;**
>   out *status*: **status_$t);**

DESCRIPTION
>   The **rpc_$listen** call dispatches incoming remote procedure call requests to manager procedures and
>   returns the responses to the client. You must issue **rpc_$use_family** or **rpc_$use_family_wk** before you
>   use **rpc_$listen**. This call normally does not return.
>
>   On systems that have Concurrent Programming Support (CPS), the RPC runtime library at the server host
>   can use CPS to handle several requests simultaneously. The *max_calls* parameter specifies how many con-
>   current requests are allowed; the RPC runtime library supports at most 10 concurrent requests; If a server
>   uses concurrency, all manager routines must be re-entrant; that is, they must maintain concurrency controls
>   on any non-local variables to prevent conflicts among the various threads of execution.
>
>   On systems that do not have CPS, *max_calls* is ignored, and the server processes only one call at a time.
>
>   *max_calls*
>   The maximum number of calls that the server is allowed to process concurrently. Regardless of
>   the value for *max_calls*, systems without CPS support only one process, and systems with CPS
>   support at most 10 concurrent processes.
>
>   *status*   The completion status.

EXAMPLE
>   The following statement listens for incoming remote procedure call requests, handling up to five con-
>   currently:
>
>       ```
>       rpc_$listen (5, &status);
>       ```

FILES
>   *idl/***rpc.idl**

SEE ALSO
>   rpc_$shutdown

NAME
>   **rpc_$name_to_sockaddr** – convert a host name and port number to a socket address (CLIENT OR SERVER)

SYNOPSIS (C)
>   #include <idl/c/rpc.h>
>
>   **void rpc_$name_to_sockaddr(**
>   **unsigned char** *name*[256],
>   **unsigned long** *nlength,*
>   **unsigned long** *port,*
>   **unsigned long** *family,*
>   **socket_$addr_t** **sockaddr,*
>   **unsigned long** **slength,*
>   **status_$t** **status*)

SYNOPSIS (PASCAL)
>   %include '/usr/include/idl/pas/rpc.ins.pas'
>
>   **procedure rpc_$name_to_sockaddr(**
>   **in** *name*: **array [0..255] of char;**
>   **in** *nlength*: **unsigned32;**
>   **in** *port*: **unsigned32;**
>   **in** *family*: **unsigned32;**
>   **out** *sockaddr*: **socket_$addr_t;**
>   **out** *slength*: **unsigned32;**
>   **out** *status*: **status_$t);**

DESCRIPTION
>   This call is obsolete. See the note below.
>
>   The **rpc_$name_to_sockaddr** call provides the socket address for a socket, given the host name, the port number, and the address family.
>
>   You can specify socket address information either by passing one text string in the *name* parameter or by passing each of the three elements in a separate parameter. In the latter case, the *name* parameter should contain only the host name.
>
>   *name*   A string that contains a host name and, optionally, a port and an address family. The format is *family:host* [*port*] , where *family:* and [*port*] are optional. If you specify a *family* as part of the *name* parameter, you must specify **socket_$unspec** in the *family* parameter. The *family* can be either **dds** or **ip**; *host* is the host name; *port* is an integer port number.
>
>   *nlength*   The number of characters in *name*.
>
>   *port*   The socket port number. This parameter should have the value **socket_$unspec_port** if you are not specifying a well-known port; in this case, the returned socket address will specify the Local Location Broker (LLB) forwarding port at *host*. If you specify the port number in the *name* parameter, this parameter is ignored.

family   The address family to use for the socket address. This value corresponds to the communications protocol used to access the socket and determines how the *sockaddr* is expressed. The **rpc_$intro** section describes possible values. If you specify the address family in the *name* parameter, this parameter must have the value **socket_$unspec**.

sockaddr   The socket address corresponding to *name*, *port*, and *family*.

slength   The length, in bytes, of *sockaddr*.

status   The completion status.

NOTE

This call has been superseded by the **socket_$from_name** call.

FILES

idl/**rpc.idl**

SEE ALSO

rpc_$sockaddr_to_name, socket_$from_name

NAME
>   rpc_$register – register an interface (SERVER ONLY)

SYNOPSIS (C)
>   #include <idl/c/rpc.h>
>
>   void rpc_$register(
>   rpc_$if_spec_t *ifspec,
>   rpc_$epv_t epv,
>   status_$t *status)

SYNOPSIS (PASCAL)
>   %include '/usr/include/idl/pas/rpc.ins.pas'
>
>   procedure rpc_$register(
>   in ifspec: rpc_$if_spec_t;
>   in epv: rpc_$epv_t;
>   out status: status_$t);

DESCRIPTION
>   This call is obsolete. See the note below.
>
>   The rpc_$register call registers an interface with the RPC runtime library. After an interface is registered, the RPC runtime library will dispatch requests for that interface to the server.
>
>   You can call rpc_$register several times with the same interface (for example, from various subroutines of the same server), but each call must specify the same EPV. Each registration increments a reference count for the registered interface; you must call rpc_$unregister an equal number of times to unregister the interface.
>
>   To generate stubs for an application whose server uses rpc_$register, specify the –s option of the NIDL Compiler when you compile the interface definition.
>
>   ifspec   The interface being registered.
>
>   epv   The entry point vector (EPV) for the operations in the interface. The EPV is normally defined in the server stub that is generated by the NIDL Compiler from an interface definition.
>
>   status   The completion status.

ERRORS
>   **rpc_$too_many_ifs**
>   The maximum number of interfaces is already registered with the server.
>
>   **rpc_$illegal_register**
>   You are trying to register an interface that is already registered, and you are specifying an EPV different from the one specified when the interface was first registered.

NOTE
>   This call has been superseded by the rpc_$register_mgr and rpc_$register_object calls, which enable a server to export more than one version of an interface and to implement an interface for more than one type.

To generate stubs for an application whose server uses **rpc_$register_mgr** and **rpc_$register_object**, specify the **-m** option of the NIDL Compiler when you compile the interface definition.

FILES

idl/**rpc.idl**

SEE ALSO

rpc_$register_mgr, rpc_$register_object, rpc_$unregister

NAME

rpc_$register_mgr – register a manager (SERVER ONLY)

SYNOPSIS (C)

#include <idl/c/rpc.h>

void rpc_$register_mgr(
        uuid_$t *type,
        rpc_$if_spec_t *ifspec,
        rpc_$generic_epv_t sepv,
        rpc_$mgr_epv_t mepv,
        status_$t *status)

SYNOPSIS (PASCAL)

%include '/usr/include/idl/pas/rpc.ins.pas'

procedure rpc_$register_mgr(
        in type: uuid_$t;
        in ifspec: rpc_$if_spec_t;
        in sepv: rpc_$generic_epv_t;
        in mepv: rpc_$mgr_epv_t;
        out status: status_$t);

DESCRIPTION

The **rpc_$register_mgr** call registers the set of manager procedures that implement a specified interface for a specified type.

This call and **rpc_$register_object** supersede the obsolete **rpc_$register** call.

Servers can invoke this call several times with the same interface (*ifspec*) and generic EPV (*sepv*) but with a different object type (*type*) and manager EPV (*mepv*) on each invocation. This technique allows a server to export several implementations of the same interface.

Servers that export several versions of the same interface (but not different implementations for different types) must also use **rpc_$register_mgr**, not **rpc_$register**. Such servers can supply **uuid_$nil** as the *type* to **rpc_$register_mgr**.

If a server uses **rpc_$register_mgr** to register a manager for a specific interface and a specific non-nil type, the server must use **rpc_$register_object** to register an object.

To generate stubs for an application whose server uses **rpc_$register_mgr** and **rpc_$register_object**, specify the –m option of the NIDL Compiler when you compile the interface definition.

type   The UUID of the type being registered.

ifspec   The interface being registered.

sepv   The generic EPV, a vector of pointers to server stub procedures.

mepv   The manager EPV, a vector of pointers to manager procedures.

status   The completion status.

EXAMPLE

The following statement from *examples*/**stacks**/**server.c**, the **stacks** example server program, registers a manager for array-based stacks:

```
rpc_$register_mgr (&astackt, &stacks_v1$if_spec, stacks_v1$server_epv,
    (rpc_$mgr_epv_t)&stacks_v1$amanager_epv, &st);
```

FILES

idl/**rpc.idl**

SEE ALSO

rpc_$register, rpc_$register_object, rpc_$unregister

NAME

    rpc_$register_object – register an object (SERVER ONLY)

SYNOPSIS (C)

    #include <idl/c/rpc.h>

    void rpc_$register_object(
        uuid_$t *_object_**,**
        uuid_$t *_type_**,**
        status_$t *_status_**)**

SYNOPSIS (PASCAL)

    %include '/usr/include/idl/pas/rpc.ins.pas'

    procedure rpc_$register_object(
        in _object_**: uuid_$t;**
        in _type_**: uuid_$t;**
        out _status_**: status_$t);**

DESCRIPTION

The **rpc_$register_object** call declares that a server supports operations on a particular object and declares the type of that object.

This call and **rpc_$register_mgr** supersede the obsolete **rpc_$register** call.

A server must register objects via **rpc_$register_object** only if it registers interfaces via **rpc_$register_mgr**. When a server receives a call, the RPC runtime library searches for the object identified in the call (that is, the object that the client specified in the handle) among the objects registered by the server. If the object is found, the type of the object determines which of the manager EPVs should be used to operate on the object.

To generate stubs for an application whose server uses **rpc_$register_mgr** and **rpc_$register_object**, specify the **–m** option of the NIDL Compiler when you compile the interface definition.

object   The UUID of the object being registered.

type   The UUID of the type of the object.

status   The completion status.

EXAMPLE

The following statement from _examples_/**stacks**/**server.c**, the **stacks** example server program, registers an array-based stack object:

```
rpc_$register_object (&astack, &astackt, &st);
```

FILES

    idl/**rpc.idl**

SEE ALSO

    rpc_$register, rpc_$register_mgr, rpc_$unregister

NAME

   rpc_$set_async_ack – set or clear asynchronous-ack mode (CLIENT ONLY)

SYNOPSIS (C)

   #include <idl/c/rpc.h>

   void rpc_$set_async_ack(
   unsigned long *on*)

SYNOPSIS (PASCAL)

   %include '/usr/include/idl/pas/rpc.ins.pas'

   procedure rpc_$set_async_ack(
   in *on*: **unsigned32);**

DESCRIPTION

   The **rpc_$set_async_ack** call sets or clears asynchronous-ack mode (see the "Background" section below)
   in a client.

   on   If "true" (nonzero), asynchronous-ack mode is set. If "false" (zero), synchronous-ack mode is
              set.

   ### MS-DOS Systems and Systems with CPS

   On MS-DOS systems and on systems that have Concurrent Programming Support, **rpc_$set_async_ack**
   has no effect. These systems always use asynchronous-ack mode.

   ### Other Systems

   On other systems, synchronous-ack mode is the default. Calling **rpc_$set_async_ack** with a nonzero
   value for *on* sets asynchronous-ack mode. Calling it with *on* zero sets synchronous-ack mode.

   ### Background

   After a client makes a remote procedure call and receives a reply from a server, the RPC runtime library at
   the client acknowledges its receipt of the reply. This "reply ack" can occur either synchronously (before
   the runtime library returns to the caller) or asynchronously (after the runtime library returns to the caller)

   It is generally good to allow asynchronous reply acks. Asynchronous-ack mode can save the client runtime
   library from making explicit reply acks, because after a client receives a reply, it may shortly issue another
   call that can act as an implicit ack.

   Asynchronous-ack mode requires that an "alarm" be set to go off sometime after the remote procedure call
   returns. Unfortunately, setting the alarm can cause two problems: (1) There may be only one alarm that
   can be set, and the application itself may be trying to use it. (2) If at the time the alarm goes off the application is blocked in a UNIX system call that is doing I/O to a "slow device" (such as a terminal), the system call will return an error (with the EINTR errno); the application may not be coded to expect this error.
   If neither of these problems obtains, the application should set asynchronous-ack mode to get greater
   efficiency.

FILES

   idl/**rpc.idl**

NAME
    rpc_$set_binding – bind an RPC handle to a server (CLIENT ONLY)

SYNOPSIS (C)
    #include <idl/c/rpc.h>

    void rpc_$set_binding(
        handle_t *handle*,
        socket_$addr_t *sockaddr,
        unsigned long *slength*,
        status_$t *status)

SYNOPSIS (PASCAL)
    %include '/usr/include/idl/pas/rpc.ins.pas'

    procedure rpc_$set_binding(
        in *handle*: **handle_t;**
        in *sockaddr*: **socket_$addr_t;**
        in *slength*: **unsigned32;**
        out *status*: **status_$t);**

DESCRIPTION
    The **rpc_$set_binding** call sets the binding of an RPC handle to the specified socket address. You can use this call either to set the binding in an unbound handle or to replace the existing binding in a fully bound or bound-to-host handle.

    If you supply a fully specified *sockaddr*, *handle* becomes a fully bound handle, one whose location information identifies a particular port at a particular host. When a client uses a fully bound handle to make a remote procedure call, the RPC runtime library delivers the call directly to the host and port identified in the handle.

    If the port number in *sockaddr* is **socket_$unspec_port**, *handle* becomes a bound-to-host handle, one whose location information identifies a host, but not a port. When a client uses a bound-to-host handle to make a remote procedure call, the RPC runtime library sends the call to the host identified in the handle; unless the requested interface specifies a well-known port, the call is sent to the Local Location Broker (LLB) forwarding port, and the LLB forwards the call to the server.

    handle   An RPC handle.

    sockaddr The socket address of the server with which the handle is being associated.

    slength   The length, in bytes, of *sockaddr*.

    status   The completion status.

EXAMPLE
    The following statement sets the binding on the handle **h** to the first server in the *lbresults* array, which was returned by a previous Location Broker lookup call:

```
rpc_$set_binding (h, &lbresults[0].saddr, lbresults[0].saddr_len, &st);
```

FILES
      idl/**rpc.idl**

SEE ALSO
      rpc_$alloc_handle, rpc_$clear_binding, rpc_$clear_server_binding

NAME

rpc_$set_fault_mode – set the fault-handling mode for a server (SERVER ONLY)

SYNOPSIS (C)

#include <idl/c/rpc.h>

unsigned long rpc_$set_fault_mode(
  unsigned long *on*)

SYNOPSIS (PASCAL)

%include '/usr/include/idl/pas/rpc.ins.pas'

function rpc_$set_fault_mode(
  in *on*: **unsigned32): unsigned32;**

DESCRIPTION

The **rpc_$set_fault_mode** function controls the handling of faults that occur in server routines.

In the default mode, the server reflects faults back to the client and continues processing. Calling **rpc_$set_fault_mode** with a nonzero value for *on* sets the fault-handling mode so that the server sends an **rpc_$comm_failure** fault back to the client and exits. (In a tasking environment on a system with Concurrent Programming Support, the distinguished task is signaled.) Calling **rpc_$set_fault_mode** with *on* zero resets the fault-handling mode to the default.

This function returns the previous setting of the fault-handling mode.

on   If "true" (nonzero), the server exits when a fault occurs. If "false" (zero), the server reflects faults back to the client.

FILES

*idl/*rpc.idl

NAME
>   **rpc_$set_short_timeout** – set or clear short-timeout mode (CLIENT ONLY)

SYNOPSIS (C)
>   **#include <idl/c/rpc.h>**
>
>   **unsigned long rpc_$set_short_timeout(**
>   **handle_t** *handle,*
>   **unsigned long** *on,*
>   **status_$t ****status*)

SYNOPSIS (PASCAL)
>   **%include '/usr/include/idl/pas/rpc.ins.pas'**
>
>   **function rpc_$set_short_timeout(**
>   **in** *handle*: **handle_t;**
>   **in** *on*: **unsigned32;**
>   **out** *status*: **status_$t): unsigned32;**

DESCRIPTION
>   The **rpc_$set_short_timeout** function sets or clears short-timeout mode on a handle. If a client uses a handle in short-timeout mode to make a remote procedure call, but the server shows no signs of life, the call fails quickly. As soon as the server shows signs of being alive, standard timeouts take effect and apply for the remainder of the call.
>
>   Calling **rpc_$set_short_timeout** with a nonzero value for *on* sets short-timeout mode. Calling it with *on* zero sets standard timeouts. Standard timeouts are the default.
>
>   This function returns the previous setting of the timeout mode.
>
>   *handle*   An RPC handle.
>
>   *on*   If "true" (nonzero), short-timeout mode is set on *handle*. If "false" (zero), standard timeouts are set.
>
>   *status*   The completion status.

FILES
>   *idl*/**rpc.idl**

NAME

>**rpc_$shutdown** – shut down a server (SERVER ONLY)

SYNOPSIS (C)

>**#include <idl/c/rpc.h>**
>
>**void rpc_$shutdown(**
>>**status_$t ****status*)

SYNOPSIS (PASCAL)

>**%include '/usr/include/idl/pas/rpc.ins.pas'**
>
>**procedure rpc_$shutdown(**
>>**out** *status*: **status_$t);**

DESCRIPTION

>The **rpc_$shutdown** call shuts down a server. When this call is executed, the server stops processing incoming calls, and **rpc_$listen** returns. On a system with Concurrent Programming Support, if the server is running in a tasking environment, this call kills all "listen tasks."
>
>If **rpc_$shutdown** is called from within a remote procedure, that procedure completes and the server shuts down after replying to the caller.
>
>*status*   The completion status.

FILES

>*idl/***rpc.idl**

SEE ALSO

>rpc_$allow_remote_shutdown, rrpc_$shutdown

NAME
    rpc_$sockaddr_to_name – convert a socket address to a host name and port number (CLIENT OR SERVER)

SYNOPSIS (C)
    #include <idl/c/rpc.h>

    void rpc_$sockaddr_to_name(
            socket_$addr_t **sockaddr,*
            unsigned long *slength,*
            unsigned char *name*[256],
            unsigned long **nlength,*
            unsigned long **port,*
            status_$t **status*)

SYNOPSIS (PASCAL)
    %include '/usr/include/idl/pas/rpc.ins.pas'

    procedure rpc_$sockaddr_to_name(
            in *sockaddr*: **socket_$addr_t;**
            in *slength*: **unsigned32;**
            out *name*: **array [0..255] of char;**
            in out *nlength*: **unsigned32;**
            out *port*: **unsigned32;**
            out *status*: **status_$t);**

DESCRIPTION
    This call is obsolete. See the note below.

    The **rpc_$sockaddr_to_name** call provides the address family, the host name, and the port number identified by the specified socket address.

    sockaddr   A socket address.

    slength   The length, in bytes, of *sockaddr*.

    name   A string that contains the host name and the address family. The format is *family:host*, where *family* can be either **dds** or **ip**.

    nlength   On input, *nlength* is the length of the *name* buffer. On output, *nlength* is the number of characters returned in the *name* parameter.

    port   The socket port number.

    status   The completion status.

NOTE
    This call has been superseded by the **socket_$to_name** call.

FILES
    *idl/***rpc.idl**

SEE ALSO
    rpc_$name_to_sockaddr, socket_$to_name

NAME

rpc_$unregister – unregister an interface (SERVER ONLY)

SYNOPSIS (C)

#include <idl/c/rpc.h>

void rpc_$unregister(
        rpc_$if_spec_t **ifspec,*
        status_$t **status*)

SYNOPSIS (PASCAL)

%include '/usr/include/idl/pas/rpc.ins.pas'

procedure rpc_$unregister(
        in *ifspec*: **rpc_$if_spec_t;**
        out *status*: **status_$t);**

DESCRIPTION

The **rpc_$unregister** call unregisters an interface that the server previously registered with the RPC run-time library. After an interface is unregistered, the RPC runtime library will not pass requests for that interface to the server.

If a server uses several **rpc_$register** or **rpc_$register_mgr** calls to register an interface more that once, then it must call **rpc_$unregister** an equal number of times to unregister the interface.

ifspec   An interface specifier. The interface being unregistered.

status   The completion status.

EXAMPLE

The following statement from *examples*/**stacks/server.c**, the **stacks** example server program, unregisters the **stacks** interface from the RPC runtime library:

```
rpc_$unregister (&stacks_v1$if_spec, &stat);
```

FILES

idl/**rpc.idl**

SEE ALSO

rpc_$register, rpc_$register_mgr, rpc_$register_object

NAME
>   **rpc_$use_family** – create a socket of a specified address family for an RPC server (SERVER ONLY)

SYNOPSIS (C)
>   **#include <idl/c/rpc.h>**
>
>   **void rpc_$use_family(**
>   **unsigned long** *family,*
>   **socket_$addr_t** ***sockaddr,*
>   **unsigned long** ***slength,*
>   **status_$t** ***status)*

SYNOPSIS (PASCAL)
>   **%include '/usr/include/idl/pas/rpc.ins.pas'**
>
>   **procedure rpc_$use_family(**
>   **in** *family*: **unsigned32;**
>   **out** *sockaddr*: **socket_$addr_t;**
>   **out** *slength*: **unsigned32;**
>   **out** *status*: **status_$t);**

DESCRIPTION
>   The **rpc_$use_family** call creates a socket for a server without specifying its port number. The RPC run-time library assigns an opaque port number. If a server must listen on a particular well-known port, use **rpc_$use_family_wk** to create the socket.
>
>   A server can listen on more than one socket. However, a server ordinarily listens on only one socket per address family, regardless of how many interfaces it exports. Therefore, most servers should make this call once per address family.
>
>   *family*   The address family of the socket to be created. This value corresponds to the communications protocol used to access the socket and determines how the socket address is expressed. The **rpc_$intro** section describes possible values.
>
>   *sockaddr* The socket address of the socket on which the server will listen.
>
>   *slength*   The length, in bytes, of *sockaddr*.
>
>   *status*   The completion status.

ERRORS
>   **rpc_$cant_create_sock**
>   The RPC runtime library could not create a socket.
>
>   **rpc_$cant_bind_sock**
>   The RPC runtime library created a socket but could not bind it to a socket address.
>
>   **rpc_$too_many_sockets**
>   The server is trying to use more than the maximum number of sockets that is allowed; it has called **rpc_$use_family** or **rpc_$use_family_wk** too many times.

EXAMPLE

The following statement from *examples*/**binoplu/server.c**, the **binoplu** example server program, creates a socket for the server:

```
rpc_$use_family (family, &loc, &llen, &st);
```

FILES

idl/**rpc.idl**

SEE ALSO

rpc_$use_family_wk

NAME

rpc_$use_family_wk – create a socket with a well-known port for an RPC server (SERVER ONLY)

SYNOPSIS (C)

#include <idl/c/rpc.h>

void rpc_$use_family_wk(
        unsigned long *family*,
        rpc_$if_spec_t **ifspec*,
        socket_$addr_t **sockaddr*,
        unsigned long **slength*,
        status_$t **status*)

SYNOPSIS (PASCAL)

%include '/usr/include/idl/pas/rpc.ins.pas'

procedure rpc_$use_family_wk(
        in *family*: unsigned32;
        in *ifspec*: rpc_$if_spec_t;
        out *sockaddr*: socket_$addr_t;
        out *slength*: unsigned32;
        out *status*: status_$t);

DESCRIPTION

The **rpc_$use_family_wk** call creates a socket that uses the port specified via the *ifspec* parameter. Use this call to create a socket only if a server must listen on a particular well-known port. Otherwise, use **rpc_$use_family**.

Most servers that use well-known ports should make this call once per address family.

family The address family of the socket to be created. This value corresponds to the communications protocol used to access the socket and determines how the socket address is expressed. The **rpc_$intro** section describes possible values.

ifspec The interface that will be registered by the server. Typically, this parameter is the *interface*$if_spec generated by the NIDL Compiler from the interface definition; the well-known port is specified as an interface attribute.

sockaddr The socket address of the socket on which the server will listen.

slength The length, in bytes, of *sockaddr*.

status The completion status.

ERRORS

rpc_$cant_create_sock
        The RPC runtime library could not create a socket.

rpc_$cant_bind_sock
        The RPC runtime library created a socket but could not bind it to a socket address.

rpc_$too_many_sockets
        The server is trying to use more than the maximum number of sockets that is allowed; it has called **rpc_$use_family** or **rpc_$use_family_wk** too many times.

rpc_$addr_in_use
>The specified address and port are already in use. This is caused by multiple calls to **rpc_$use_family_wk** with the same well-known port.

EXAMPLE
>The following statement from *examples*/**binopwk/server.c**, the **binopwk** example server program, creates a socket for the server:

```
rpc_$use_family_wk (family, &binopwk_v1$if_spec, &loc, &llen, &st);
```

FILES
>*idl*/**rpc.idl**

SEE ALSO
>rpc_$use_family

Chapter 14

rrpc_$ Calls

Contents

NAME
>   rrpc_$intro – Remote Remote Procedure Call interface

SYNOPSIS (C)
>   **#include <idl/c/rrpc.h>**

SYNOPSIS (PASCAL)
>   **%include '/sys/ins/rrpc.ins.pas';**

DESCRIPTION
>   The **rrpc_$** calls enable a client to request information about a server or to shut down a server.
>
>   The **rrpc_** interface is defined by the file *idl/rrpc.idl*, where the symbol *idl* denotes the system **idl** direc-
>   tory. On Apollo workstations and other UNIX systems, *idl* is **/usr/include/idl**.
>
>   If you are using the **rrpc_** interface on Apollo systems, see Appendix B for more information.

CONSTANTS
>   **rrpc_$mod**
>
> >   A module code indicating the Remote RPC module. See the description of the **status_$t** type.
>
>   The **rrpc_$sv** constants are indexes for elements in an **rrpc_$stat_vec_t** array. Each element is a 32-bit
>   integer representing a statistic about a server. The following list describes the statistic indexed by each
>   **rrpc_$sv** constant:
>
> >   **rrpc_$sv_calls_in**
> > >   The number of calls processed by the server.
> >
> >   **rrpc_$sv_rcvd**
> > >   The number of packets received by the server.
> >
> >   **rrpc_$sv_sent**
> > >   The number of packets sent by the server.
> >
> >   **rrpc_$sv_calls_out**
> > >   The number of calls made by the server.
> >
> >   **rrpc_$sv_frag_resends**
> > >   The number of fragments sent by the server that duplicated previous sends.
> >
> >   **rrpc_$sv_dup_frags_rcvd**
> > >   The number of duplicate fragments received by the server.

DATA TYPES
>   The following data types are used in **rpc_$** calls:
>
>   **handle_t** An RPC handle.
>
>   **rrpc_$interface_vec_t**
> >   An array of **rpc_$if_spec_t**, RPC interface specifiers.
>
>   **rrpc_$stat_vec_t**
> >   An array of 32-bit integers, indexed by **rrpc_$sv** constants, representing statistics about a
> >   server.

status_$t A status code. Most of the NCS calls supply their completion status in this format. The **status_$t** type is defined as a structure containing a long integer:

```
struct status_$t {
    long all;
    }
```

However, the calls can also use **status_$t** as a set of bit fields. To access the fields in a returned status code, you can assign the value of the status code to a union defined as follows:

```
typedef union {
    struct {
        unsigned fail : 1,
                 subsys : 7,
                 modc : 8;
        short    code;
    } s;
    long all;
} status_u;
```

all   All 32 bits in the status code. If **all** is equal to **status_$ok**, the call that supplied the status was successful.

fail   If this bit is set, the error was not within the scope of the module invoked, but occurred within a lower-level module.

subsys This indicates the subsystem that encountered the error.

modc   This indicates the module that encountered the error.

code   This is a signed number that identifies the type of error that occurred.

STATUS CODES
rrpc_$shutdown_not_allowed
Remote shutdown of the server is not allowed. Either the server does not ever allow remote shutdown or the server executed a check function that returned "false."

status_$ok
The call was successful.

FILES
idl/**rrpc.idl**

NAME

   rrpc_$are_you_there – check whether a server is answering requests

SYNOPSIS (C)

   #include <idl/c/rrpc.h>

   void rrpc_$are_you_there(
   handle_t *handle,*
   status_$t **status*)

SYNOPSIS (PASCAL)

   %include '/usr/include/idl/pas/rrpc.ins.pas'

   procedure rrpc_$are_you_there(
   in *handle*: **handle_t;**
   out *status*: **status_$t);**

DESCRIPTION

   The **rrpc_$are_you_there** call checks whether a server is answering requests. If the server is answering requests, the completion status of this call is **status_$ok.**

   handle   An RPC handle.

   status   The completion status.

FILES

   *idl/***rrpc.idl**

NAME

   rrpc_$inq_interfaces – obtain a list of the interfaces that a server exports

SYNOPSIS (C)

   #include <idl/c/rrpc.h>

   void rrpc_$inq_interfaces(
        handle_t handle,
        unsigned long max_ifs,
        rrpc_$interface_vec_t ifs,
        unsigned long *l_if,
        status_$t *status)

SYNOPSIS (PASCAL)

   %include '/usr/include/idl/pas/rrpc.ins.pas'

   procedure rrpc_$inq_interfaces(
        in handle: handle_t;
        in max_ifs: unsigned32;
        out ifs: univ rrpc_$interface_vec_t;
        out l_if: unsigned32;
        out status: status_$t);

DESCRIPTION

   The rrpc_$inq_interfaces call returns an array of RPC interface specifiers.

   handle   An RPC handle.

   max_ifs   The maximum number of elements in the array of interface specifiers.

   ifs   An array of rpc_$if_spec_t.

   l_if   The index of the last element in the returned array.

   status   The completion status.

FILES

   idl/rrpc.idl

NAME

rrpc_$inq_stats – obtain statistics about a server

SYNOPSIS (C)

#include <idl/c/rrpc.h>

void rrpc_$inq_stats(
        handle_t *handle*,
        unsigned long *max_stats*,
        rrpc_$stat_vec_t *stats*,
        unsigned long *l_stat*,
        status_$t *status*)

SYNOPSIS (PASCAL)

%include '/usr/include/idl/pas/rrpc.ins.pas'

procedure rrpc_$inq_stats(
        in *handle*: handle_t;
        in *max_stats*: unsigned32;
        out *stats*: univ rrpc_$stat_vec_t;
        out *l_stat*: unsigned32;
        out *status*: status_$t);

DESCRIPTION

The **rrpc_$inq_stats** call returns an array of integer statistics about a server.

handle   An RPC handle.

max_stats The maximum number of elements in the array of statistics.

stats   An array of 32-bit integers representing statistics about the server. A set of **rrpc_$sv** constants defines indexes for the elements in this array. The following list describes the statistic indexed by each **rrpc_$sv** constant:

rrpc_$sv_calls_in
        The number of calls processed by the server.

rrpc_$sv_rcvd
        The number of packets received by the server.

rrpc_$sv_sent
        The number of packets sent by the server.

rrpc_$sv_calls_out
        The number of calls made by the server.

rrpc_$sv_frag_resends
        The number of fragments sent by the server that duplicated previous sends.

rrpc_$sv_dup_frags_rcvd
        The number of duplicate fragments received by the server.

l_stat   The index of the last element in the returned array.

status   The completion status.

FILES

idl/**rrpc.idl**

NAME
       rrpc_$shutdown – shut down a server

SYNOPSIS (C)
       #include <idl/c/rrpc.h>

       void rrpc_$shutdown(
               handle_t *handle*,
               **status_$t *****status*)

SYNOPSIS (PASCAL)
       %include '/usr/include/idl/pas/rrpc.ins.pas'

       procedure rrpc_$shutdown(
               in *handle*: **handle_t;**
               out *status*: **status_$t);**

DESCRIPTION
       The **rrpc_$shutdown** call shuts down a server, if the server allows it. A server can use the
       rpc_$allow_remote_shutdown call to allow or disallow remote shutdown.

       handle   An RPC handle.

       status   The completion status.

FILES
       idl/**rrpc.idl**

SEE ALSO
       rpc_$allow_remote_shutdown, rpc_$shutdown

Chapter 15

socket_$ Calls

Contents

NAME
>   socket_$intro – operations on socket addresses

SYNOPSIS (C)
>   #include <idl/c/socket.h>

SYNOPSIS (PASCAL)
>   %include '/sys/ins/socket.ins.pas';

DESCRIPTION
>   The **socket_$** calls manipulate socket addresses. Unlike the calls provided in some operating systems, the **socket_$** calls operate on addresses of any protocol family.
>
>   The **socket_** interface is defined by the file *idl*/**socket.idl**, where the symbol *idl* denotes the system **idl** directory. On Apollo workstations and other UNIX systems, *idl* is **/usr/include/idl**.

CONSTANTS
>   The following constants are used in **socket_$** calls:
>
>   **socket_$addr_module_code**
>   >   A module code indicating the socket address module. See the description of the **status_$t** type.
>
>   The **socket_$eq** constants are flags indicating the fields to be compared in a **socket_$equal** call.
>
>   >   **socket_$eq_hostid**
>   >   >   Indicates that the host IDs are to be compared.
>   >
>   >   **socket_$eq_netaddr**
>   >   >   Indicates that the network addresses are to be compared.
>   >
>   >   **socket_$eq_port**
>   >   >   Indicates that the port numbers are to be compared.
>   >
>   >   **socket_$eq_network**
>   >   >   Indicates that the network IDs are to be compared.
>
>   The following 16-bit-integer constants are values for the **socket_$addr_family_t** type, used to specify the address family in a **socket_$addr_t** structure. Note that several of the **rpc_$** and **socket_$** calls use the 32-bit-integer equivalents of these values.
>
>   >   **socket_$unspec**
>   >   >   Address family is unspecified.
>   >
>   >   **socket_$internet**
>   >   >   Internet Protocols (IP).
>   >
>   >   **socket_$dds**
>   >   >   Domain protocols (DDS).
>
>   **socket_$unspec_port**
>   >   A port number indicating that no port is specified.

The following 16-bit-integer constant is a value for the **socket_$wk_ports_t** type, used to specify a well-known port. Note that several of the **socket_$** calls use the 32-bit-integer equivalent of this value.

> **socket_$wk_fwd**
>> The Local Location Broker forwarding port.

DATA TYPES

The following data types are used in **socket_$** calls:

socket_$addr_family_t
> An enumerated type for specifying an address family. The "CONSTANTS" section lists values for this type.

socket_$addr_list_t
> An array of socket addresses in **socket_$addr_t** format.

socket_$addr_t
> A structure that uniquely identifies a socket address. This structure consists of a **socket_$addr_family_t** specifying an address family and 14 bytes specifying a socket address.

socket_$host_id_t
> A structure that uniquely identifies a host. This structure consists of a **socket_$addr_family_t** specifying an address family and 12 bytes specifying a host.

socket_$len_list_t
> An array of unsigned 32-bit integers, the lengths of socket addresses in a **socket_$addr_list_t**.

socket_$local_sockaddr_t
> An array of 50 characters, used to store a socket address in a format native to the local host.

socket_$net_addr_t
> A structure that uniquely identifies a network address. This structure consists of a **socket_$addr_family_t** specifying an address family and 12 bytes specifying a network address. It contains both a host ID and a network ID.

socket_$string_t
> An array of 100 characters, used to store the string representation of an address family or a socket address.
>
> The string representation of an address family is a textual name such as **dds**, **ip**, or **unspec**.
>
> The string representation of a socket address has the format *family*:*host* [*port*], where *family* is the textual name of an address family, *host* is either a textual host name or a numeric host ID preceded by a #, and *port* is a port number.

socket_$wk_ports_t
> An enumerated type for specifying a well-known port. The "CONSTANTS" section lists values for this type.

status_$t A status code. Most of the NCS calls supply their completion status in this format. The **status_$t** type is defined as a structure containing a long integer:

```
struct status_$t {
     long all;
     }
```

However, the calls can also use **status_$t** as a set of bit fields. To access the fields in a returned status code, you can assign the value of the status code to a union defined as follows:

```
typedef union {
    struct {
        unsigned fail : 1,
                 subsys : 7,
                 modc : 8;
        short    code;
    } s;
    long all;
} status_u;
```

all   All 32 bits in the status code. If **all** is equal to **status_$ok**, the call that supplied the status was successful.

fail   If this bit is set, the error was not within the scope of the module invoked, but occurred within a lower-level module.

subsys   This indicates the subsystem that encountered the error.

modc   This indicates the module that encountered the error.

code   This is a signed number that identifies the type of error that occurred.

STATUS CODES

The following are status codes returned by **socket_$** calls:

socket_$bad_numeric_name
        A specified name in numeric format is invalid.

socket_$buff_too_large
        A specified buffer size (for example, the length of a name) is too large.

socket_$buff_too_small
        A specified buffer size (for example, the length of a name) is too small.

socket_$cant_create_socket
        A socket could not be created.

socket_$cant_cvrt_addr_to_name
        A specified address could not be converted to a name.

socket_$cant_find_name
        A specified name could not be resolved to an address.

socket_$cant_get_if_config
        The interface configuration list for the local host could not be obtained.

socket_$cant_get_local_name
> The name of the local host could not be obtained.

socket_$family_not_valid
> The specified address family is not valid for the local host.

socket_$internal_error
> An internal error.

socket_$invalid_name_format
> The format of a specified name is invalid.

status_$ok
> The call was successful.

FILES
> *idl*/**socket.idl**

NAME

    socket_$equal – compare two socket addresses

SYNOPSIS (C)

    #include <idl/c/socket.h>

    boolean socket_$equal(
        socket_$addr_t *sockaddr1,
        unsigned long *s1length,*
        socket_$addr_t *sockaddr2,
        unsigned long *s2length,*
        unsigned long *flags,*
        status_$t *status)

SYNOPSIS (PASCAL)

    %include '/usr/include/idl/pas/socket.ins.pas'

    function socket_$equal(
        in *sockaddr1*: **socket_$addr_t;**
        in *s1length*: **unsigned32;**
        in *sockaddr2*: **socket_$addr_t;**
        in *s2length*: **unsigned32;**
        in *flags*: **unsigned32;**
        out *status*: **status_$t): boolean;**

DESCRIPTION

    The **socket_$equal** call compares two socket addresses. The *flags* parameter determines which fields of the socket addresses are compared. The call returns "true" (nonzero) if all of the fields compared are equal, "false" (zero) if not.

sockaddr1
    A socket address.

s1length   The length, in bytes, of *sockaddr1*.

sockaddr2
    A socket address.

s2length   The length, in bytes, of *sockaddr2*.

flags   The logical OR of values selected from the following:

    socket_$eq_hostid
        Indicates that the host IDs are to be compared.

    socket_$eq_netaddr
        Indicates that the network addresses are to be compared.

    socket_$eq_port
        Indicates that the port numbers are to be compared.

    socket_$eq_network
        Indicates that the network IDs are to be compared.

status   The completion status.

EXAMPLE

The following call compares the network and host IDs in the socket addresses **sockaddr1** and **sockaddr2**:

```
if (socket_$equal (&sockaddr1, s1length, &sockaddr2, s2length,
        socket_$eq_network | socket_$eq_hostid, &st))
    printf ("sockaddrs have equal network and host IDs\n");
```

FILES

idl/**socket.idl**

NAME
        socket_$family_from_name – convert an address family name to an integer

SYNOPSIS (C)
        #include <idl/c/socket.h>

        unsigned long socket_$family_from_name(
                socket_$string_t *name*,
                unsigned long *nlength*,
                status_$t *status*)

SYNOPSIS (PASCAL)
        %include '/usr/include/idl/pas/socket.ins.pas'

        function socket_$family_from_name(
                in *name*: **socket_$string_t;**
                in *nlength*: **unsigned32;**
                out *status*: **status_$t): unsigned32;**

DESCRIPTION
        The **socket_$family_from_name** call returns the integer representation of the address family specified in
        the text string *name*.

        name   The textual name of an address family. Possible values include **dds** and **ip**.

        nlength   The length, in bytes, of *name*.

        status   The completion status.

EXAMPLE
        The server program for the **binoplu** example, *examples*/**binoplu/server.c**, accepts a textual family name as
        its first argument. The program uses the following **socket_$family_from_name** call to convert this name
        to the corresponding integer representation:

```
family = socket_$family_from_name ((ndr_$char *)argv[1],
    (long)strlen(argv[1]), &st);
```

FILES
        idl/**socket.idl**

SEE ALSO
        socket_$family_to_name, socket_$from_name, socket_$to_name

NAME
          socket_$family_to_name – convert an integer address family to a textual name

SYNOPSIS (C)
          #include <idl/c/socket.h>

          void socket_$family_to_name(
                    unsigned long *family*,
                    socket_$string_t *name*,
                    unsigned long *nlength*,
                    status_$t *status*)

SYNOPSIS (PASCAL)
          %include '/usr/include/idl/pas/socket.ins.pas'

          procedure socket_$family_to_name(
                    in *family*: unsigned32;
                    out *name*: socket_$string_t;
                    in out *nlength*: unsigned32;
                    out *status*: status_$t);

DESCRIPTION
          The **socket_$family_to_name** call converts the integer representation of an address family to a textual
          name for the family.

          family   The integer representation of an address family.

          name   The textual name of *family*.

          nlength   On input, the maximum length, in bytes, of the name to be returned. On output, the actual
                        length of the returned name.

          status   The completion status.

EXAMPLE
          The following statement converts the integer representation of an address family (**i**) to the corresponding
          textual name (**name**):

          ```
          socket_$family_to_name (i, (ndr_$char *)name, &namelen, &st);
          ```

FILES
          idl/**socket.idl**

SEE ALSO
          socket_$family_from_name, socket_$from_name, socket_$to_name

NAME

    socket_$from_local_rep – convert from a local representation of a socket address to a **socket_$addr_t**

SYNOPSIS (C)

    #include <idl/c/socket.h>

    void socket_$from_local_rep(
        socket_$addr_t *sockaddr,
        socket_$local_sockaddr_t *local_sockaddr*,
        status_$t *status)

SYNOPSIS (PASCAL)

    %include '/usr/include/idl/pas/socket.ins.pas'

    procedure socket_$from_local_rep(
        in out *sockaddr*: **socket_$addr_t;**
        in *local_sockaddr*: **socket_$local_sockaddr_t;**
        out *status*: **status_$t);**

DESCRIPTION

    The **socket_$from_local_rep** call converts a socket address from the format native to the local host into NCS **socket_$addr_t** format. This call is useful only on systems with non-standard socket address structure layouts, and even then, only if NCS-based applications need to use the native socket primitives on NCS **socket_$addr_t** structures.

    sockaddr The representation of *local_sockaddr* in NCS **socket_$addr_t** format.

    local_sockaddr

        A socket address in the format native to the local host.

    status The completion status.

FILES

    idl/**socket.idl**

SEE ALSO

    socket_$to_local_rep

NAME

     socket_$from_name – convert a name and port number to a socket address

SYNOPSIS (C)

     #include <idl/c/socket.h>

     void socket_$from_name(
          unsigned long *family*,
          socket_$string_t *name*,
          unsigned long *nlength*,
          unsigned long *port*,
          socket_$addr_t **sockaddr*,
          unsigned long **slength*,
          status_$t **status*)

SYNOPSIS (PASCAL)

     %include '/usr/include/idl/pas/socket.ins.pas'

     procedure socket_$from_name(
          in *family*: **unsigned32;**
          in *name*: **socket_$string_t;**
          in *nlength*: **unsigned32;**
          in *port*: **unsigned32;**
          out *sockaddr*: **socket_$addr_t;**
          in out *slength*: **unsigned32;**
          out *status*: **status_$t);**

DESCRIPTION

     The **socket_$from_name** call converts a textual address family, host name, and port number to a socket address. The address family and the port number can be either specified as separate parameters or included in the *name* parameter.

     family   The integer representation of an address family. If the *family* parameter is **socket_$unspec**, then the *name* parameter is scanned for a prefix of *family:* (for example, **ip:**).

     name   A string in the format *family:host* [*port*] , where *family:*, *host*, and [*port*] are all optional.

              The *family* is an address family. Possible values include **dds** and **ip**. If you specify a *family* as part of the *name* parameter, you must specify **socket_$unspec** in the *family* parameter.

              The *host* is a host name. A leading **#** can be used to indicate that the host name is in the standard numeric form (for example, **#192.9.8.7** or **#464a.465c**). If *host* is omitted, the local host name is used.

              The *port* is a port number. If you specify a *port* as part of the *name* parameter, the *port* parameter is ignored.

     nlength   The length, in bytes, of *name*.

     port   A port number. If you specify a port number in the *name* parameter, this parameter is ignored.

     sockaddr   A socket address.

slength   The length, in bytes, of *sockaddr*.

status   The completion status.

EXAMPLE

The client program for the **binopfw** example, *examples*/**binopfw/client.c**, accepts as its first argument a string identifying a server host, in the format *family:host*. The client program does not require the server port number because it sends its first remote procedure call to the Local Location Broker forwarding port at the specified host. The program uses the following **socket_$from_name** call to convert this string to a socket address:

```
socket_$from_name ((long)socket_$unspec, (ndr_$char *)argv[1],
    (long)strlen(argv[1]), (long)socket_$unspec_port, &loc, &llen, &st);
```

FILES

idl/**socket.idl**

SEE ALSO

socket_$family_from_name, socket_$to_name

NAME

    socket_$inq_broad_addrs – return a list of broadcast addresses

SYNOPSIS (C)

    #include <idl/c/socket.h>

    void socket_$inq_broad_addrs(
        unsigned long *family*,
        unsigned long *port*,
        socket_$addr_list_t *brd_addrs*,
        socket_$len_list_t *brd_lens*,
        unsigned long **length*,
        status_$t **status*)

SYNOPSIS (PASCAL)

    %include '/usr/include/idl/pas/socket.ins.pas'

    procedure socket_$inq_broad_addrs(
        in *family*: **unsigned32;**
        in *port*: **unsigned32;**
        out *brd_addrs*: **univ socket_$addr_list_t;**
        out *brd_lens*: **univ socket_$len_list_t;**
        in out *length*: **unsigned32;**
        out *status*: **status_$t);**

DESCRIPTION

    The **socket_$inq_broad_addrs** call returns a list of all broadcast addresses that the local host can use in the specified address family.

    If a host has network interfaces to several networks in *family*, this call returns a socket address for each interface that supports broadcasting. IP interfaces via serial lines, for example, do not support broadcasting, so no addresses are returned for such interfaces.

    family   The integer representation of an address family.

    port   The value to be used as the port number in the returned addresses.

    brd_addrs
        An array of the socket addresses in *family* to which the host can send broadcasts.

    brd_lens An array of the lengths of the *brd_addrs*.

    length   On input, the maximum number of addresses to be returned in *brd_addrs*. On return, the number of addresses actually returned.

    status   The completion status.

FILES

    idl/**socket.idl**

NAME
     socket_$inq_hostid – return the host ID part of a socket address

SYNOPSIS (C)
     #include <idl/c/socket.h>

     void socket_$inq_hostid(
          socket_$addr_t **sockaddr,*
          unsigned long *slength,*
          socket_$host_id_t **hostid,*
          unsigned long **hlength,*
          status_$t **status*)

SYNOPSIS (PASCAL)
     %include '/usr/include/idl/pas/socket.ins.pas'

     procedure socket_$inq_hostid(
          in *sockaddr*: **socket_$addr_t;**
          in *slength*: **unsigned32;**
          out *hostid*: **socket_$host_id_t;**
          in out *hlength*: **unsigned32;**
          out *status*: **status_$t);**

DESCRIPTION
     The **socket_$inq_hostid** call returns the host ID part of a socket address.

     sockaddr   A socket address.

     slength   The length, in bytes, of *sockaddr.*

     hostid   The host ID part of *sockaddr.*

     hlength   The length, in bytes, of *hostid.*

     status   The completion status.

FILES
     *idl/***socket.idl**

SEE ALSO
     socket_$set_hostid

NAME

      socket_$inq_my_netaddr – return the primary network address for the local host

SYNOPSIS (C)

      #include <idl/c/socket.h>

      void socket_$inq_my_netaddr(
          unsigned long *family,*
          socket_$net_addr_t **netaddr,*
          unsigned long **nlength,*
          status_$t **status)*

SYNOPSIS (PASCAL)

      %include '/usr/include/idl/pas/socket.ins.pas'

      procedure socket_$inq_my_netaddr(
          in *family*: **unsigned32;**
          out *netaddr*: **socket_$net_addr_t;**
          in out *nlength*: **unsigned32;**
          out *status*: **status_$t);**

DESCRIPTION

      The **socket_$inq_my_netaddr** call returns the primary network address for the local host in the specified family.

      family   The integer representation of an address family.

      netaddr   The network address for the local host in *family*.

      nlength   The length, in bytes, of *netaddr*.

      status   The completion status.

FILES

      *idl/***socket.idl**

SEE ALSO

      socket_$inq_netaddr, socket_$set_netaddr

NAME
        socket_$inq_netaddr – return the network address part of a socket address

SYNOPSIS (C)
        #include <idl/c/socket.h>

        void socket_$inq_netaddr(
                socket_$addr_t **sockaddr*,
                unsigned long *slength*,
                socket_$net_addr_t **netaddr*,
                unsigned long **nlength*,
                status_$t **status*)

SYNOPSIS (PASCAL)
        %include '/usr/include/idl/pas/socket.ins.pas'

        procedure socket_$inq_netaddr(
                in *sockaddr*: **socket_$addr_t;**
                in *slength*: **unsigned32;**
                out *netaddr*: **socket_$net_addr_t;**
                in out *nlength*: **unsigned32;**
                out *status*: **status_$t);**

DESCRIPTION
        The **socket_$inq_netaddr** call returns the network address part of a socket address.

        sockaddr A socket address.

        slength   The length, in bytes, of *sockaddr*.

        netaddr   The network address part of *sockaddr*.

        nlength   The length, in bytes, of *netaddr*.

        status   The completion status.

FILES
        *idl/***socket.idl**

SEE ALSO
        socket_$inq_my_netaddr, socket_$set_netaddr

NAME

   socket_$inq_port – return the port number part of a socket address

SYNOPSIS (C)

   #include <idl/c/socket.h>

   unsigned long socket_$inq_port(
   socket_$addr_t **sockaddr,*
   unsigned long *slength,*
   status_$t **status)*

SYNOPSIS (PASCAL)

   %include '/usr/include/idl/pas/socket.ins.pas'

   function socket_$inq_port(
   in *sockaddr*: **socket_$addr_t;**
   in *slength*: **unsigned32;**
   out *status*: **status_$t): unsigned32;**

DESCRIPTION

   The **socket_$inq_port** call returns the port number part of a socket address.

   sockaddr   A socket address.

   slength   The length, in bytes, of *sockaddr*.

   status   The completion status.

EXAMPLE

   The following call returns the port number in the socket address **sockaddr**:

   ```
   port = socket_$inq_port (&sockaddr, slen, &st);
   ```

FILES

   idl/**socket.idl**

SEE ALSO

   socket_$inq_my_netaddr, socket_$inq_netaddr, socket_$set_port

NAME

   socket_$max_pkt_size – return the maximum packet size for an address family

SYNOPSIS (C)

   #include <idl/c/socket.h>

   unsigned long socket_$max_pkt_size(
      unsigned long *family*,
      status_$t *status)

SYNOPSIS (PASCAL)

   %include '/usr/include/idl/pas/socket.ins.pas'

   function socket_$max_pkt_size(
      in *family*: **unsigned32;**
      out *status*: **status_$t): unsigned32;**

DESCRIPTION

   The **socket_$max_pkt_size** call returns the maximum packet size, in bytes, for the specified address family.

   family The integer representation of an address family. Possible values include **socket_$internet** and **socket_$dds**.

   status The completion status.

FILES

   idl/**socket.idl**

NAME
>   socket_$set_hostid – set the host ID part of a socket address

SYNOPSIS (C)
>   #include <idl/c/socket.h>
>
>   void socket_$set_hostid(
>   socket_$addr_t *sockaddr,
>   unsigned long *slength,
>   socket_$host_id_t *hostid,
>   unsigned long hlength,
>   status_$t *status)

SYNOPSIS (PASCAL)
>   %include '/usr/include/idl/pas/socket.ins.pas'
>
>   procedure socket_$set_hostid(
>   in out sockaddr: socket_$addr_t;
>   in out slength: unsigned32;
>   in hostid: socket_$host_id_t;
>   in hlength: unsigned32;
>   out status: status_$t);

DESCRIPTION
>   The socket_$set_hostid call sets the host ID in a socket address to the specified value.
>
>   *sockaddr*   A socket address.
>
>   *slength*   The length, in bytes, of *sockaddr*.
>
>   *hostid*   A host ID.
>
>   *hlength*   The length, in bytes, of *hostid*.
>
>   *status*   The completion status.

FILES
>   *idl*/**socket.idl**

SEE ALSO
>   socket_$inq_hostid

NAME

   socket_$set_netaddr – set the network address part of a socket address

SYNOPSIS (C)

   #include <idl/c/socket.h>

   void socket_$set_netaddr(
           socket_$addr_t **sockaddr,*
           unsigned long **slength,*
           socket_$net_addr_t **netaddr,*
           unsigned long *nlength,*
           status_$t **status)*

SYNOPSIS (PASCAL)

   %include '/usr/include/idl/pas/socket.ins.pas'

   procedure socket_$set_netaddr(
           in out *sockaddr*: **socket_$addr_t;**
           in out *slength*: **unsigned32;**
           in *netaddr*: **socket_$net_addr_t;**
           in *nlength*: **unsigned32;**
           out *status*: **status_$t);**

DESCRIPTION

   The **socket_$set_netaddr** call sets the network address in a socket address to the specified value.

   sockaddr A socket address.

   slength   The length, in bytes, of *sockaddr*.

   netaddr   A network address.

   nlength   The length, in bytes, of *netaddr*.

   status   The completion status.

SEE ALSO

   socket_$inq_netaddr

NAME

   socket_$set_port – set the port number in a socket address

SYNOPSIS (C)

   #include <idl/c/socket.h>

   void socket_$set_port(
      socket_$addr_t **sockaddr,*
      unsigned long **slength,*
      unsigned long *port,*
      status_$t **status*)

SYNOPSIS (PASCAL)

   %include '/usr/include/idl/pas/socket.ins.pas'

   procedure socket_$set_port(
      in out *sockaddr*: **socket_$addr_t;**
      in out *slength*: **unsigned32;**
      in *port*: **unsigned32;**
      out *status*: **status_$t);**

DESCRIPTION

   The **socket_$set_port** call sets the port number in a socket address to the specified value.

   sockaddr   A socket address.

   slength   The length, in bytes, of *sockaddr*.

   port   The value to which the port number in *sockaddr* will be set.

   status   The completion status.

EXAMPLE

   The following call sets the port number in **sockaddr** to **port**:

   ```
   socket_$set_port (&sockaddr, &slen, port, &st);
   ```

SEE ALSO

   socket_$inq_port, socket_$set_netaddr, socket_$set_wk_port

NAME

socket_$set_wk_port – set the port number in a socket address to a well-known value

SYNOPSIS (C)

#include <idl/c/socket.h>

void socket_$set_wk_port(
       socket_$addr_t *_sockaddr_,
       unsigned long *_slength_,
       unsigned long _port_,
       status_$t *_status_)

SYNOPSIS (PASCAL)

%include '/usr/include/idl/pas/socket.ins.pas'

procedure socket_$set_wk_port(
       in out _sockaddr_: socket_$addr_t;
       in out _slength_: unsigned32;
       in _port_: unsigned32;
       out _status_: status_$t);

DESCRIPTION

The **socket_$set_wk_port** call sets the port number in a socket address to the specified well-known value.

sockaddr A socket address.

slength   The length, in bytes, of _sockaddr_.

port   A value of the enumerated type **socket_$wk_ports_t**. The well-known value to which the port number in _sockaddr_ will be set.

status   The completion status.

EXAMPLE

The Local Location Broker daemon listens on the LLB forwarding port, which has the well-known port number **socket_$wk_fwd**. The daemon uses the following call to set the port number in its socket address:

```
socket_$set_wk_port (&saddr, &slen, (unsigned long) socket_$wk_fwd, &st);
```

SEE ALSO

socket_$inq_port, socket_$set_netaddr, socket_$set_port

NAME

   socket_$to_local_rep – convert a **socket_$addr_t** to a local representation

SYNOPSIS (C)

   #include <idl/c/socket.h>

   void socket_$to_local_rep(
       socket_$addr_t **sockaddr,*
       socket_$local_sockaddr_t *local_sockaddr,*
       status_$t **status*)

SYNOPSIS (PASCAL)

   %include '/usr/include/idl/pas/socket.ins.pas'

   procedure socket_$to_local_rep(
       in *sockaddr:* **socket_$addr_t;**
       in out *local_sockaddr:* **socket_$local_sockaddr_t;**
       out *status:* **status_$t);**

DESCRIPTION

   The **socket_$to_local_rep** call converts a socket address from NCS **socket_$addr_t** format into a format usable by the socket primitives native to the local host. This call is useful only on systems with non-standard socket address structure layouts, and even then, only if NCS-based applications need to use the native socket primitives on NCS **socket_$addr_t** structures.

   sockaddr A socket address in NCS **socket_$addr_t** format.

   local_sockaddr

       The representation of *sockaddr* in a format native to the local host.

   status The completion status.

FILES

   idl/**socket.idl**

SEE ALSO

   socket_$from_local_rep

NAME

socket_$to_name – convert a socket address to a name and port number

SYNOPSIS (C)

#include <idl/c/socket.h>

void socket_$to_name(
        socket_$addr_t *sockaddr,
        unsigned long slength,
        socket_$string_t name,
        unsigned long *nlength,
        unsigned long *port,
        status_$t *status)

SYNOPSIS (PASCAL)

%include '/usr/include/idl/pas/socket.ins.pas'

procedure socket_$to_name(
        in sockaddr: socket_$addr_t;
        in slength: unsigned32;
        out name: socket_$string_t;
        in out nlength: unsigned32;
        out port: unsigned32;
        out status: status_$t);

DESCRIPTION

The socket_$to_name call converts a socket address to a textual address family, host name, and port number.

sockaddr   A socket address.

slength   The length, in bytes, of *sockaddr*.

name   A string in the format *family:host*, where *family* is the address family and *host* is the host name; *host* may be in the standard numeric form (for example, **#192.1.2.3** or **#499d.488a**) if a textual host name cannot be obtained.

nlength   On input, the maximum length, in bytes, of the name to be returned. On output, the actual length of the name returned.

port   The port number.

status   The completion status.

EXAMPLE

The client program for the **binoplu** example, *examples*/**binoplu/client.c**, uses the following call to convert the socket address for its server to a textual name:

```
socket_$to_name (&loc, llen, name, &namelen, &port, &st);
```

FILES

      idl/**socket.idl**

SEE ALSO

      socket_$family_to_name, socket_$from_name, socket_$to_numeric_name

NAME

   socket_$to_numeric_name – convert a socket address to a numeric name and port number

SYNOPSIS (C)

   #include <idl/c/socket.h>

   void socket_$to_numeric_name(
           socket_$addr_t *sockaddr,
           unsigned long *slength*,
           socket_$string_t *name*,
           unsigned long *nlength,
           unsigned long *port,
           status_$t *status)

SYNOPSIS (PASCAL)

   %include '/usr/include/idl/pas/socket.ins.pas'

   procedure socket_$to_numeric_name(
           in *sockaddr*: **socket_$addr_t;**
           in *slength*: **unsigned32;**
           out *name*: **socket_$string_t;**
           in out *nlength*: **unsigned32;**
           out *port*: **unsigned32;**
           out *status*: **status_$t);**

DESCRIPTION

   The **socket_$to_numeric_name** call converts a socket address to a textual address family, a numeric host name, and a port number.

   sockaddr A socket address.

   slength   The length, in bytes, of *sockaddr*.

   name   A string in the format *family*:*host*, where *family* is the address family and *host* is the host name in the standard numeric form (for example, **#192.7.8.9** for an IP address or **#840c.940f** for a DDS address).

   nlength   On input, the maximum length, in bytes, of the numeric name to be returned. On output, the actual length of the name returned.

   port   The port number.

   status   The completion status.

FILES

   idl/**socket.idl**

SEE ALSO

   socket_$family_to_name, socket_$from_name, socket_$to_name

NAME

socket_$valid_families – obtain a list of valid address families

SYNOPSIS (C)

#include <idl/c/socket.h>

void socket_$valid_families(
  unsigned long *max_families,*
  socket_$addr_family_t *families*[],
  status_$t **status*)

SYNOPSIS (PASCAL)

%include '/usr/include/idl/pas/socket.ins.pas'

procedure socket_$valid_families(
  in out *max_families*: **unsigned32;**
  out *families*: **array [1..*] of socket_$addr_family_t;**
  out *status*: **status_$t);**

DESCRIPTION

The **socket_$valid_families** call returns a list of the address families that are valid for the NCK implementation on the calling host.

max_families
  The maximum number of families that can be returned.

families An array of **socket_$addr_family_t**. Possible values for this type are enumerated in *idl*/**nbase.idl**.

status   The completion status. A status of **socket_$buff_too_small** indicates that the *families* array is not long enough to hold all the valid families.

EXAMPLE

The following call returns a list of at most two valid address families:

```
socket_$valid_families (2, &families, $st);
```

FILES

idl/**socket.idl**

SEE ALSO

socket_$valid_family

NAME

socket_$valid_family – check whether an address family is valid

SYNOPSIS (C)

#include <idl/c/socket.h>

boolean socket_$valid_family(
    unsigned long *family*,
    status_$t **status*)

SYNOPSIS (PASCAL)

%include '/usr/include/idl/pas/socket.ins.pas'

function socket_$valid_family(
    in *family*: unsigned32;
    out *status*: status_$t): boolean;

DESCRIPTION

The **socket_$valid_family** call returns "true" if the specified address family is valid for the NCK implementation on the calling host, "false" if not.

family   The integer representation of an address family, as enumerated in *idl*/**nbase.idl**.

status   The completion status.

EXAMPLE

The following call checks whether **socket_$internet** is a valid address family:

```
internetvalid = socket_$valid_family (socket_$internet, &st);
```

FILES

idl/**socket.idl**

SEE ALSO

socket_$valid_families

Chapter 16

uuid_$ Calls

Contents

NAME
uuid_$intro – operations on Universal Unique Identifiers

SYNOPSIS (C)
#include <idl/c/uuid.h>

SYNOPSIS (PASCAL)
%include '/sys/ins/uuid.ins.pas';

DESCRIPTION
The **uuid_$** calls operate on UUIDs (Universal Unique Identifiers).

The **uuid_** interface is defined by the file *idl/***uuid.idl,** where the symbol *idl* denotes the system **idl** directory. On Apollo workstations and other UNIX systems, *idl* is **/usr/include/idl**.

Apollo software also uses UIDs (Unique Identifiers) as identifiers. On Apollo systems, we supply two additional operations that convert UUIDs to UIDs and vice versa, and we define these operations in the file *idl/***uuid_uid.idl**.

EXTERNAL VARIABLES
The following external variables are used in **uuid_$** calls:

uid_$nil An external **uid_$t** variable that is preassigned the value of the nil UID. Do not change the value of this variable.

uuid_$nil

An external **uuid_$t** variable that is preassigned the value of the nil UUID. Do not change the value of this variable.

DATA TYPES
The following data types are used in **uuid_$** calls.

status_$t A status code. Most of the NCS calls supply their completion status in this format. The **status_$t** type is defined as a structure containing a long integer:

```
struct status_$t {
    long all;
    }
```

However, the calls can also use **status_$t** as a set of bit fields. To access the fields in a returned status code, you can assign the value of the status code to a union defined as follows:

```
typedef union {
    struct {
        unsigned fail : 1,
                 subsys : 7,
                 modc : 8;
        short    code;
    } s;
    long all;
} status_u;
```

all   All 32 bits in the status code. If **all** is equal to **status_$ok**, the call that supplied the status was successful.

fail   If this bit is set, the error was not within the scope of the module invoked, but occurred within a lower-level module.

subsys   This indicates the subsystem that encountered the error.

modc   This indicates the module that encountered the error.

code   This is a signed number that identifies the type of error that occurred.

uid_$t   A 64-bit value that uniquely identifies objects and types on Apollo systems.

uuid_$string_t

A string of 37 characters (including a null terminator) that is an ASCII representation of a UUID. The format is *cccccccccccc.ff.h1.h2.h3.h4.h5.h6.h7*, where *cccccccccccc* is the timestamp, *ff* is the address family, and *h1 ... h7* are the seven bytes of host identifier. Each character in these fields is a hexadecimal digit.

uuid_$t A 128-bit value that uniquely identifies an object, type, or interface for all time. The **uuid_$t** type is defined as follows:

```
typedef struct uuid_$t {
    unsigned long time_high;
    unsigned short time_low;
    unsigned short reserved;
    unsigned char family;
    unsigned char (host)[7];
} uuid_$t;
```

time_high
                The high 32 bits of a 48-bit unsigned time value which is the number of 4-microsecond intervals that have passed between 1 January 1980 00:00 GMT and the time of UUID creation.

time_low The low 16 bits of the 48-bit time value.

reserved 16 bits of reserved space.

family   8 bits identifying an address family.

host   7 bytes identifying the host on which the UUID was created. The format of this field depends on the address family.

STATUS CODES

status_$ok
                The call was successful.

FILES

*idl/***uuid.idl**

NAME

    uuid_$decode – convert a character-string representation of a UUID into a UUID

    #include <idl/c/uuid.h>

    void uuid_$decode(
        uuid_$string_t *s,*
        uuid_$t **uuid,*
        status_$t *status)

SYNOPSIS (PASCAL)

    %include '/usr/include/idl/pas/uuid.ins.pas'

    procedure uuid_$decode(
        in *s*: **uuid_$string_t;**
        out *uuid*: **uuid_$t;**
        out *status*: **status_$t);**

DESCRIPTION

    The **uuid_$decode** call returns the UUID corresponding to a valid character-string representation of a UUID.

    s   The character-string representation of a UUID.

    uuid   The UUID that corresponds to *s*.

    status   A **status_$t**. The completion status.

EXAMPLE

    The following call returns as **leek_uuid** the UUID corresponding to the character-string representation in **leek_uuid_rep**:

```
uuid_$decode (leek_uuid_rep, &leek_uuid, &status);
```

FILES

    *idl/***uuid.idl**

SEE ALSO

    uuid_$encode

NAME

uuid_$encode – convert a UUID into its character-string representation

SYNOPSIS (C)

#include <idl/c/uuid.h>

void uuid_$encode(
    uuid_$t *uuid,
    uuid_$string_t s)

SYNOPSIS (PASCAL)

%include '/usr/include/idl/pas/uuid.ins.pas'

procedure uuid_$encode(
    in uuid: uuid_$t;
    out s: uuid_$string_t);

DESCRIPTION

The **uuid_$encode** call returns the character-string representation of a UUID.

uuid   A UUID.

s   The character-string representation of *uuid*.

EXAMPLE

The following call returns as **shallot_uuid_rep** the character-string representation for the UUID **shallot_uuid**:

```
uuid_$encode (&shallot_uuid, shallot_uuid_rep);
```

FILES

idl/**uuid.idl**

SEE ALSO

uuid_$decode

NAME
>   **uuid_$equal** – compare two UUIDs

SYNOPSIS (C)
>   **#include <idl/c/uuid.h>**
>
>   **boolean uuid_$equal(**
>   **uuid_$t *u1,**
>   **uuid_$t *u2)**

SYNOPSIS (PASCAL)
>   **%include '/usr/include/idl/pas/uuid.ins.pas'**
>
>   **function uuid_$equal(**
>   **in u1: uuid_$t;**
>   **in u2: uuid_$t): boolean;**

DESCRIPTION
>   The **uuid_$equal** call compares the UUIDs *u1* and *u2*. It returns "true" if they are equal, "false" if they are not.
>
>   *u1*   A UUID.
>
>   *u2*   Another UUID.

EXAMPLE
>   The following code compares the UUIDs **cilantro_uuid** and **coriander_uuid**:

```
if (uuid_$equal (&cilantro_uuid, &coriander_uuid))
    printf ("cilantro and coriander UUIDs are equal\n");
else
    printf ("cilantro and coriander UUIDs are not equal\n");
```

FILES
>   *idl*/**uuid.idl**

NAME

uuid_$from_uid – convert a Domain UID into a UUID (APOLLO SYSTEMS ONLY)

SYNOPSIS (C)

#include <idl/c/uuid_uid.h>

void uuid_$from_uid(
        uid_$t *uid,
        uuid_$t *uuid)

SYNOPSIS (PASCAL)

%include '/usr/include/idl/pas/uuid_uid.ins.pas'

procedure uuid_$from_uid(
        in uid: uid_$t;
        out uuid: uuid_$t);

DESCRIPTION

The **uuid_$from_uid** call returns the 128-bit NCS UUID corresponding to a 64-bit Domain UID. This call is available only on Apollo systems.

uid   A Domain Unique Identifier (UID).

uuid   The UUID corresponding to uid.

EXAMPLE

The following call returns as **onion_uuid** the UUID corresponding to the UID **onion_uid**:

```
uuid_$from_uid (&onion_uid, &onion_uuid);
```

FILES

idl/**uuid.idl**

SEE ALSO

uuid_$to_uid

NAME
  uuid_$gen – generate a new UUID

SYNOPSIS (C)
  #include <idl/c/uuid.h>

  void uuid_$gen(
      uuid_$t *_uuid_)

SYNOPSIS (PASCAL)
  %include '/usr/include/idl/pas/uuid.ins.pas'

  procedure uuid_$gen(
      out _uuid_: **uuid_$t);**

DESCRIPTION
  The **uuid_$gen** call returns a new UUID.

  uuid   A UUID.

EXAMPLE
  The following call returns as **newid** a new UUID:

```
uuid_$gen (&newid);
```

FILES
  idl/**uuid.idl**

NAME

       uuid_$to_uid – convert a UUID into a Domain UID (APOLLO SYSTEMS ONLY)

SYNOPSIS (C)

       #include <idl/c/uuid_uid.h>

       void uuid_$to_uid(
              uuid_$t **uuid,*
              uid_$t **uid,*
              status_$t **status*)

SYNOPSIS (PASCAL)

       %include '/usr/include/idl/pas/uuid_uid.ins.pas'

       procedure uuid_$to_uid(
              in *uuid*: **uuid_$t;**
              out *uid*: **uid_$t;**
              out *status*: **status_$t);**

DESCRIPTION

       The **uuid_$to_uid** call returns the 64-bit Domain UID corresponding to a 128-bit NCS UUID. This call is available only on Apollo systems. It is not guaranteed to work, since not all UUIDs correspond to UIDs.

       uuid   A UUID.

       uid   The Domain Unique Identifier (UID) corresponding to *uuid*.

       status   A **status_$t**. The completion status.

EXAMPLE

       The following call returns as **scallion_uid** the UID corresponding to the UUID **scallion_uuid**:

```
uuid_$to_uid (&scallion_uuid, &scallion_uid, &st);
```

FILES

       idl/**uuid.idl**

SEE ALSO

       uuid_$from_uid

Chapter 17

Daemons and Utilities

Contents

NAME

intro – NCS daemons and utilities

DESCRIPTION

This chapter describes the NCS daemons and utilities.

The appendixes indicate the directories where these utilities reside.

NAME
>   **drm_admin** – Data Replication Manager Administrative Tool

SYNOPSIS
>   **drm_admin** [**–version**]

DESCRIPTION
>   The **drm_admin** tool administers servers based on the Data Replication Manager (DRM) such as **glbd**, the
>   replicated version of the Global Location Broker (GLB).
>
>   With **drm_admin**, you can inspect or modify replica lists, merge databases to force convergence among
>   replicas, stop servers, and delete replicas.
>
>   The role of **drm_admin** is to administer the replication of databases, not to change the data they contain.
>   For instance, you can use **drm_admin** to merge two replicas of the GLB database, but you must use
>   **lb_admin** to add a new entry to the database. Also, although **drm_admin** can stop or delete a GLB
>   replica, you must invoke **glbd** directly if you want to start or create a replica.
>
>   Once invoked, **drm_admin** enters an interactive mode, in which it accepts the commands described below.

OPTIONS
>   **–version** Display the version of NCK that this **drm_admin** belongs to, but do not start the tool.

COMMANDS
>   Most **drm_admin** commands operate on a default object (*default_obj*) at a default host (*default_host*).
>   Together, *default_obj* and *default_host* specify a default replica. Defaults are established by the **set** com-
>   mand and are remembered until changed by another **set**.
>
>   Currently, the only known object is **glb**.
>
>   Some **drm_admin** commands operate on a host other than the default. We identify this host as *other_host*.
>
>   The host name you supply as a *default_host* or an *other_host* takes the form *family:host*, where the host can
>   be specified either by its name or by its network address. For example, **dds://jeeves**, **dds:#101a.57f95**,
>   **ip:bertie**, and **ip:#192.5.5.5** are acceptable host names.
>
>   **addrep** *other_host*
>>   Add *other_host* to the replica list at *default_host*. The replica at *default_host* will propagate
>>   *other_host* to all other replica lists for *default_obj*.
>
>   **chrep –from** *other_host* **–to** *new_other_host*
>>   Change the network address for *other_host* in the replica list at *default_host* to *new_other_host*.
>>   The replica at *default_host* will propagate this change to all other replica lists for *default_obj*.
>>   The **chrep** command will fail if a replica of *default_obj* is running at *other_host* or if *other_host*
>>   is not on the replica list at *default_host*.
>
>   **delrep** *other_host*
>>   Delete the replica of *default_obj* at *other_host*. The **delrep** command tells the replica at
>>   *other_host*
>>
>>   1. To propagate all of the entries in its propagation queue
>>
>>   2. To propagate a delete request to all other replicas, causing *other_host* to be deleted from all
>>   other replica lists for *default_obj*

3. To delete its copy of *default_obj*

4. To stop running

The **delrep** command returns you immediately to the **drm_admin** prompt, but the actual deletion of the replica can take a long time in configurations that are not stable and intact. You can check whether the daemon for the deleted replica has stopped by listing the processes running on its host.

info   Get status information about the replica for *default_obj* at *default_host*.

lrep [−**d**] [−**clocks**] [−**na**]

List replicas for *default_obj* as stored in the replica list at *default_host*.

The −**d** option lists deleted as well as existing replicas.

The −**clocks** option shows the current time on each host and indicates clock skew among the replicas.

The −**na** option lists the network address of each host.

merge { −**from** | −**to** } *other_host*

The **merge** command copies entries in the *default_obj* database and replica list from one replica to another. It copies an entry if no corresponding entry exists in the destination database or if the corresponding entry in the destination database bears an earlier timestamp.

A merge does not cause entries to be propagated. The database and replica list at the origination are not changed.

The −**from** option copies entries from the *default_obj* database and replica list at *other_host* to the *default_obj* database and replica list at *default_host*.

The −**to** option copies entries from the database and replica list at *default_host* to the database and replica list at *other_host*.

A **merge** −**from** followed by a **merge** −**to** causes the replicas at the two hosts to converge.

merge_all

The **merge_all** command uses *default_host* as the hub for a global merge of all replicas for *default_obj*. For each host on the replica list at *default_host*, a **merge_all** first does a **merge** −**from,** then does a **merge** −**to.** All replicas of *default_obj* are thereby forced into a consistent state. The **merge_all** operation does not cause any entries to be propagated.

You should do a **merge_all**

- When a replica is purged
- When a replica is reset
- When a replica has been incommunicado for two weeks or more
- When a replica "dies" (for example, when its database is destroyed by a disk failure)

monitor [−**r** *n*]

This command causes **drm_admin** to read the clock of each replica of *default_obj* every *n* minutes and to report any clock skews or non-answering replicas. If you do not specify −**r**, the period is 15 minutes.

purgerep *other_host*

The **purgerep** command purges *other_host* from the replica list at *default_host*. The replica at *default_host* then propagates a delete request to the replicas at the hosts remaining on its list, thereby removing *other_host* from all other replica lists for *default_obj*. The delete request is not sent to *other_host*.

A **purgerep** can cause data to be lost and should only be used when a replica has "died." We recommend strongly that you do a **merge_all** operation after the **purgerep** to prevent the remaining replicas of the *default_obj* database from becoming inconsistent. If the purged replica is still running, it should be **reset**.

We recommend that you use **chrep** (rather than **addrep** and **purgerep**) to change entries on the replica list.

quit   Quit the **drm_admin** session.

reset *other_host*

Reset the replica of *default_obj* at *other_host*.

The **reset** command tells the replica at *other_host* to delete its copy of *default_obj* and to stop running. It does not cause *other_host* to be deleted from any other replica lists. This command can cause data to be lost unless a successful **merge_all** is done first.

set [−o *obj_name*] −h *host_name*

Set the default object and host. All subsequent commands will operate on *obj_name*. Subsequent commands that do not specify a host will be sent to *host_name*. If you do not specify the −o option, **drm_admin** keeps the current *default_obj*.

If you use **set** with the −o option, **drm_admin** checks the clocks at all hosts with replicas of the specified object.

stop   Stop the server for *default_obj* that is running at *default_host*.

EXAMPLE

The following example starts **drm_admin**, sets the default object to **glb**, and sets the default host to **//mars**:

```
$ /etc/ncs/drm_admin
drm_admin: set -o glb -h dds://mars
        Default object: glb  default host: dds://mars   state: in service
        Checking clocks of glb replicas
        dds://mars              1987/04/09.17:09
        dds://pluto             1987/04/09.17:09
        dds://mercury           1987/04/09.17:07
```

SEE ALSO

glbd, lb_admin
Managing NCS Software

NAME

glbd – Global Location Broker Daemon

SYNOPSIS

glbd [–**create** { –**first** [–**family** *family_name*] | –**from** *host_name* }]
[–**change_family** *family_name*] [–**listen** *family_list*] [–**version**]

DESCRIPTION

The Global Location Broker (GLB), part of the Network Computing System (NCS), helps clients to locate servers on a network or internet. The GLB database stores the locations (that is, the network addresses and port numbers) where server processes are running. A daemon maintains this database and provides access to it.

There are two versions of the GLB daemon: **glbd** and **nrglbd**. We provide the replicatable version, **glbd**, only for Apollo, SunOS, and ULTRIX systems. For other systems, we provide the non-replicatable version, **nrglbd**.

Here, we describe only **glbd**.

You can replicate the GLB database to increase its availability. Copies of the database can exist on several hosts, with a **glbd** running on each of those hosts to maintain the consistency of the database replicas. (In an internet, at least one **glbd** must run in each network.) Each replica of the GLB keeps a list of all the other GLB replicas. The **drm_admin** tool administers the replication of the GLB database and of the replica list.

Currently, **glbd** supports both the DARPA IP and Domain DDS network protocols. A GLB replica can allow access to its database from both IP and DDS clients. However, when communicating with each other to maintain replication of the GLB database, GLB replicas should use only one protocol family. You choose which family the GLBs will use. In an internet, all routing nodes must support this family.

If a set of GLB replicas includes any SunOS or ULTRIX systems, all replicas must use IP protocols to communicate with each other. A replica running on an Apollo system can communicate with other replicas via IP protocols but still provide lookup and update services to its clients via both IP and DDS protocols.

The following subsections briefly describe **glbd** startup on various systems. See *Managing NCS Software* for more detailed information.

Running glbd on SR10 Apollo Systems

If the GLB is to communicate via IP protocols, either with clients or with other GLB replicas, a TCP daemon (**tcpd**) must be running on the local host when **glbd** is started. Also, regardless of which protocol **glbd** uses, a Local Location Broker daemon (**llbd**) must be running on the local host when **glbd** is started.

The TCP and Location Broker daemons should be started in this order: **tcpd**, **llbd**, **glbd**. The daemons will start automatically in the correct order at boot time if the files **/etc/daemons/tcpd**, **/etc/daemons/llbd**, and **/etc/daemons/glbd** exist. Use **touch** or **crf** to create these files.

Running glbd on SR9 Apollo Systems

If the GLB is to communicate via IP protocols, either with clients or with other GLB replicas, a TCP server (**tcp_server**) must be running on the local host when **glbd** is started. Also, regardless of which protocol **glbd** uses, a Local Location Broker daemon (**llbd**) must be running on the local host when **glbd** is started.

The TCP server and the Location Broker daemons should be started in this order: **tcp_server**, **llbd**, **glbd**. Typically, processes are started by the file `**node_data/startup.***suffix*, where *suffix* indicates the display type.

Running glbd on SunOS and ULTRIX Systems

On SunOS and ULTRIX systems, the GLB communicates only via IP protocols. A Local Location Broker daemon (**llbd**) must be running on the local host when **glbd** is started.

Typically, the **llbd** and **glbd** processes are started in background at boot time from **/etc/rc**. If you start the daemons by hand, you must be root.

OPTIONS

−create Create a replica of the GLB. This option creates a GLB database in addition to starting a broker process. It must be used with either **−first** or **−from**.

−first This option can be used only with the **−create** option. Use it to create the first replica (that is, the very first instance) of the GLB on your network or internet.

−family *family_name*

This option can be used only in conjunction with the **−first** option. It specifies the address family that the first GLB replica will use to identify itself on the replica list. Any subsequently created replicas must use this family to communicate with this replica. Currently, *family_name* can be either **dds** or **ip**. If this option is not used, the replica will be identified on the replica list by its DDS address.

−from *host_name*

This option can be used only with the **−create** option. Use it to create additional replicas of the GLB. A replica of the GLB must exist at *host_name*. The database and replica list for the new replica are initialized from those at *host_name*. The replica at *host_name* adds an entry for the new replica to its replica list and propagates the entry to the other GLB replicas.

A *host_name* takes the form *family:host*, where the host can be specified either by its name or by its network address. For example, **dds://jeeves**, **dds:#959a.940f**, **ip:bertie**, and **ip:#192.5.5.5** are acceptable host names.

The new replica will use the same address family as *host_name* in identifying itself on the replica list. For example, if *host_name* is an IP address, the new replica will be listed by its IP address on the replica list.

−change_family *family_name*

Use this option only if network reconfigurations require that you change the address family of every GLB replica; see the discussion in the "DESCRIPTION" section. Currently, *family_name* can be either **dds** or **ip**.

For a procedure to change all of your GLB replicas from one address family to another, see *Managing NCS Software*.

−listen *family_list*

This option restricts the address families on which a GLB listens. Use it only if you are creating a special configuration where access to a GLB is restricted to a subset of hosts in the network or internet.

The *family_list* is a list of the address families on which the GLB will listen. Names in this list are separated by spaces. Possible family names include **dds** and **ip**.

The GLB will always listen for requests from the family by which it is listed on the replica list, even if that family is not specified in *family_list*.

If **glbd** is started without the **−listen** option, the GLB will listen on all address families that are supported both by NCS and by the local host. On Apollo systems, this set of families always includes **dds** and may also include **ip**. On most other systems, **ip** is currently the only family.

−version   Display the version of NCK that this **glbd** belongs to, but do not start the daemon.

EXAMPLES

These examples give commands suitable for use on Apollo SR10 systems. On Apollo SR9 systems, use the Display Manager **cps** command to start **glbd** as a server process. On other UNIX systems, you must be root to start **glbd** and you should use **&** to place the daemon in background. *Managing NCS Software* contains detailed procedures for starting Location Brokers.

1. Create and start for the first time the first replica of the GLB on this network or internet:

$ **/etc/server /etc/ncs/glbd −create −first −family dds &**

2. Start for the first time a subsequent replica of the GLB, initializing its database from host //**jeeves**:

$ **/etc/server /etc/ncs/glbd −create −from dds://jeeves &**

3. Restart an existing replica of the GLB:

$ **/etc/server /etc/ncs/glbd &**

4. Restart an existing replica of the GLB on remote host //**bertie**:

$ **crp −on //bertie /etc/server //bertie/etc/ncs/glbd &**

FILES

On Apollo systems, **glbd** writes diagnostic output to the file \`**node_data/system_logs/glb_log**. On other UNIX systems, the log file is **/etc/ncs/glb_log**.

SEE ALSO

drm_admin, lb_admin, llbd, nrglbd, glb_obj.txt, glb_site.txt
Managing NCS Software

NAME

lb_admin – Location Broker Administrative Tool

SYNOPSIS

lb_admin [**−nq**] [**−version**]

DESCRIPTION

The **lb_admin** tool administers the registrations of NCS-based servers in Global Location Broker (GLB) or Local Location Broker (LLB) databases. A server registers Universal Unique Identifiers (UUIDs) specifying an object, a type, and an interface, along with a socket address specifying its location. A client can locate servers by issuing lookup requests to GLBs and LLBs. Using the **lb_admin** tool, you can look up information, add new entries, and delete existing entries in a specified database.

The **lb_admin** tool is useful for inspecting the contents of Location Broker databases and for correcting database errors. For example, if a server terminates abnormally without unregistering itself, you can use **lb_admin** to manually remove its entry from the GLB database.

In accepting input or displaying output, **lb_admin** uses either character strings or descriptive textual names to identify objects, types, and interfaces. A character string directly represents the data in a UUID in the format $xxxxxxxxxxxx.xx.xx.xx.xx.xx.xx.xx.xx$, where each x is a hexadecimal digit. Descriptive textual names are associated with UUIDs in the **uuidname.txt** file.

With **lb_admin**, you examine or modify only one database at a time, which we refer to as the "current database." The **use_broker** command selects the type of Location Broker database, GLB or LLB. The **set_broker** command selects the host whose GLB or LLB database is to be accessed. Of course, if you modify one replica of a replicated GLB database, your modifications will be propagated to the other replicas of that database.

On Apollo systems, **lb_admin** presents both a Domain/Dialogue window-oriented user interface and a terminal-oriented interface. On other systems, it presents only the terminal-oriented interface. Here we describe the terminal-oriented interface to **lb_admin**. For information on the Domain/Dialogue interface, use the HELP key or the right mouse button, or see *Managing NCS Software*.

OPTIONS

−nq   Do not query for verification of wildcard expansions in **unregister** operations.

−version Display the version of NCK that this **lb_admin** belongs to, but do not start the tool.

COMMANDS

In **lookup**, **register**, and **unregister** commands, the *object*, *type*, and *interface* arguments can be either character strings representing UUIDs or textual names corresponding to UUIDs, as described earlier.

a[dd]   Synonym for **register**.

c[lean] Find and delete obsolete entries in the current database.

      When you issue this command, **lb_admin** attempts to contact each server registered in the database. If the server responds, the entry for its registration is left intact in the database. If the server does not respond, **lb_admin** tries to look up its registration in the LLB database at the host where the server is located, tells you the result of this lookup, and asks whether you want to delete the entry. If a server responds, but its UUIDs do not match the entry in the database, **lb_admin** tells you this result and asks whether you want to delete the entry.

There are two situations in which it is likely that a database entry should be deleted:

- The server does not respond, **lb_admin** succeeds in contacting the LLB at the host where the server is located, and the server is not registered with that LLB. The server is probably no longer running.

- A server responds, but its UUIDs do not match the entry in the database. The server that responded is not the one that registered the entry.

Entries that meet either of these conditions are probably safe to delete and are considered eligible for "automatic deletion" (described in the next paragraph). In other situations, it is best not to delete the entry unless you can verify directly that the server is not running (for example, by listing the processes running on its host).

When **lb_admin** asks whether you want to delete an entry, you have four ways to respond. A **y**[es] response deletes the entry. A **n**[o] response leaves the entry intact in the database. After a **yes** or a **no**, **lb_admin** proceeds to check the next entry in the current database. A **g**[o] response invokes automatic deletion, in which all eligible entries are deleted and all ineligible entries are left intact, without your being queried, until all entries have been checked. A **q**[uit] response terminates the **clean** operation.

d[elete]   Synonym for **unregister**.

h[elp] *[command]* or **?** *[command]*

> Display a description of the specified *command* or, if none is specified, list all of the **lb_admin** commands.

l[ookup] *object type interface*

> Look up and display all entries with matching *object*, *type*, and *interface* fields in the current database. You can use asterisks as wildcards for any of the arguments. If all the arguments are wildcards, **lookup** displays the entire database.

q[uit]   Exit the **lb_admin** session.

r[egister] *object type interface location annotation* [*flag*]

> Add the specified entry to the current database. You can use an asterisk to represent the nil UUID in the *object*, *type*, and *interface* fields.

> The *location* is a string in the format *family:host* [*port*] , where *family* is an address family, *host* is a host name, and *port* is a port number. Possible values for *family* include **dds** and **ip**. You can use a leading **#** to indicate that a host name is in the standard numeric form. For example, **dds://salzburg[515]**, **dds:#575d.542e[452]**, **ip:vienna[1756]**, and **ip:#192.5.5.5[1791]** are all acceptable *location* specifiers.

> The *annotation* is a string of up to 64 characters annotating the entry. Use double quotation marks to delimit a string that contains a space or contains no characters. To embed a double quotation mark in the string, precede it with a backslash.

> The *flag* is either **local** (the default) or **global**, indicating whether the entry should be marked for local registration only or for registration in both the LLB and GLB databases. The *flag* is a field that is stored with the entry; it does not affect where the entry is registered. The **set_broker** and **use_broker** commands select the particular LLB or GLB database for registration.

s[et_broker] [*broker_switch*] *host*

> Set the host for the current LLB or GLB. If you specify **global** as the *broker_switch*, **set_broker** sets the current GLB; otherwise, it sets the current LLB. The *host* is a string in the format *family*:*host*, where *family* is an address family and *host* is a host name. Possible values for *family* include **dds** and **ip**. You can use a leading # to indicate that a host name is in the standard numeric form. For example, **dds://linz**, **dds:#499d.590f**, ip·prague, and ip·#192.5.5.5 are all acceptable *host* specifiers.
>
> Issue **use_broker**, not this command, to determine whether subsequent operations will access the LLB or the GLB.

set_t[imeout] [**short** | **long**]

> Set the timeout period used by **lb_admin** for all of its operations. With an argument of **short** or **long**, **set_timeout** sets the timeout accordingly. With no argument, it displays the current timeout value.

u[nregister] *object type interface location*

> Delete the specified entry from the current database.
>
> The *location* is a string in the format *family*:*host* [*port*] , where *family* is an address family, *host* is a host name, and *port* is a port number. Possible values for *family* include **dds** and **ip**. You can use a leading # to indicate that a host name is in the standard numeric form. For example, **dds://salzburg[515]**, **dds:#575d.542e[452]**, **ip:vienna[1756]**, and **ip:#192.5.5.5[1791]** are all acceptable *location* specifiers.
>
> You can use an asterisk as a wildcard in the *object*, *type*, and *interface* fields to match any value for the field. Unless you have suppressed queries by invoking **lb_admin** with the −**nq** option, **unregister** asks you whether to delete each matching entry. A **y**[es] response deletes the entry. A **n**[o] response leaves the entry in the database. A **g**[o] response deletes all remaining database entries that match, without your being queried. A **q**[uit] response terminates the **unregister** operation, without deleting any more entries.

us[e_broker] [*broker_switch*]

> Select the type of database that subsequent operations will access, GLB or LLB. The *broker_switch* is either **global** or **local**. If you do not supply a *broker_switch*, **use_broker** tells whether the current database is global or local.
>
> Use **set_broker** to select the host whose GLB or LLB is to be accessed.

SEE ALSO

drm_admin, glbd, llbd, nrglbd, uuidname.txt
Managing NCS Software

NAME
   llbd – Local Location Broker Daemon

SYNOPSIS
   llbd [−**version**]

DESCRIPTION
   The Local Location Broker daemon (**llbd**) is part of the Network Computing System (NCS). It manages the Local Location Broker (LLB) database, which stores information about NCS-based server programs running on the local host.

   A host must run **llbd** if it is to support the Location Broker forwarding function or to allow remote access (for example, by the **lb_admin** tool) to the LLB database. In general, any host that runs NCS-based servers should run an **llbd**, and **llbd** should be running before any such servers are started. Additionally, any network or internet supporting NCS activity should have at least one host running a Global Location Broker daemon (**glbd** or **nrglbd**).

   (On MS-DOS systems, which can run only one process at a time, **llbd** functionality is automatically incorporated into every NCS-based server.)

   The following subsections briefly describe **llbd** startup on various systems. See *Managing NCS Software* for more detailed information.

Running llbd on SR10 Apollo Systems
   If the LLB is to support remote access from hosts in the IP address family, a TCP daemon (**tcpd**) must be running on the local node when **llbd** is started.

   To start **llbd** on a node that is already running, become root and type the following at a shell prompt:

   $ **/etc/server /etc/ncs/llbd**

   To have **llbd** start every time a node boots, use **touch** or **crf** to create the file **/etc/daemons/llbd**.

Running llbd on SR9 Apollo Systems
   If the LLB is to support remote access from hosts in the IP address family, a TCP server (**tcp_server**) must be running on the local node when **llbd** is started.

   To start **llbd** on a node that is already running, become root and type the following at a Display Manager prompt:

   Command: **cps /sys/ncs/llbd**

   To have **llbd** start every time a node boots, add the following line to the file `node_data/startup.*suffix*, where *suffix* indicates the display type:

   cps /sys/ncs/llbd

Running llbd on SunOS and ULTRIX Systems
   On SunOS and ULTRIX systems, **llbd** is typically started by a line in **/etc/rc** such as the following:

   /etc/ncs/llbd

   To start **llbd** by hand on one of these systems, you must be root.

Running llbd on VMS Systems

On VMS systems, **llbd** is typically started by a line in the **systartup.com** startup file. To start **llbd** by hand on one of these systems, you need special privileges which are described in *Managing NCS Software*.

OPTIONS

−listen *family_list*

This option restricts the address families on which an LLB listens. Use it only if you are creating a special configuration where access to an LLB is restricted to a subset of hosts in the network or internet.

The *family_list* is a list of the address families on which the LLB will listen. Names in this list are separated by spaces. Possible family names include **dds** and **ip**.

If **llbd** is started without the **−listen** option, the LLB will listen on all address families that are supported both by NCS and by the local host. On Apollo systems, this set of families always includes **dds** and may also include **ip**. On most other systems, **ip** is currently the only family.

−version   Display the version of NCK that this **llbd** belongs to, but do not start the daemon.

SEE ALSO

glbd, lb_admin, nrglbd
Managing NCS Software

NAME

nidl – Network Interface Definition Language Compiler

SYNOPSIS

nidl *idl_file* –m|–s [*other options*]

DESCRIPTION

nidl is a compiler for the Network Interface Definition Language (NIDL).

The *idl_file* argument is the pathname of an interface definition file, written in either the C syntax or the Pascal syntax of NIDL.

The NIDL Compiler generates a header file, a client stub file, a server stub file, and a client switch file, all in C source code. The Compiler derives the names of these output files from *idl_file* by replacing the suffix (the rightmost period and all subsequent characters) with extensions for the client stub, server stub, and client switch.

OPTIONS

–bug *i* [*j* ...]

Generate stubs as though the NIDL Compiler bugs designated *i, j, ...* had not been fixed. See the "BUGS" section of this reference description for more information.

–confirm Display the options chosen but do not compile anything or generate any output files. The –confirm option is useful for viewing the "idir list" and for viewing the default values of other options.

In displaying information about –idir, the Compiler constructs the list of all directories it would use to resolve relative pathnames of imported files, not just the ones explicitly supplied. (If the list is empty, the Compiler uses only the current directory.)

–cpp *pathname*

Run the specified program instead of the default C preprocessor. You can use the –confirm option to view the default pathname. This option is valid only on Apollo workstations and other UNIX systems.

–def *def1* [*def2* ...]

Pass the specified definitions to the C preprocessor. A definition can take either of two forms: *symbol* or *symbol=value*. This option is valid only on Apollo workstations and other UNIX systems.

–exts *cstub-ext, sstub-ext, cswtch-ext*

Set the extensions that the Compiler uses to name the stub and switch files it generates. The text strings *cstub-ext*, *sstub-ext*, and *cswtch-ext* must be separated by commas, with no spaces; they are used as extensions for the client stub, the server stub, and the client switch, respectively. These extensions have different defaults on different operating systems. You can use the –confirm option to view the defaults.

–f77c Generate client switch code that is compatible with the UNIX f77 compiler. The NIDL Compiler appends an underscore (_) character to the name of each client switch routine so that the routines can be called from FORTRAN programs generated by the f77 compiler.

–f77s Generate server stub code that is compatible with the UNIX f77 compiler. The NIDL Compiler appends an underscore (_) character to the name of each manager routine that the stub calls so that the stub can call routines generated by the f77 compiler.

−idir *directory1* [*directory2* ...]

Use the specified directories as paths from which to resolve relative pathnames of imported files. The Compiler generates an ordered list of these directories. By default, it prepends to this list your current working directory and appends to the list the system **idl** directory. You can suppress this default by supplying the **−no_def_idir** option.

−m

Support multiple versions and/or multiple managers within a single server. This option allows a server to export more than one version of an interface ("multiple versions") and to implement an interface for more than one type ("multiple managers").

If invoked with **−m**, the Compiler appends the version number to the interface name when it generates identifiers in the stub and header files. For example, the interface specifier for version 3 of the **leonore** interface would be **leonore_v3$if_spec**.

The server for an interface compiled with **−m** must use **rpc_$register_mgr** to register its managers. The server supplies the name of a manager EPV to **rpc_$register_mgr**; the manager code defines this EPV. If the server supports objects of several types, it must use **rpc_$register_object** to register each object. These registrations enable the RPC runtime library at the server host to dispatch incoming requests to the correct version of the correct manager.

The multiple version and multiple manager capabilities require that the server host have NCK software of Version 1.5 or later vintage.

If you do not specify either **−m** or its counterpart, **−s**, the Compiler assumes **−s** and issues a warning. However, this default may be removed or changed in the future. Even if your server exports only one version of its interface and contains only one manager, we recommend that you use the **−m** option, so that it will be easy for you to incorporate multiple versions and multiple managers later.

−nobug *i* [*j* ...]

Generate stubs whose behavior reflects fixes to the NIDL Compiler bugs designated *i, j, ...* . See the "BUGS" section of this reference description for more information.

−no_cpp Do not run the C preprocessor on the input file. This option is valid only on Apollo workstations and other UNIX systems. On these systems, the NIDL Compiler by default runs a C preprocessor on its input file. If you specify **−no_cpp**, the C preprocessor will not be invoked, and any C preprocessor directives (such as **#include** directives) in the interface definition will produce errors.

−no_def_idir

Do not prepend the current working directory or append the system **idl** directory to the list of directories constructed from **−idir** arguments. If you specify **−no_def_idir** without **−idir**, the Compiler resolves pathnames of imported files only relative to the current working directory.

−no_stubs

Do not generate any stub or switch files. The Compiler generates only header files and (if the **−pascal** option is specified) insert files.

−no_warn

Suppress warning messages.

−out *directory*
> Place the generated files in *directory*. The default is the current working directory.

−pascal   Generate a Pascal insert (**.ins.pas**) file in addition to a C header (**.h**) file. The default is to generate only a C header file.

> The NIDL Compiler cannot generate Pascal source code to represent a variant record with an **otherwise** case (in the Pascal syntax) or a union with a **default** case (in the C syntax). Interface definitions containing such records or unions are thus incompatible with the **−pascal** option.

−s   Allow a server to export only a single version of an interface and to implement an interface for only a single type. This option requests the behavior of NIDL Compilers before Version 1.5.1, which added support for multiple versions and multiple interfaces. (See **−m**.)

> The server for an interface compiled with **−s** must use **rpc_$register** to register its interfaces.

> If you do not specify either **−s** or its counterpart, **−m**, the Compiler assumes **−s** and issues a warning. However, this default may be removed or changed in future NIDL Compilers. Even if your server exports only one version of its interface and contains only one manager, we recommend that you use the **−m** option, so that it will be easy for you to incorporate multiple versions and multiple managers later.

−space_opt
> Reduce the size of generated stub code, possibly at the expense of slower data marshalling.

−version   Display the version number of the NIDL Compiler but do not compile anything or generate any output files.

BUGS

Fixes to NIDL Compiler bugs can change the way data is represented in network messages, introducing backward incompatibilities. The **−bug** and **−nobug** options enable you to choose, for each bug fix that introduces incompatibilities, between the old incorrect behavior (**−bug**) and the new correct behavior (**−nobug**). Supply the designated bug number with the **−bug** or **−nobug** option.

Following are NIDL Compiler bugs whose fixes have introduced potential incompatibilities:

Bug 1   This bug, fixed in Version 1.5.1 of the NIDL Compiler, causes stubs generated by the Compiler to marshall incorrectly open arrays whose *last* is such that no elements are marshalled.

> The NIDL Compiler assumes **−nobug 1** as a default.

If you have an application that exhibits a bug listed in this section, you should try to rebuild all clients and servers at the same time, to take advantage of the bug fix while maintaining compatibility. However, in situations where you cannot rebuild everything simultaneously, you need to create servers that export two versions of each affected interface, as follows:

1. Create a new version of the interface definition with a different **version** attribute in the interface header.

2. Compile the new definition with the **−nobug** option and the old definition with the **−bug** option.

3. Build servers that export both versions of the interface.

4. When you build new clients or rebuild old clients, use stub and header files generated for the new version of the interface.

5. After all clients are updated to the new version of the interface, remove support for the old interface from the servers.

EXAMPLES

The following examples illustrate use of the NIDL Compiler on UNIX systems.

1. Show the default values for all options:

$ nidl –confirm
```
Should specify -s or -m; assuming -s.
Options table:
    bug
    cpp                     /usr/lib/cpp
    def
    exts                    _cstub.c,_sstub.c,_cswtch.c
    f77c                    No
    f77s                    No
    idir                    .        /usr/include/idl
    m                       No
    no_bug
    no_cpp                  No
    no_def_idir             No
    no_stubs                No
    no_warn                 No
    out
    pascal                  No
    s                       No
    space_opt               No
    version                 No
```

2. Request support for multiple managers and multiple interface versions, turn off filtering through the C preprocessor, specify **/alternate/idl** as the only "idir," and confirm values for all options:

```
$ nidl –confirm –m –no_cpp –idir /alternate/idl –no_def_idir
Options table:
     bug
     cpp                   /usr/lib/cpp
     def
     exts                  _cstub.c,_sstub.c,_cswtch.c
     f77c                  No
     f77s                  No
     idir                  /alternate/idl
     m                     Yes
     no_bug
     no_cpp                Yes
     no_def_idir           Yes
     no_stubs              No
     no_warn               No
     out
     pascal                No
     s                     No
     space_opt             No
     version               No
```

3. Compile the interface definition **egmont.idl**:

$ **nidl egmont.idl –m –no_cpp**

4. Compile **egmont.idl**, requesting compatibility with old programs that have the bug designated as Bug 1:

$ **nidl egmont.idl –m –no_cpp –bug 1**

SEE ALSO
     uuid_gen

NAME
nrglbd – Non-Replicatable Global Location Broker Daemon

SYNOPSIS
nrglbd [**−version**]

DESCRIPTION
The Global Location Broker (GLB), part of the Network Computing System (NCS), helps clients to locate servers on a network or internet. The GLB database stores the locations (that is, the network addresses and port numbers) where server processes are running. A daemon maintains this database and provides access to it.

There are two versions of the GLB daemon, **glbd** and **nrglbd**. We provide the replicatable version, **glbd**, only for Apollo, SunOS, and ULTRIX systems. For other systems, we provide the non-replicatable version, **nrglbd**.

Here, we describe only **nrglbd**.

Typically, **nrglbd** is started in background at boot time. Unless the host is an MS-DOS system, a Local Location Broker daemon (**llbd**) must be running on the local host when **nrglbd** is started.

On MS-DOS systems that use DDS network protocols, **nrglbd** uses DDS protocols; on other systems, it uses IP protocols.

You should run only one **nrglbd** on a network or internet, and you should not run an **nrglbd** and a **glbd** on the same network or internet.

See *Managing NCS Software* for more information about Location Broker configuration.

OPTIONS
−version Display the version of NCK that this **nrglbd** belongs to, but do not start the daemon.

SEE ALSO
glbd, lb_admin, llbd
Managing NCS Software

NAME

stcode – translate a hexadecimal status code value to a textual message

SYNOPSIS

stcode *hex_stat_code*

DESCRIPTION

stcode prints the textual message associated with a hexadecimal status code. This command is useful when a program produces a hexadecimal status code instead of a textual message.

stcode processes predefined status codes. No provision is currently made to add user-defined status codes to the error text database.

hex_stat_code   The hexadecimal status code to be translated.

EXAMPLES

Translate the hexadecimal status code 1c010003:

$ stcode 1c010003
```
unknown interface (network computing system/RPC runtime)
```

NAME
    uuid_gen – UUID generating program

SYNOPSIS
    uuid_gen [−c] [−p] [−C] [−P] [−t] [−version]

DESCRIPTION
    The **uuid_gen** program generates Universal Unique Identifiers (UUIDs).

    Without options, **uuid_gen** generates the character-string representation of a UUID. The −c and −p options enable you to generate templates for Network Interface Definition Language (NIDL) files. The −C and −P options enable you to generate source-code representations of UUIDs, suitable for initializing variables of type **uuid_$t**.

    You can specify several options at once to generate several representations for the same UUID. To generate the default character-string representation as well as one of the optional representations, use the −t option.

OPTIONS
    −C   Generate the C source-code representation of a UUID.

    −c   Generate a template, including a UUID attribute, for an interface definition in the C syntax of NIDL.

    −P   Generate the Pascal source-code representation of a UUID.

    −p   Generate a template, including a UUID attribute, for an interface definition in the Pascal syntax of NIDL.

    −t   Generate the character-string representation of a UUID. This option allows you to request the default output of **uuid_gen** while also requesting optional output forms.

    −version   Display the version of NCK that this **uuid_gen** belongs to, but do not generate a UUID.

EXAMPLES
    1. Generate the character-string representation of a UUID:

    $ **/etc/ncs/uuid_gen**
    ```
    34dc23469000.0d.00.00.7c.5f.00.00.00
    ```

    2. Generate a template for an interface definition in the C syntax of NIDL:

    $ **/etc/ncs/uuid_gen** −c
    ```
    %c
    [
    uuid(34dc239ec000.0d.00.00.7c.5f.00.00.00),
    version(1)
    ]
    interface INTERFACENAME {

    }
    ```

3. Generate the C source-code representation of a UUID:

$ /etc/ncs/uuid_gen –C

```
= { 0x34dc23af,
    0xf000,
    0x0000,
    0x0d,
    {0x00, 0x00, 0x7c, 0x5f, 0x00, 0x00, 0x00} };
```

4. Generate both the character-string representation and the C source-code representation of a UUID:

$ /etc/ncs/uuid_gen –t –C

```
450ccaed6000.0d.00.02.18.cb.00.00.00
= { 0x450ccaed,
    0x6000,
    0x0000,
    0x0d,
    {0x00, 0x02, 0x18, 0xcb, 0x00, 0x00, 0x00} };
```

Chapter 18

Files

Contents

NAME

intro – NCS configuration files

DESCRIPTION

This chapter describes configuration files used by NCS software. The "SYNOPSIS" section in each description lists the pathnames for the file on various systems.

NAME

glb_obj.txt – file specifying the object UUID of the Global Location Broker

SYNOPSIS

/etc/ncs/glb_obj.txt (Apollo workstations at SR10.2 or later)
/etc/ncs/glb_obj.txt (other UNIX systems)
ncs$exe:glb_obj.txt (VMS systems)
\ncs\glb_obj.txt (MS DOS systems)

DESCRIPTION

The Global Location Broker (GLB) is an object identified by a Universal Unique Identifier (UUID). This UUID has a default value. The **glb_obj.txt** file allows you to override the default value by specifying a different GLB object UUID for a particular host.

The **glb_obj.txt** file is used only in special configurations that require several disjoint GLB databases (each of which is possibly replicated). In most networks and internets, there is only one GLB database (possibly replicated), and hosts do not need to have a **glb_obj.txt** file.

If a host has a **glb_obj.txt** file, the UUID in the file identifies the GLB object to which that host will direct lookups and updates. If the host runs a GLB daemon (**glbd** or **nrglbd**), the UUID also identifies the GLB object managed by that daemon, and the daemon will accept lookups and updates only for that object. By specifying different GLB object UUIDs on different sets of hosts, you can partition a network or internet into Location Broker "cells."

Location Broker cells have independent GLB databases. Each cell can be serviced by one **glbd**, one **nrglbd**, or a set of **glbd** replicas. All hosts in a cell use the same GLB object UUID. Cells need not correspond in any way to physical or logical network topology.

Managing NCS Software describes how to set up a configuration that uses Location Broker cells.

A **glb_obj.txt** file consists of one line containing the textual representation of a UUID, such as is generated by the **uuid_gen** utility. The contents of **glb_obj.txt** are identical on all hosts in a cell.

If a host does not have a **glb_obj.txt** file, it will use the default value for the GLB object UUID.

EXAMPLE

The following is a sample **glb_obj.txt** file:

```
437f28e72000.0d.00.00.fb.40.00.00.00
```

SEE ALSO

glbd, nrglbd, uuid_gen
Managing NCS Software

NAME

   glb_site.txt – file listing possible Global Location Broker sites

SYNOPSIS

   /etc/ncs/glb_site.txt (Apollo workstations at SR10.2 or later)
   /etc/ncs/glb_site.txt (other UNIX systems)
   ncs$exe:glb_site.txt (VMS systems)
   \ncs\glb_site.txt (MS-DOS systems)

DESCRIPTION

   The **glb_site.txt** file lists the network addresses of hosts where a Global Location Broker (GLB) daemon
   may be running.

   There are two versions of the GLB daemon: **glbd** and **nrglbd**. We provide the replicatable version, **glbd**,
   only for Apollo, SunOS, and ULTRIX systems. For other systems, we provide the non-replicatable version, **nrglbd**.

   Ordinarily, programs contact a GLB by broadcasting on the local network. However, some systems do not
   support broadcasting. Also, in certain internet configurations, not every network can have a GLB. (This
   typically occurs in internets that use **nrglbd**, but it can also occur in an internet that uses **glbd** if not all networks include a host that can run a **glbd**.) For hosts that cannot locate a GLB via broadcast, the
   glb_site.txt file provides a list of addresses where the host can try to directly contact a GLB.

   Each line in **glb_site.txt** contains a network address where a GLB may be running. Hosts that have a
   glb_site.txt file try these addresses in order. Each address has the following form:

   family:host

   The *family* is the textual name of an address family. Possible values include **ip** and **dds**.

   The *host* is a host name. A leading # can be used to indicate that the host name is in the standard numeric
   form (for example, **#192.9.8.7** or **#515c.111g**).

   Blank lines and lines beginning with # are ignored.

   If a host has a **glb_site.txt** file but does not find a GLB at any of the addresses listed in the file, the host
   then tries to locate one via broadcast.

   See *Managing NCS Software* for information about Location Broker configuration.

EXAMPLE

   The following are sample **glb_site.txt** files for the IP and DDS address families:

```
ip:piglet
ip:#192.9.8.7

dds://owl
dds:#135f.132a
```

SEE ALSO

   glbd, nrglbd
   Managing NCS Software

NAME

uuidname.txt – file associating names with UUIDs

SYNOPSIS

Public file:

/sys/ncs/uuidname.txt (SR9 Apollo workstations)

/etc/ncs/uuidname.txt (SR10 Apollo workstations and other UNIX systems)

ncs$exe:uuidname.txt (VM3 systems)

\ncs\uuidname.txt (MS-DOS systems)

Private file:

¯/uuidname.txt (Apollo workstations and other UNIX systems)

DESCRIPTION

A **uuidname.txt** file associates textual names with UUIDs (Universal Unique Identifiers). The **lb_admin** administrative tool can use these names to identify objects, types, and interfaces; it accepts names as input and displays names as output whenever possible.

System-wide associations of names with UUIDs are defined in a public **uuidname.txt** file on the host where **lb_admin** is invoked. On Apollo workstations and other UNIX systems, user-specific associations can also be defined in a private **uuidname.txt** file in the home directory of the user who invokes **lb_admin**. The **lb_admin** tool reads these files (first the public file, then the private file, if it exists) when it starts up, and it uses the names defined in the files for the duration of the session.

Each UUID in a **uuidname.txt** file appears at the beginning of a line. Names associated with that UUID occupy the remainder of the line, separated by spaces or tabs. Names that contain spaces or tabs must be delimited by double quotation marks. Blank lines and lines beginning with # are ignored. A **#include** construct supports inclusion of other files in this format.

More than one name can be associated with a UUID if several names appear on one line of a **uuidname.txt** file, if a UUID appears on several lines of one file, or if a UUID appears in several files. The first name encountered by **lb_admin** when it starts up is treated as the "primary name" for the UUID, and all subsequent names are treated as "aliases." Any primary names or aliases can be entered as input to **lb_admin**, but the tool always uses primary names for output.

If an undefined name is entered as input, **lb_admin** treats the input as a wildcard.

Note that this mechanism for associating names with UUIDs may be superseded by a more general naming service in a future software release.

EXAMPLE

The following is part of a sample **uuidname.txt** file:

```
333b91c50000.0d.00.00.87.84.00.00.00    glb/object
333b91de0000.0d.00.00.87.84.00.00.00    glb/type
333b2e690000.0d.00.00.87.84.00.00.00    glb/interface
34b45208a000.0d.00.00.87.84.00.00.00    rgy/object
```

SEE ALSO

lb_admin

Managing NCS Software

Appendix A

Using NCS with
FORTRAN Programs

NCS allows you to write distributed applications in FORTRAN. You define interfaces in NIDL. The NIDL Compiler generates C source code for client stubs, client switches, and server stubs; you use a C compiler to compile these modules. You write client and server application code in FORTRAN, compile it with a FORTRAN compiler, and link it with the stubs and switches.

This appendix describes considerations that apply to FORTRAN in general and to UNIX f77 FORTRAN in particular. If you are building an application from source code both in FORTRAN and in C or Pascal, consult the language documentation for your system for more information on cross-language communication.

A.1 Declaring Operations

FORTRAN programs pass all parameters by reference. Therefore, in the NIDL declaration for any operation called from or implemented in FORTRAN, you must specify that the stubs are to pass parameters by reference.

If you write your interface definition in the C syntax of NIDL, prefix all parameters with an asterisk (*), the indirection operator.

If you use the Pascal syntax of NIDL, specify the **in ref** parameter attributes for all input parameters; the NIDL Compiler assumes that all output parameters are passed by reference, so they require no special treatment.

A.2 Invoking NCS Calls

A FORTRAN program cannot directly invoke a call that expects any parameters to be passed by value. To circumvent this limitation, we provide FORTRAN **interlude routines**, or **language bindings**, for all of the documented NCS calls. These routines coexist with the real calls in the NCK runtime software. The interludes accept input parameters by reference, invoke the real calls (passing parameters by value where necessary), and return output parameters by reference.

The name of each interlude routine is formed by appending an underscore character (_) to the name of the corresponding call. For example, the FORTRAN interlude routine for **rpc_$bind** is named **rpc_$bind_**.

A.2.1 Invoking Interlude Routines from f77

The UNIX f77 compiler appends an underscore to any external name. For example, if a client written in f77 invokes **rpc_$bind**, the f77 compiler changes the spelling of the call to **rpc_$bind_**. For NCS calls, the f77 spelling exactly matches that of the FORTRAN interlude, so f77 programs can invoke the calls by their ordinary names, and the calls will pass through the interludes transparently.

A.2.2 Invoking Interlude Routines from Other Versions of FORTRAN

Most other FORTRAN compilers, including the Apollo Domain FORTRAN compiler, do not append underscores to external names. In order to use NCS calls, programs must explicitly invoke the interlude routines by their extended names.

A.3 Using the NIDL Compiler f77 Options

As we explained in Section A.2, the UNIX f77 compiler appends an underscore character to all external names. For example, if your source code defines or references an operation named **db$lookup**, the compiler changes the name to **db$lookup_**. If an application is generated entirely from FORTRAN source, this renaming is transparent. However, if some program modules are written in another language such as C or Pascal, that source code must explicitly terminate with an underscore any names that will be referenced or defined by a FORTRAN program.

The NIDL Compiler provides two options, **−f77c** and **−f77s**, that cause the Compiler to generate stubs with names that conform to the f77 naming convention. If you use these options, you can write interface definitions without appending underscores to any names. The **−f77c** and **−f77s** options also make it easier to write an application in which the client is written in FORTRAN and the server is written in C or Pascal, or vice versa.

Use the **−f77c** option if the client is written in FORTRAN and will be compiled by a UNIX f77 compiler. This option causes the NIDL Compiler to use f77-compatible names (with underscores appended) for the client switch routines.

Use the **−f77s** option if the server manager routines (the routines that actually implement the operations in an interface) are written in FORTRAN and will be compiled by a UNIX f77 compiler. This option causes the NIDL Compiler to generate server stub code that calls the manager routines by f77-compatible names.

Appendix B
Using NCS on Apollo Systems

This appendix describes how to use NCS on an Apollo system.

B.1 Organization of NCS Software

Table B-1 shows the directories where NCS software resides on SR10.*x* and SR9.7 Apollo systems. The table includes software from both NCK, which is part of standard operating system software, and NIDL, which is an optional product.

Table B-1. Organization of NCS Software on Apollo Systems

Directory	Contents
/etc/ncs (SR10.*x*) /sys/ncs (SR9.7)	NCK daemons and utilities: **glbd** Global Location Broker Daemon **llbd** Local Location Broker Daemon **lb_admin** Location Broker Administrative Tool **drm_admin** DRM Administrative Tool **uuid_gen** UUID Generating Tool configuration files: **glb_obj.txt** file specifying GLB object UUID **glb_site.txt** file listing possible GLB sites **uuidname.txt** file mapping UUIDs to names
/usr/apollo/bin (SR10.*x*) /com (SR9.7)	**nidl** NIDL Compiler **stcode** status code translator
/lib	**ddslib** NCK global library
/usr/include/idl	system **idl** files: interface definitions distributed by Apollo
/usr/include/idl/c	system header files: **.h** files generated from the system **idl** files
/usr/include/idl/pas	system insert files: **.ins.pas** files generated from the system **idl** files
/usr/include (SR10.2 and later)	**ppfm.h** Portable PFM header file
/usr/include/apollo (SR10.*x*)	**pfm.h** PFM header file
/domain_examples/ncs	examples
/usr/man (BSD environment) /usr/catman (SysV environment) /sys/help (Aegis environment)	online reference documentation

In our documentation, we sometimes refer to **/usr/include/idl** as *idl* and refer to
/domain_examples/ncs as *examples*.

B.2 Location Broker Configuration

For Apollo systems, we supply **glbd** (the replicatable Global Location Broker daemon) rather than **nrglbd** (the non-replicatable GLB daemon). If your network or internet contains any Apollo systems, we recommend that you run **glbd** on one or more of the Apollo hosts rather than **nrglbd** on another host.

See *Managing NCS Software* (formerly *Managing the NCS Location Broker*) for more information about Location Broker configuration.

B.3 Using the rrpc_$ Calls

On Apollo systems with operating system software earlier than SR10.2, the **ddslib** global library lacks client support for the **rrpc_** interface. To use **rrpc_$** calls on such systems, you must

1. Run the NIDL Compiler to compile *idl*/**rrpc.idl** and generate **rrpc_** stub and switch source code modules.

2. Run a C Compiler to generate **rrpc_** client stub and switch object modules.

3. Link the **rrpc_** client stub and switch object modules with your client.

Beginning at SR10.2, you can use the **rrpc_$** calls transparently, as on other systems.

B.4 Building Applications

On Apollo systems, the NCS runtime software is part of the **ddslib** global library, so there is no need to specify a library when you link client and server programs. Beginning at the SR10.2 software release, we supply a dummy **libnck.a** library so that your makefiles and build scripts can specify the **–lnck** linker option on Apollo workstations as well as on other UNIX systems.

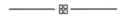

Appendix C

Using NCS on
SunOS Systems

This appendix describes how to use NCS on a SunOS system.

C.1 Organization of NCS Software

Table C–1 shows the directories where NCS software resides on SunOS systems. The table includes software from both NCS products, NCK and NIDL.

Table C-1. Organization of NCS Software on SunOS Systems

Directory	Contents
/etc/ncs	NCK daemons and utilities: **glbd** Global Location Broker Daemon **llbd** Local Location Broker Daemon **lb_admin** Location Broker Administrative Tool **drm_admin** DRM Administrative Tool **uuid_gen** UUID generating tool **stcode** status code translator configuration files: **glb_obj.txt** file specifying GLB object UUID **glb_sites** file listing possible GLB sites **uuidname.txt** file mapping UUIDs to names
/usr/local/bin	**nidl** NIDL Compiler
/usr/lib	**libnck.a** NCK library
/usr/include/idl	system **idl** files: interface definitions distributed by Apollo
/usr/include/idl/c	system header files: **.h** files generated from the system **idl** files
/usr/include	miscellaneous header files: **ppfm.h** portable PFM header file
NCS/**nidl/examples**	examples
/usr/man	online reference documentation

In our documentation, we sometimes refer to the systems **idl** directory as *idl* and refer to the online examples directory as *examples*. The examples typically reside in the directory *NCS*/**nidl/examples**, where *NCS* is the directory into which NIDL software was read from the distribution media.

The *Release Document* for each NCS product describes any prerequisites that apply and any diagnostic utilities that are available.

C.2 Location Broker Configuration

For SunOS systems, we supply **glbd** (the replicatable Global Location Broker daemon) rather than **nrglbd** (the non-replicatable GLB daemon). If your network or internet contains any systems that can run **glbd**, we recommend that you run **glbd** on one or more of these hosts rather than **nrglbd** on another host.

See *Managing NCS Software* (formerly *Managing the NCS Location Broker*) for more information about Location Broker configuration.

C.3 Building Applications

When you build NCS-based applications on SunOS systems, specify the **–lnck** option to the compiler or linker.

Appendix D

Using NCS on
ULTRIX Systems

This appendix describes how to use NCS on an ULTRIX system.

D.1 Organization of NCS Software

Table D-1 shows the directories where NCS software resides on ULTRIX systems. The table includes software from both NCS products, NCK and NIDL.

Table D-1. Organization of NCS Software on ULTRIX Systems

Directory	Contents
/etc/ncs	NCK daemons and utilities: **glbd** Global Location Broker Daemon ~~**llbd** Local Location Broker Daemon~~ **lb_admin** Location Broker Administrative Tool **drm_admin** DRM Administrative Tool **uuid_gen** UUID generating tool **stcode** status code translator configuration files: **glb_obj.txt** file specifying GLB object UUID **glb_sites** file listing possible GLB sites **uuidname.txt** file mapping UUIDs to names
/usr/local/bin	**nidl** NIDL Compiler
/usr/lib	**libnck.a** NCK library
/usr/include/idl	system **idl** files: interface definitions distributed by Apollo
/usr/include/idl/c	system header files: .h files generated from the system **idl** files
/usr/include	miscellaneous header files: **ppfm.h** portable PFM header file
NCS/**nidl/examples**	examples
/usr/man	online reference documentation

In our documentation, we sometimes refer to the systems **idl** directory as *idl* and refer to the online examples directory as *examples*. The examples typically reside in the directory *NCS*/**nidl/examples**, where *NCS* is the directory into which NIDL software was read from the distribution media.

The *Release Document* for each NCS product describes any prerequisites that apply and any diagnostic utilities that are available.

D.2 Location Broker Configuration

For ULTRIX systems, we supply **glbd** (the replicatable Global Location Broker daemon) rather than **nrglbd** (the non-replicatable GLB daemon). If your network or internet contains any systems that can run **glbd**, we recommend that you run **glbd** on one or more of these hosts rather than **nrglbd** on another host.

See *Managing NCS Software* (formerly *Managing the NCS Location Broker*) for more information about Location Broker configuration.

D.3 Building Applications

When you build NCS-based applications on VAX/ULTRIX systems, specify the **-lnck** option to the compiler or loader. You should also specify use of VAX G floating-point instructions by supplying the **-Mg** option to the compiler and the **-lcg -lmg** options to the compiler or loader.

Appendix E

Using NCS on VMS Systems

This appendix describes how to use NCS on a VAX/VMS system. We assume that you know how to build C programs under VMS.

E.1 Organization of NCS Software

Table E-1 shows the directories where NCS software resides on VMS systems. These directories have logical names that are typically defined in **systartup.com,** the system startup script. The table includes software from both of the NCS products, NCK and NIDL.

ncs$exe names the directory that contains NCS executables and configuration files, usually **sys$sysdevice:[ncs.exe]**.

ncs$lib names the directory that contains NCS libraries, usually **sys$sysdevice:[ncs.lib]**.

ncs$idl names the system **idl** directory, usually **sys$sysdevice:[ncs.idl]**.

ncs$idl_c names the directory that contains header files generated from the standard interface definition files, usually **sys$sysdevice:[ncs.idl.c]**.

ncs$include names the directory that contains miscellaneous NCS header files, usually **sys$sysdevice:[ncs.include]**.

ncs$man names the directory that contains online reference documentation, usually **sys$sysdevice:[ncs.man]**.

Table E-1. Organization of NCS Software on VMS Systems

Logical Name	Directory	Contents
ncs$exe	[ncs.exe]	executables: **nrglbd.exe** Global Location Broker Daemon **llbd.exe** Local Location Broker Daemon **lb_admin.exe** LB Administrative Tool **uuid_gen.exe** UUID generating tool **stcode.exe** status code translator **nidl.exe** NIDL Compiler configuration files: **glb_obj.txt** file specifying GLB object UUID **glb_site.txt** file listing possible GLB sites **uuidname.txt** file mapping UUIDs to names
ncs$lib	[ncs.lib]	**libnck.opt** generic linker options **libtwg.opt** linker options for Wollongong hosts **libexcelan.opt** linker options for Excelan hosts **libnck.olb** generic library **libtwg.olb** library for Wollongong hosts **libexcelan.olb** library for Excelan hosts
ncs$idl	[ncs.idl]	system **idl** files: interface definitions distributed by Apollo
ncs$idl_c	[ncs.idl.c]	system header files: .h files generated from the system **idl** files
ncs$include	[ncs.include]	miscellaneous header files: **ppfm.h** portable PFM header file
none	[.nidl.examples]	examples
ncs$man	[ncs.man]	online reference documentation

In our documentation, we sometimes refer to **ncs$idl** as *idl* and refer to [**.nidl.examples**] as *examples*. The pathname [**.nidl.examples**] is relative to the directory into which NIDL software was read from the distribution media.

The *Release Document* for each NCS product describes any prerequisites that apply and any diagnostic utilities that are available.

E.2 Configuring the Location Broker

We supply **nrglbd** (the non-replicatable GLB daemon) for VMS systems. However, if your network or internet has a host that can run **glbd**, we recommend that you run **glbd** on that host rather than **nrglbd** on your VMS system.

See *Managing NCS Software* (formerly *Managing the NCS Location Broker*) for more information about Location Broker configuration.

E.3 Network Interface Support

NCS applications on VMS systems use IP protocols with either Wollongong WIN/TCP products or Excelan EXOS products.

The NCK runtime software consists of two parts: a library that is independent of the network interface (**libnck.olb**) and libraries that are specific to each network interface (**libtwg.olb** and **libexcelan.olb**).

E.4 Building Applications

On VMS systems, the NIDL Compiler expects pathnames in UNIX format and cannot parse pathnames in VMS format.

E.4.1 Compiling

When you compile source code modules for a distributed application, you should supply **ncs$include** and **ncs$idl_c** as directories from which the VAX C compiler will resolve the targets of **#include** directives, and you should supply the **g_float** compiler option to specify the use of VAX G floating-point instructions. Use a command line of the form

```
$ cc/debug/lis/g_float/include=(ncs$include:, ncs$idl_c:) sourcefile
```

E.4.2 Linking

Once you have successfully compiled the source modules of your application, you need to link it with the NCS object library and the Wollongong or Excelan libraries. We provide linker options files which you can use as input to the linker.

On hosts with Wollongong network interfaces, use a command line of the form

$ link *objfile*, ..., **ncs$lib:libnck.opt/opt, ncs$lib:libtwg.opt/opt**

On hosts with Excelan network interfaces, use a command line of the form

$ link *objfile*, ..., **ncs$lib:libnck.opt/opt, ncs$lib:libexcelan.opt/opt**

The subdirectories of **[.nidl.examples]** contain **build.com** files that illustrate procedures for building applications.

———— 🔡 ————

Appendix F

Using NCS on MS-DOS Systems

This appendix describes how to use NCS on an MS-DOS system. We assume that you are using Microsoft® C Version 5.1 with the large memory model and Microsoft Librarian Version 3.11.

F.1 Organization of NCS Software

Table F–1 shows the directories where NCS software resides on MS-DOS systems. The table includes software from both of the NCS products, NCK and NIDL.

Table F-1. Organization of NCS Software on MS-DOS Systems

Directory	Contents
\ncs	configuration files: **ddshosts.txt** mapping of DDS node IDs to host names **glb_obj.txt** file specifying GLB object UUID **glb_site.txt** file listing possible GLB sites **uuidname.txt** file mapping UUIDs to names
\ncs\bin	executables: **stcode.exe** status code translator **nidl.exe** NIDL Compiler
\ncs\bin\dds	executables for Domain/PCI DDS implementation: **nrglbd.exe** Global Location Broker Daemon **lb_admin.exe** Location Broker Administrative Tool **uuid_gen.exe** UUID generating tool
\ncs\bin\xln	executables for Excelan IP implementation: **nrglbd.exe** Global Location Broker Daemon **lb_admin.exe** Location Broker Administrative Tool **uuid_gen.exe** UUID generating tool
\ncs\lib	NCK runtime software: **nck.lib** network independent software **nck_dds.lib** software for DPCI DDS implementation **nck_xln.lib** software for Excelan IP implementation
\ncs\include\idl	system **idl** files: interface definitions distributed by Apollo
\ncs\include\idl\c	system header files: **.h** files generated from the system **idl** files
\ncs\include	miscellaneous header files: **ppfm.h** portable PFM header file
\ncs\examples	examples
\ncs\man	online reference documentation

In our documentation, we sometimes refer to **\ncs\include\idl** as *idl* and refer to **\ncs\examples** as *examples*.

The *Release Document* for each NCS product describes any prerequisites that apply and any diagnostic utilities that are available.

F.2 Network Protocol Support

NCS applications on MS-DOS systems can use either DDS protocols (with Apollo Domain/PCI products) or IP protocols (with Excelan LAN WorkPlace products).

The NCK runtime software consists of two parts: a library that is independent of the network protocol implementation (**nck.lib**) and libraries that are specific to each protocol implementation (**nck_dds.lib** and **nck_xln.lib**).

The NIDL Compiler and the **stcode** utility are independent of the network protocol implementation; they reside in **\ncs\bin**. The executables **nrglbd, lb_admin,** and **uuid_gen** exist in versions specific to each protocol implementation; Domain/PCI versions reside in **\ncs\bin\dds** and Excelan versions reside in **\ncs\bin\xln**.

F.2.1 Using NCS with Domain/PCI Products

For each DDS socket that is opened, the runtime software in **nck_dds.lib** allocates eight 1-kilobyte buffers from the heap.

The **socket_$from_name** and **socket_$to_name** system calls perform conversions between host names and numeric IDs. The implementations of these calls in the **nck_dds.lib** library read the **c:\ncs\ddshosts.txt** file. This file lists all accessible DDS hosts; it must be kept up to date in order for the **socket_$** routines to work.

Each line of the **ddshosts.txt** file contains the hexadecimal node ID and the node name of a host, separated by spaces or tabs. Blank lines and lines beginning with **#** are ignored. Figure F-1 shows a sample **ddshosts.txt** file.

```
# a sample ddshosts.txt file
1492a arnold
10ef5 anton
224c4 alban
1789  pierre
7777  karlheinz
```

Figure F-1. A ddshosts.txt File

F.2.2 Using NCS with Excelan TCP/IP Products

For each IP socket that is opened, the runtime software in **nck_xln.lib** allocates two 1-kilobyte buffers from the heap.

The socket_$from_name and socket_$to_name system calls perform conversions between host names and numerical IDs. The implementations of these calls in the **nck_xln.lib** library invoke Excelan routines which in turn read the **\xln\tcp\hosts** file. This file must be installed and maintained correctly in order for the **socket_$** routines to work.

Applications that use Excelan TCP/IP software must be linked with the Excelan socket library **llibsock.lib** in addition to **nck.lib** and **nck_xln.lib**. However, **nck_xln.lib** references **llibsock.lib**, so you need not specify **llibsock.lib** in your **link** command if its location is specified in the **LIB** environment variable.

F.3 Configuring the Location Broker

We supply **nrglbd** (the non-replicatable GLB daemon) for MS-DOS systems. However, if your network or internet has a host that can run **glbd**, we recommend that you run **glbd** on that host rather than **nrglbd** on your MS-DOS system.

We also do not supply **llbd**, the Local Location Broker daemon, for MS-DOS systems, since NCS servers that run on MS-DOS automatically incorporate the functionality of **llbd**.

See *Managing NCS Software* (formerly *Managing the NCS Location Broker*) for more information about Location Broker configuration.

F.4 Writing Interface Definitions and Running the NIDL Compiler

This section describes considerations for using NIDL on MS-DOS systems.

F.4.1 Naming Interface Definition Files

By convention, the names of interface definition files end with the suffix **.idl**. On MS-DOS systems, the NIDL Compiler generates names for header, client stub, client switch, and server stub files by replacing this suffix with **.h**, **c.c**, **w.c**, and **s.c**. From an interface definition file named **raoul.idl**, for instance, the NIDL Compiler would generate files named **raoul.h**, **raoulc.c**, **raoulw.c**, and **raouls.c**.

MS-DOS allows at most eight characters to precede the period in a filename. Names for interface definition files should therefore contain at most seven characters before the suffix: **alceste.idl** is legal, **clotaire.idl** is not.

F.4.2 Naming Imported Files

As we stated in Sections 6.3 and 7.3, it is harmless to import a file more than once, because the NIDL Compiler ignores redundant **import** declarations. On MS-DOS, the Compiler provides this feature by making literal comparisons of the pathnames supplied in **import** declarations. If one file is imported under two names (for example, an absolute pathname and a relative pathname), the Compiler does not detect the redundancy, tries to read the file twice, and produces errors.

To avoid importing a file under two different names, we recommend that you specify only leaf names in **import** declarations and that you use the **–idir** NIDL Compiler option to specify the locations of imported files. For example, to import the file **\foie\gras.idl**, use the declaration **import gras.idl** and the option **–idir \foie**. Your interface definition file will also be free of MS-DOS notation and more easily portable to other systems.

F.4.3 Data Types

In NIDL, the **int** type is a 32-bit quantity. In Microsoft C, **int** is a 16-bit quantity. To avoid confusion, we suggest that you use the NIDL keywords **short** and **long** to declare 16-bit and 32-bit integers in interface definitions.

Source code generated by the NIDL Compiler does not make use of the Microsoft C **huge** data attribute.

F.4.4 Pascal Insert Files

When given the **–pascal** option, the NIDL Compiler generates Pascal insert files. We intend these files for use with Domain Pascal on Apollo workstations and not for any Pascal implementations on MS-DOS systems.

F.4.5 NIDL Compiler Memory Usage

When compiling very large interface definitions on MS-DOS systems, the NIDL Compiler may run out of memory.

To increase the amount of memory, remove any terminate-and-stay-resident programs (TSRs) and large device drivers, or run the Compiler directly rather than from Microsoft MAKE. If an interface definition imports a large number of other interface definition files, some memory may be taken up by operation declarations and unused type declarations in the imported files; to decrease the amount of memory used, put the type declarations you need in a separate file and import only this file.

If these techniques fail to overcome the memory limitation, run the NIDL Compiler on another machine under a different operating system, then copy the generated header, stub, and switch files to the MS-DOS machine. On any two hosts that have the same version of the NIDL Compiler and the same version of the system **idl** directory, the Compiler will generate identical C source code files.

F.5 Writing Clients and Servers

On MS-DOS systems, if you call **pfm_$init** with the **pfm_$init_signal_handlers** flag, the Microsoft C signals SIGINT, SIGILL, SIGFPE, SIGTERM and converted to PFM signals.

Application programs should terminate by calling the Microsoft C **exit** function. This allows the RPC runtime library to clean up before returning to MS-DOS. Do not use the **abort** function, as this will cause the machine eventually to crash. Robust applications should declare an MS-DOS critical error handler that terminates correctly.

F.6 Building Applications

On MS-DOS, you link client and server programs with **\ncs\lib\nck.lib** and with either **\ncs\lib\nck_dds.lib** or **\ncs\lib\nck_xln.lib**, depending on which networking protocols your application will use.

If the linker complains that there are too many segments in an application program, use the **/SE** linker switch.

Figure F–2 shows a prototypical Microsoft MAKE file for building a server program based on NCS.

```
NET = dds
LIB = c:\ncs\lib
CFLAGS = /AL /Ic:\ncs\include /Ic:\ncs\include\idl\c
NFLAGS = -idir \ncs\include\idl -m
LFLAGS = /ST:8192

### Compile user written module
foo.obj : foo.c
    cl $(CFLAGS) /c $*.c

### Run NIDL on interface spec
foos.c : foo.idl
    nidl $*.idl $(NFLAGS)

### Compile a stub file
foos.obj : foos.c
    cl $(CFLAGS) /c $*.c

### Link application with RPC libraries
foo.exe : foo.obj foos.obj
    link foo.obj foos.obj,,,$(LIB)\nck $(LIB)\nck_$(NET) $(LFLAGS);
```

Figure F–2. A Prototypical Microsoft MAKE File

The subdirectories of **\ncs\examples** contain **build.bat** files that illustrate procedures for building applications. These batch files use environment variables. When you run the batch files, you may exhaust the available space for environment strings. To increase the amount of memory reserved for environment strings, add a **COMSPEC** command to the **config.sys** file.

Glossary

address family

> A set of communications protocols that use a common addressing mechanism to identify endpoints. We use the terms "address family" and "protocol family" synonymously.

allocate a handle

> To create an RPC handle that identifies an object but not a location. Such a handle is said to be "allocated" or "unbound."

allocated handle

> An RPC handle that identifies an object but not a location. This term is synonymous with "unbound handle."

automatic binding

> A binding technique in which the client uses generic handles. Each time the client makes a remote procedure call, the client stub invokes an autobinding routine that converts the generic handle to an RPC handle. *See also* **manual binding**.

Berkeley UNIX socket abstraction

> A network programming abstraction, developed by the University of California at Berkeley, that is independent of communications protocols and is based on the concept of sending and receiving datagrams.

binding

> The representation of a server location in a handle. To bind a handle or to set its binding is to establish this representation. *See also* **binding state** and **handle**.

binding state

> A state reflecting the degree to which an RPC handle represents a server location. The three possible binding states are unbound, bound-to-host, and fully bound.

bound-to-host handle

    An RPC handle that identifies an object and a host but not a port.

bound-to-server handle

    An RPC handle that identifies an object, a host, and a port. This term is synonymous with "fully bound handle."

broadcast

    To send a remote procedure call request to all hosts in a network.

broker

    A server that provides information about resources. A Location Broker is a broker.

cell

    A subset of a network or internet in which all hosts use the same Global Location Broker object UUID. Cells have independent GLB databases. For hosts in cells that do not use the default GLB object UUID, the configuration file **glb_obj.txt** specifies an alternate UUID.

cleanup handler

    A piece of code that allows a program to terminate gracefully when it receives an error. The **pfm_$cleanup** call establishes a cleanup handler. *See also* **Process Fault Manager**.

client

    A process that uses resources. In the context of this manual, a client is a program that makes remote procedure calls. A client imports one or more interfaces. *See also* **server**.

Concurrent Programming Support (CPS)

    A set of calls that create and manage a multitasking environment within a single process. These calls are especially useful in servers that simultaneously manage multiple remote requests. CPS is implemented on only a subset of the systems for which NCS is available.

Data Replication Manager (DRM)

    A set of calls that manage weakly consistent replicated data. The replicated version of the Global Location Broker uses the DRM to manage its database.

entry point vector (EPV)

    A record of pointers to the operations in an interface.

explicit handle

    A handle that is passed as an operation parameter, rather than represented as a global variable in the client process. *See also* **implicit handle**.

export an interface

To provide the operations defined by an interface. A server exports an interface to a client. *See also* **import**.

fixed array

An array whose declaration specifies an explicit fixed length. *See also* **open array**.

forward

To dispatch a remote procedure call request to a server that exports the requested interface for the requested object. The Local Location Broker forwards remote procedure calls that are sent to the LLB forwarding port on a server host.

fully bound handle

An RPC handle that identifies an object, a host, and a port. This term is synonymous with "bound-to-server handle."

generic handle

A handle of a data type other than **handle_t**. Generic handles appear in applications that use automatic binding. *See also* **RPC handle**.

Global Location Broker (GLB)

A server that maintains global information about objects on a network or internet. There are two versions of the GLB daemon: **glbd** (the replicatable version, which uses the DRM to manage the replication of its data) and **nrglbd** (the non-replicatable version).

handle

A temporary local identifier for an object. A handle represents for a client process the object and the location of a server that exports one or more interfaces to the object. A handle always represent the same object, but it may represent different server locations at different times, or it may not represent a server location at all. *See also* **binding**.

host

A computer that is attached to a network.

host ID

An identifier that, given an address family, uniquely identifies a host but may not contain information sufficient to establish communication with the host. *See also* **network address**.

idempotent operation

An operation whose results do not affect the results of any operation. For example, an operation that reads a value is idempotent, but an operation that increments a value is not.

implement an interface

To provide the routines that execute the operations in an interface. A manager implements one interface for one type.

implicit handle

> A handle that is represented as a global variable in the client process, rather than passed as an operation parameter.

import an interface

> To request the operations defined by an interface. A client imports an interface from a server. *See also* export.

interface

> A set of operations. The Network Computing Architecture specifies a Network Interface Definition Language for defining interfaces.

interface UUID

> A UUID that identifies a particular interface. Both the RPC runtime library and the Location Broker use interface UUIDs to identify interfaces.

internet

> A set of two or more connected networks. The networks in an internet do not necessarily use the same communications protocol.

Local Location Broker (LLB)

> A server that maintains information about objects on the local host. The LLB also provides the Location Broker forwarding facility. Any host that runs NCS servers should run the LLB daemon, **llbd**.

Location Broker

> A set of software including the Local Location Broker, the Global Location Broker, and the Location Broker Client Agent. The Location Broker maintains information about the locations of objects and interfaces.

Location Broker Client Agent

> Part of the NCS Location Broker. Programs communicate with Global Location Brokers and Local Location Brokers via the Location Broker Client Agent.

manager

> A set of routines that implements the operations in one interface for objects of one type.

manual binding

> A binding technique in which the client uses RPC handles.

marshall

> To copy data into an RPC packet. Stubs perform marshalling. *See also* **unmarshall**.

network

> Data transmission media through which computers can be connected.

network address

> An identifier that, given an address family, uniquely identifies a host and contains information sufficient to establish communication with the host. A network address does not identify a port. *See also* **host ID** and **socket address**.

Network Computing Architecture

> An architecture for distributing software applications across heterogeneous collections of networks, computers, and programming environments.

Network Computing Kernel (NCK)

> The runtime components of the Network Computing System. These components include the Remote Procedure Call runtime library and the Location Broker. NCK contains all the software needed to support a distributed application.

Network Computing System (NCS)

> A set of software components, developed by Apollo Computer Inc., that conform to the Network Computing Architecture. These components include the RPC runtime library, the Location Broker, and the NIDL Compiler.

Network Data Representation (NDR)

> A protocol that defines how the structured values supplied in a call to a remote interface are encoded into byte stream format for transmission via the RPC runtime mechanism. NDR is part of the Network Computing Architecture.

Network Interface Definition Language (NIDL)

> A declarative language for defining interfaces. NIDL is part of the Network Computing Architecture. NIDL has two syntaxes, one resembling C and one resembling Pascal.

NIDL Compiler

> A compiler that takes as input an interface definition written in NIDL and generates as output C source code modules, including client and server stubs. The NIDL Compiler is a component of the Network Computing System. It is used to develop NCS-based applications.

object

> An entity that is manipulated by well-defined operations. Databases, files, directories, devices, processes, and processors are all examples of objects. Objects are accessed though interfaces. Every object has a type.

object UUID

> A UUID that identifies a particular object. Both the RPC runtime library and the Location Broker use object UUIDs to identify objects.

opaque port

A port that is dynamically assigned to a server by the RPC runtime library. The port number is said to be opaque because there is no need for either clients or servers to know the number. *See also* **well-known port.**

open array

An array whose declaration does not specify an explicit fixed length. The length of an open array is not determined until an operation that uses it is called. *See also* **fixed array.**

operation

A function or procedure through which an object is accessed.

port

A specific communications endpoint within a given host. A port is identified by a port number. *See also* **socket** and **socket address.**

port number

The part of a socket address that identifies a port within a host.

presented type

For data types with the **transmit_as** attribute, the data type that clients and servers manipulate. Stubs invoke conversion routines to convert the presented type to a transmitted type, which is passed over the network.

Process Fault Manager (PFM)

A set of calls that allow programs to manage signals, faults, and exceptions by establishing cleanup handlers. The **pfm_$** calls that we provide with the NCS software products are a portable subset of the Apollo Domain/OS **pfm_$** calls.

propagation queue

For replicated servers that use the Data Replication Manager, the queue that each server maintains for updates that it will propagate to other servers.

protocol family

A set of communications protocols, for example, the DARPA Internet Protocols. All members of a protocol family use a common addressing mechanism to identify endpoints. We use the terms "protocol family" and "address family" synonymously.

register an interface with the RPC runtime library

To make an interface known to the RPC runtime library and thereby available to clients through the RPC mechanism. Servers use the **rpc_$register_mgr** call to register interfaces; this call specifies the manager that implements a particular interface for a particular type.

register an object and an interface with the Location Broker

To enter in the Location Broker database an object and the location of a server that exports an interface for that object. Servers use the **lb_$register** call to register objects with the Location Broker. Clients can use Location Broker lookup calls to determine the locations of registered objects.

register an object with the RPC runtime library

To make an object known to the RPC runtime library and thereby available to clients through the RPC mechanism. Servers use the **rpc_$register_object** call to register objects; this call specifies an object and its type.

remote procedure call

An invocation of a remote operation. You can make remote procedure calls between processes on different hosts or on the same host.

Remote Procedure Call (RPC) runtime library

A set of calls that NCS provides to implement and support its remote procedure call mechanism.

replica

A copy of a replicated object. Replicas of an object have identical object UUIDs.

replica list

A list of all hosts on which replicas of a replicated object reside. Servers on these hosts cooperate to maintain a consistent view of the object.

replicated object

An object of which replicas are maintained. On Apollo systems, for example, the network registry is a replicated object.

replicated server

A server that provides access to a replicated object and cooperates with other servers to maintain consistency among all replicas of the object. On Apollo systems, for example, the network registry daemon is a replicated server.

RPC handle

A handle of the data type **handle_t**. RPC handles appear in applications that use manual binding. *See also* **generic handle**.

server

A process that provides resources. In the context of this manual, a server is a program containing routines that can be invoked from remote hosts. A server exports one or more interfaces. *See also* **client**.

set a binding

To set the representation of a server location in an RPC handle.

signature

The syntax of an operation, that is, its name, the data type it returns, and the order and types of its parameters. The definition of an operation specifies only its signature, not its implementation.

socket

An endpoint of communications in the form of a message queue. A socket is identified by a socket address. *See also* **Berkeley UNIX socket abstraction**.

socket address

A data structure that uniquely identifies a socket. A socket address consists of an address family identifier, a network address, and a port number.

status parameter

A parameter with the **comm_status** attribute. If an operation has a status parameter, communications errors that occur during execution of the operation are passed to the client in this parameter.

strongly consistent replicas

Replicas that are identical whenever they are accessible. *See also* **weakly consistent**.

stub

A program module that transfers remote procedure calls and responses between a client and a server. Stubs perform marshalling, unmarshalling, and data format conversion. Both clients and servers have stubs. The NIDL Compiler generates client and server stub code from an interface definition.

switch

A module in client programs that contains "public" routines whose names are those defined in an interface definition. These routines in turn invoke "private" routines through the client EPV. By eliminating conflicts in naming, this scheme makes possible the creation of replicated servers. The NIDL Compiler generates client switch code from an interface definition.

task

One of several threads of execution within a single process. Concurrent Programming Support provides calls that create and manage a multitasking environment.

transmitted type

For data types with the **transmit_as** attribute, the data type that stubs pass over the network. Stubs invoke conversion routines to convert the transmitted type to a presented type, which is manipulated by clients and servers.

type

> A class of object. All objects of a specific type can be accessed though the same interface or interfaces.

type UUID

> A UUID that identifies a particular type. Both the RPC runtime library and the Location Broker use type UUIDs to specify types.

unbound handle

> An RPC handle that identifies an object but not a location. This term is synonymous with "allocated handle."

unmarshall

> To copy data from an RPC packet. Stubs perform unmarshalling. *See also* **marshall**.

Unique Identifier (UID)

> An identifier used by Apollo systems.

Universal Unique Identifier (UUID)

> An identifier used by NCS to identify interfaces, objects, and types.

weakly consistent replicas

> Replicas that are accessible even at times when they might not be identical. *See also* **strongly consistent**.

well-known port

> A port whose port number is part of the definition of an interface. Clients of the interface always send to that port; servers always listen on that port. *See also* **opaque port**.

Index

allocated handles, 14, 363
   See also unbound handles

allocating handles, 230, 232—233

allowing remote server shutdown, 231

annotation, member of **lb_$entry_t** type, 189—190

annotations, in Location Broker database entries, 30

Apollo systems, 339—341
   default cleanup handlers, 79
   Location Broker configuration, 341
   linking client and server programs, 341
   PFM include files, 206—207, 216, 217—218
   Remote RPC interface, 341

applications
   building, 96—97
   developing, 65—97

ARPANET IMP addresses, 102

arrays
   as parameters, 61, 113
   attributes. *See* field attributes
   C syntax, 109—110, 117
   field attributes
      C syntax, 108
      Pascal syntax, 132
   fixed, 365
   multidimensional
      C syntax, 109
      Pascal syntax, 140
   open, 147—152, 368
      C syntax, 109
      examples, 150—153
      field attributes
         C syntax, 108
         Pascal syntax, 132
      in records, 141
      in structures, 109
      in unions, 109
      Pascal syntax, 141
   Pascal syntax, 140
   packed, 157—159
   run-length-encoded, 157—159
   sparse, 157—159
   subscripting
      C syntax, 109
      Pascal syntax, 140

asterisk. *See* *

asynchronous acks, 249

asynchronous faults
   enabling, 211, 212
   inhibiting, 213
      while allowing task switching, 214

at most once calling semantics, 110

attributes. *See* field attributes; interface attributes; operation attributes; parameter attributes; type attributes

audience for this book, xix

autobinding routines, 16
   examples, 161—163
   prototype, 161

automatic binding, 16, 160—164, 363
   examples, 161—164
   handle attribute
      C syntax, 106
      Pascal syntax, 130
   routines
      examples, 161—164
      prototypes, 161
   stub activity, 160

autounbinding routines, 16
   examples, 164
   prototype, 161

B

bank example, 161—164

base.idl file, 50

batch files, on MS-DOS systems, 361

Berkeley sockets, 7, 363
   See also sockets

_bind routine, 161
   examples, 161—163

binding, 13, 363
   automatic, 16, 160—164, 363
      examples, 161—164
      handle attribute
         C syntax, 106
         Pascal syntax, 130
      routines
         examples, 161—164
         prototypes, 161
      stub activity, 160
   manual, 16, 366

const declaration
    C syntax, 105
    Pascal syntax, 129

constant declarations
    C syntax, 105
    Pascal syntax, 129

constant expressions, 105

constants
    declarations. *See* constant declarations
    defined in the system **idl** directory, 50
    in interfaces with multiple versions, 173

constructed types
    C syntax, 115—117
    Pascal syntax, 138—141

conv.idl file, 51

conventions
    for names of interface definition files, 54
    for names of interfaces, 54
    for names of operations, 54
    std_$call, in PFM interfaces, 206—207
    used in this book, xx

conversion
    from UIDs to UUIDs, 303
    from UUIDs to UIDs, 305
    of address families
        from integers to names, 277
        from names to integers, 276
    of data, 18
        suppressing, 114
    of socket addresses
        from local representations to
          socket_$addr_t, 278
        from names to **socket_$addr_t**,
          279—280
        from **socket_$addr_t** to local
          representations, 291
        from **socket_$addr_t** to names, 292
        from **socket_$addr_t** to numeric
          names, 294
    of status codes to error messages, 186
    of types. *See* **transmit_as** attribute; type
      conversion
    of UUIDs
        from character strings to **uuid_$t**, 300
        from **uuid_$t** to character strings, 301

copying handles, 236

CPS, 3, 364
    asynchronous acks, 249
    documentation, xix
    duplicate handles for tasks, 236

creating handles
    fully bound, 232—233
    unbound, 230

creating sockets, 257—258
    with well-known ports, 259—260

creating UUIDs, 301

D

daemons, 307—328
    See also **glbd**; **llbd**; **nrglbd**

data
    conversion, 18
        suppressing, 114
    replication, 6, 11
    representation, 18

Data Replication Manager, 364
    See also **DRM**; **drm_admin**

databases
    distributed, 1
    Location Broker, 30—31
    merging, 310
        globally, 310
    SR10 Domain/OS registry, 1

Datakit protocols, 102

DDS protocols, 7
    on MS-DOS systems, 357
    socket address structure, 8

ddshosts.txt file, 357

ddslib library, 341

DEC. *See* ULTRIX systems; VMS systems

declarations. *See* constant declarations;
  import declarations; operation declarations;
  type declarations

decoding. *See* **sparse** example; type conversion

definitions, of interfaces, 3
    See also interface definitions

delete, command in **lb_admin**, 316

delrep, command in **drm_admin**, 309

diagnostic messages. *See* error messages

Digital Equipment Corporation. *See* ULTRIX
  systems; VMS systems

directional attributes
    C syntax, 112
    Pascal syntax, 135

disallowing remote server shutdown, 231

discriminators, in unions, 116

distributed databases, 1

dollar sign. *See* $

Domain C. *See* header files

Domain Pascal, 136
    See also insert files

Domain protocols. *See* DDS protocols

Domain systems. *See* Apollo systems

Domain/OS
    network root directory, 6
    registry, 1, 6

Domain/PCI products, 357

DOS. *See* MS-DOS systems

double type
    C syntax, 114
    Pascal syntax, 137

DPCI products, 357

DRM, 364
    See also **drm_admin**

drm_admin, 41, 309—311

dummies. *See* skeletal interface definitions

duplicating handles, 236

dynamic assignment of ports, 9

E

ECMA protocols, 102

ellipsis points. *See* ...

enabling asynchronous faults
    after **pfm_$inhibit**, 211
    after **pfm_$inhibit_faults**, 212

encoding. *See* **sparse** example; type conversion

entry point vectors, 21, 364
    See also EPVs

enum type, 115

enumerations
    C syntax, 115
    Pascal syntax, 138

epv_t types, 21

EPVs, 21, 364
    client, 22
    manager
        defining, 90
        names, 90
        with multiple interface versions, 171
        with multiple managers, 180

error messages
    calls, 183—186
    conversion from status codes, 186
    translation from hexadecimal status codes,
        41, 326

error_$ calls, 48, 183—186
    error_$c_get_text, 185
    error_$c_text, 186
    types used in, 184

errors, 75—76
    communications errors, 75
    in status codes, 185
    interface mismatches, 76
    server crashes, 76

examples directory, xx, 19
    on Apollo systems, 340
    on MS-DOS systems, 356
    on SunOS systems, 344
    on ULTRIX systems, 348
    on VMS systems, 352

Excelan EXOS products, 353

Excelan LAN WorkPlace products, 358

exceptions. *See* faults; PFM

execution, of remote procedure calls, 10

exit function, Microsoft C, 360

exiting
    cleanup handlers, 219, 223
    programs, 223

EXOS products, 353

explicit handles, 15, 364
    in operation declarations
        C syntax, 112
        Pascal syntax, 135

exporting interfaces, 11, 365

extern declaration, 82

external variables, **uuid_$nil**, 6

F

f77, 335—337
  NIDL Compiler options, 336—337

fail, member of **status_$t** type, 184

false, Boolean value, 115

families. *See* address families; DDS protocols; IP protocols

faults
  See also PFM
  asynchronous
    enabling, 211, 212
    inhibiting, 213
      while allowing task switching, 214
  setting server mode, 252
  signaling, 219

field attributes, 148—150
  examples, 150
  in operation declarations
    C syntax, 112
    Pascal syntax, 135—136
  in records, 139
  in structures, 116
  in type declarations
    C syntax, 108
    Pascal syntax, 132
  last_is
    C syntax, 108, 112
    Pascal syntax, 132, 135
  max_is
    C syntax, 108, 112
    Pascal syntax, 132, 135

fields
  See also parameters; records; structures
  attributes. *See* field attributes

files, Location Broker configuration, 41, 329—333

fixed arrays, 365

flags, in Location Broker database entries, 30

flags, member of **lb_$entry_t** type, 189—190

float type, 114

floating-point instructions, VAX G
  on ULTRIX systems, 349
  on VMS systems, 353

floating-point numbers
  data representation formats, 18
  types
    C syntax, 114
    Pascal syntax, 137

flow
  of cleanup handler execution, 77
  of local procedure calls, 10
  of remote procedure calls, 10

fonts, conventions used in this book, xx

formats, data representation, 18

FORTRAN, 335—337
  interlude routines, 336
  language bindings, 336
  operations called from or implemented in, 335

forwarding, 14, 32, 66, 365
  example. *See* **binopfw** example

_free routine, 153
  examples, 156, 159

_free_xmit_rep routine, 153
  examples, 156, 159

freeing handles, 237

_from_xmit_rep routine, 153
  examples, 156, 159

fully bound handles, 14, 365
  creating, 232—233
  from bound-to-host handles, 250—251
  from unbound handles, 250—251
  how to use, 72

function declaration, 134
  See also operation declarations

functions, 134
  See also operations

G

garbage collection, of Location Broker databases, 315—316

generating UUIDs, 304

generic handles, 13, 16, 160—164, 365
  handle attribute
    C syntax, 106
    Pascal syntax, 130

GLB, 365
  See also Global Location Broker

handles (*continued*)
    RPC, 13, 16, 369
        figure, 13
        handle_t type
            C syntax, 117
            Pascal syntax, 141
    representation, 15
    server side, 15
    setting bindings, 250—251
    unbound, 14, 371
        creating, 230
        disadvantages, 74
        from fully bound handles, 234
        how to use, 74

header files
    corresponding to imported interface
        definitions, 104, 128
    corresponding to system **idl** files, 51
    idl_base.h, 51
    ppfm.h, 51

heading, of an interface definition
    C syntax, 100
    examples, 55
    Pascal syntax, 124
    writing, 54—55

help, command in **lb_admin**, 316

heterogeneity, 1, 18
    NDR scalar types, 67

host IDs, 8, 365
    extracting from socket addresses, 282
    numeric, 9
    on MS-DOS systems, 357, 358
    setting in socket addresses, 287

host names, 9
    on MS-DOS systems, 357, 358

hosts, 365

hosts file, Excelan LAN WorkPlace, 358

huge attribute, Microsoft C, 359

hyper type, 114

I

IBM
    See also MS-DOS systems
    SNA protocols, 102

idempotent operation attribute
    C syntax, 110
    Pascal syntax, 133

identifiers
    See also UIDs; UUIDs
    host. *See* host IDs; host names
    NIDL syntaxes
        C syntax, 100
        Pascal syntax, 123
    network. *See* network IDs

idl directory, xx, 50—51
    on Apollo systems, 340
    on MS-DOS systems, 356
    on SunOS systems, 344
    on ULTRIX systems, 348
    on VMS systems, 352

.idl files. *See* interface definitions; system **idl**
directory

idl_base.h file, 51
    NDR scalar types, 67

if_spec interface specifiers, 21

IMP addresses, 102

implicit handles, 15, 366
    limitations, 16
    specifying in interface definitions
        C syntax, 103
        Pascal syntax, 127

implicit_handle attribute
    C syntax, 103
    Pascal syntax, 127

import declarations
    C syntax, 104
    Pascal syntax, 128

importing interfaces, 11, 366
    declarations. *See* import declarations

in parameter attribute
    C syntax, 112
    Pascal syntax, 135

include files, PFM, 206—207, 216, 217—218

#include directives, in generated header files,
104—105, 128—129

%include directives, in generated insert files,
104—105, 128—129

info, command in **drm_admin**, 310

inhibiting asynchronous faults, 213
    while allowing task switching, 214

initializing the PFM package, 215

.ins.pas files. *See* insert files

insert files, corresponding to system **idl** files, 51

int type, 114
    on MS-DOS systems, 359

L

multidimensional arrays
    C syntax, 109
    open
        C syntax, 109
        Pascal syntax, 141
    Pascal syntax, 140

multiple interface versions, 165—173
    changing operations, 171—172
    constants, 173
    examples, 165—171
    types, 173

multiple managers, 174—182
    examples, 174—182

multitasking, 3

multithreading, 3

N

named types
    C syntax, 105—109, 118
    Pascal syntax, 129—132, 141

names
    associations with UUIDs, 333
    conventions used in this book, xx
    of files generated by the NIDL Compiler,
        21, 54
        on MS-DOS systems, 358—359
    of files in import declarations, on MS-DOS
        systems, 359
    of interface definition files, 54
        on MS-DOS systems, 358—359
        on VMS systems, 353
    of interfaces, 54
    of manager EPVs, 90
    of manager routines, 90
    of operations, 54

National Bureau of Standards (NBS) protocols,
    102

nbase.idl file, 50

NBS protocols, 102

NCA, 367
    See also Network Computing Architecture

ncastat.idl file, 50

NCK, 2, 367
    product, 39
        technical changes in Version 1.5.1,
            xviii

NCS, 367
    administration
        documentation, xix
        tools, 41
            See also drm_admin; lb_admin
    components, 2
    configuration files, 41, 329—333
    daemons, 40—41, 307—328
        See also glbd; llbd; nrglbd
    on Apollo systems, 339—341
    on MS-DOS systems, 355—361
    on SunOS systems, 343—345
    on ULTRIX systems, 347—349
    on VMS systems, 351—354
    products, 39
        See also NCK; NIDL
        technical changes in Version 1.5.1,
            xviii
    software, 39—51
        organization
            on Apollo systems, 339—340
            on MS-DOS systems, 355—356
            on SunOS systems, 343—344
            on ULTRIX systems, 347—348
            on VMS systems, 351—352
    utilities, 40—41, 307—328
        See also nidl; stcode; uuid_gen

NDR, 367
    scalar types, 67

ndr_$ types, 67

network addresses, 8, 367
    changing in replica lists, 309
    extracting from socket addresses, 284
    for local host, 283
    setting in socket addresses, 288

Network Computing Architecture, 1, 5, 367
    documentation, xix

Network Computing Kernel, 2, 367
    See also NCK

Network Computing System, 367
    See also NCS

Network Data Representation, 367
    scalar types, 67

Network Interface Definition Language, 367
    See also NIDL

network interfaces, support on VMS systems,
    353

network protocols. See protocols

network root directory, Domain/OS, 6

pointers
  as parameters, 60, 113
  C syntax, 109, 117
  in structures, 116
  in unions, 117
  null, 117
  Pascal syntax, 140
  restrictions, 60, 117

port interface attribute
  C syntax, 102—103
  Pascal syntax, 126—127

port numbers, 8, 368
  extracting from socket addresses, 285
  setting in socket addresses, 289
    to well-known values, 290
  specifying in interface definitions
    C syntax, 102—103
    Pascal syntax, 126—127

portability, 2, 82, 96
  of cleanup handlers, 79
  of data types, 67

portable PFM interface, 206—207

ports, 8, 368
  opaque, 9, 368
    creating sockets for, 257—258
    setting in socket addresses, 289
  well-known, 9, 32, 371
    creating sockets for, 259—260
    examples, 23—29
    setting in socket addresses, 290
    specifying in interface definitions
      C syntax, 102—103
      Pascal syntax, 126—127

pound sign. *See* #

ppfm.h file, 51, 206—207

presented types, 368
  See also **transmit_as** attribute;
    type conversion
  storage for, 153

primes example, 150—153
  client, 151
  interface definition, 150
  manager, 152

procedure declaration, 134
  See also operation declarations

procedures, 134
  See also operations

Process Fault Manager, 368
  See also PFM

products, NCS, 39
  See also NCK; NIDL

propagation queues, 368

protocol families, 8, 368
  See also address families; DDS protocols;
    IP protocols

protocols, 7
  DDS, 7
    socket address structure, 8
  IP, 7
    socket address structure, 8
  supported on MS-DOS systems, 357—358

PUP protocols, 102

purgerep, command in **drm_admin**, 311

Q

queues
  message, 7
  propagation, 368

quit
  command in **drm_admin**, 311
  command in **lb_admin**, 316

R

real type, 137

records, 139
  See also structures; unions
  variant, 139—140
    See also unions
    containing arrays, 141
    representation in generated code, 142—145
    tags, 140, 142—145

ref parameter attribute, 135

reference, passing parameters by
  FORTRAN considerations, 335
  in PFM interfaces, 206—207
  input parameters, 113
  records containing open arrays, 139
  structures containing open arrays, 116

register, command in **lb_admin**, 316

socket_$ types (continued)
    socket_$len_list_t, 271
    socket_$local_sockaddr_t, 271
    socket_$net_addr_t, 271
    socket_$string_t, 271
    socket_$wk_ports_t, 271

socket.idl file, 50

sockets, 7, 363, 370
    See also socket addresses; **socket_$** calls
    calls, 269—296
    creating, 87, 257—258
        with well-known ports, 259—260

sparse arrays, 157—159

sparse example, 157—159
    conversion routines, 158—159
    interface definition, 157—158

specifications, Network Computing Architecture, xix

specifiers, for interfaces, 21

stacks example, 174—182
    client, 175—177
    header file, 175
    interface definition, 174
        compiling, 174
    managers, 180—182
    server, 178—179

star. *See* *

statistics, about servers, 266—267

status codes
    See also **status_$t** type
    calls, 183—186
    conversion to error messages, 186
    extraction of subsystem, module, and error, 185
    hexadecimal, translation, 326
    status_$ok, 184
    translation, 41, 326

status parameters, 80—81, 370
    checking, 80—81
        example, 80
    in interface definitions, 80
        C syntax, 112
        example, 80
        Pascal syntax, 135
    initializing, 81, 91
        example, 81

status_$ok status code, 184

status_$t type, 184—185

stcode, 41, 326

std_$call calling convention, in PFM interfaces, 206—207

stop, command in **drm_admin**, 311

strings
    constants
        C syntax, 105
        Pascal syntax, 129
    types
        C syntax, 116
        Pascal syntax, 139

strong consistency, 6, 370

structures, 116
    See also records
    containing open arrays, 109
    containing pointers, 116

stubs, 3, 17—18, 370
    client. *See* client stubs
    server. *See* server stubs

subranges, 138

subsys, member of **status_$t** type, 184

subsystems, in status codes, 185

SunOS systems, 343—345
    Location Broker configuration, 345
    linking client and server programs, 345

switches, 22—23, 370

synchronous acks, 249

syntax
    conventions used in this book, xx
    identifiers
        C syntax, 100
        Pascal syntax, 123

systartup.com, VMS startup script, 351

system administration
    documentation, xix
    tools, 41

system **idl** directory, 50—51
    on Apollo systems, 340
    on MS-DOS systems, 356
    on SunOS systems, 344
    on ULTRIX systems, 348
    on VMS systems, 352

T

tagged_union generic name
in C representations of unions, 120
in C representations of variant records, 144

tags
in unions, 116, 118
in variant records, 140, 142

tasks, 3, 370
duplicate handles, 236
switching, 214

TCP/IP. *See* IP protocols

templates. *See* skeletal interface definitions

threads. *See* tasks

timeouts, setting
in client handles, 253
in **lb_admin**, 317

_to_xmit_rep routine, 153
examples, 155, 158

tools, 40—41, 307—328
See also **drm_admin**; **lb_admin**

translation. *See* conversion

transmit_as type attribute
C syntax, 106—107
examples, 154—155, 157—158
Pascal syntax, 130—131
restrictions, 160

transmitted types, 370
See also **transmit_as** attribute;
type conversion
storage for, 153

transparency, 7, 10, 17

true, Boolean value, 115

type attributes
C syntax, 105—107
handle
C syntax, 106
Pascal syntax, 130
Pascal syntax, 130—131
transmit_as
C syntax, 106—107
examples, 154—155, 157—158
Pascal syntax, 130—131
restrictions, 160

type conversion, 153—160
examples, 154—156, 157—159
for efficiency, 157—159

restrictions, 160
routines
examples, 155—156, 158—159
prototypes, 153
to pass complex types, 154—156

type declaration, 129—132

type declarations
C syntax, 105—109
Pascal syntax, 129—132

type managers. *See* managers

type UUIDs, 6, 371
in Location Broker database entries, 30

typedef declaration, 105—109

types, 5, 371
aggregate. *See* constructed types
arrays
C syntax, 109, 117
Pascal syntax, 140
attributes. *See* type attributes
Boolean
C syntax, 115
Pascal syntax, 138
bitset, 115
byte
C syntax, 114
Pascal syntax, 137
C syntax, 114—121
character
C syntax, 115
Pascal syntax, 137
complex, 106, 130
See also **transmit_as** attribute;
type conversion
constructed
C syntax, 115—117
Pascal syntax, 138—141
conversion. *See* **transmit_as** attribute;
type conversion
declarations. *See* type declarations
declarators, C syntax, 109
defined in the system **idl** directory, 50
double
C syntax, 114
Pascal syntax, 137
enum, 115
enumerations
C syntax, 115
Pascal syntax, 138

unions, 116
 See also variant records
 containing open arrays, 109
 containing pointers, 117
 discriminators, 116
 representation in generated code, 118—121
 tags, 116, 118—121

Unique Identifiers, 371
 See also UIDs

Universal Unique Identifiers, 371
 See also UUIDs

UNIX pipes, 102

unmarshalling, 18, 371

unregister, command in **lb_admin**, 317

unregistering
 with the Location Broker, 89, 204
  via **lb_admin**, 317
 with the RPC runtime library, 89, 256

unsigned integer types
 C syntax, 114
 Pascal syntax, 137

use of this book, xix

use_broker, command in **lb_admin**, 317

utilities, 41, 307—328
 See also **nidl**; **stcode**; **uuid_gen**

uuid interface attribute
 C syntax, 101
 Pascal syntax, 125

uuid_$ calls, 48, 297—305
 external variables used in, 298
 status codes used in, 299—300
 types used in, 298—299
 uuid_$decode, 300
 uuid_$encode, 301
 uuid_$equal, 302
 uuid_$from_uid, 303
 uuid_$gen, 304
 uuid_$to_uid, 305

uuid_$ types
 uuid_$string_t, 299
 uuid_$t, 299

uuid_$nil external variable, 6, 298

uuid.idl file, 50

uuid_gen, 6, 40, 327—328

uuid_uid.idl file, 50

uuidname.txt file, 333

UUIDs, 6, 371
 associations with names, 333
 calls, 48, 297—305
  See also **uuid_$** calls
 comparison, 302
 conversion
  from character strings to **uuid_$t**, 300
  from UIDs, 303
  from **uuid_$t** to character strings, 301
  to UIDs, 305
 data structure, 6
 generation, 40, 304, 327—328
 nil, 6
  See also **uuid_$nil** external variable
 string representation, 6

V

var declaration, 129

variant records, 139—140
 containing arrays, 141
 representation in generated code, 142—145
 tags, 140, 142—145

VAX C
 globaldef declaration, 96
 globalref declaration, 82

VAX G floating-point instructions
 on ULTRIX systems, 349
 on VMS systems, 353

VAX/ULTRIX. *See* ULTRIX systems

VAX/VMS. *See* VMS systems

version interface attribute
 C syntax, 102
 Pascal syntax, 125—126

versions
 of interfaces
  See also multiple interface versions
  checking, 168
  specifying in interface definitions
   C syntax, 102
   Pascal syntax, 125—126
  version number appended to interface
   name, 21, 166—167
 of Microsoft products, 355
 of NCS products, xviii
 of PFM include files, 206—207, 216,
  217—218